THE STRUGGLE FOR DEMOCRACY
IN GERMANY

THE STRUGGLE
FOR DEMOCRACY
IN GERMANY

Edited by

GABRIEL A. ALMOND

Eugene N. Anderson	Wolfgang H. Kraus
Gabriel A. Almond	Fred H. Sanderson
Hans Meyerhoff	Vera F. Eliasberg

Clara Menck

NEW YORK

RUSSELL & RUSSELL · INC

1965

50954

Preface

IN THE FIRST MONTHS after the defeat of Germany it appeared, at least on the surface, that the primary criterion for the solution of the German question was the elimination of Germany's physical and psychological capacity to make war. This was the spirit of the Potsdam Agreement, concluded in the flush of victory, and in the mood of Allied amity which followed. Western opinion has experienced a profound disillusionment in the three years which have followed this era of sanguine expectations. Each phase of the peace settlement and each step in the program of bringing international politics within the framework of effective law and organization has been assimilated to the over-all struggle between East and West. The collapse of the Conference of Foreign Ministers at London in November, 1947 put an end to hopes that a peaceful and stable German settlement could be reached in the present state of international relations. Subsequent developments indicate that the division of Germany has become a practical if not a juridical reality.

The solution to the German question contemplated in the Potsdam accords and earlier agreements, rested on the expectation of a stable "concert of power" in the postwar period. It was assumed that the German problem could be settled largely in its own terms— that of destroying once and for all Germany's capacity to make war and laying the basis for a peaceful and democratic polity. Three years after Potsdam finds us subordinating these problems to the more urgent question of whether German power is to be included in the Soviet orbit or integrated with the surviving democratic strength of Western Europe.

This shift in emphasis in the German question confronts us with a very real danger. In the atmosphere of tension between the Soviet Union and the Western powers there is an obvious temptation to attempt to maximize anti-Soviet strength regardless of its character and consequences. Thus, a reactionary and nationalist Western Germany would be more anti-Communist than a moderate democratic one and might therefore seem more desirable from a security point of view. But the development of such a Western Germany would endanger the American interest in Europe in at least three ways: (1) such a Germany might be provocatively hostile to the Soviet Union and might force the hand of American policy; (2) the emergence of a new German nationalism would create disunity in the Western camp by raising the spectre of German aggression and expansionism; (3) a reactionary and nationalist Western Germany would be opposed by a substantial proportion of the German population and consequently would be vulnerable to Communist infiltration and Soviet propaganda.

These considerations suggest that the general change in the international situation should not be permitted to suppress the original aims of the German occupation. Our primary concern ought still to be German "democratization." But it is necessary to face the threat to democracy in Germany on two fronts: (1) the threat of historic German authoritarianism and nationalism; (2) the threat of Communist infiltration and Soviet expansionism.

To counteract this twofold threat the earlier primarily negative approach to the German problem has had to give way to a positive and constructive emphasis in which the key concept is "integration." If the larger part of German strength is to be employed in the interest of the democratic and liberal world the postwar status of Germany and Germans will have to be revised. Perhaps the main objective of such a policy would be to give the Germans a sense of participation in the values and programs of the Western community of nations. The main problem of German politics is that most of the Germans, and particularly the youth, are "hold-outs." The present strength of the moderate Socialist and Christian parties is largely a surface manifestation. To the historic political indifference of the German masses there has been added a widespread mood of bitterness and futility, a mood which deprives the existing party elites of any right to speak with full authority for Germany, and which provides extremists and authoritarians of a right or left coloration with the kind of spiritual vacuum which has always facilitated their success.

The United States has a very real security interest in integrating that part of Germany which we can influence into the Western community of effort. This is not merely the economic question of utilizing German resources, equipment, and manpower in the European Recovery Program, although that is an important part of it. American policy should add social, cultural, and psychological reintegration, to its present economic emphasis.

Two objectives are suggested here: (1) the elimination of the moral *cordon sanitaire;* and (2) the initiation of steps that will hasten the processes of social integration. In connection with the first objective, German representation in the various Western European organizations will constitute a symbolic modification of the pariah status to which postwar Germans have been condemned. Equally important, a substantial program of cultural interchange and exchange of personnel, might be undertaken on a collaborative basis between the interested Western powers. Such measures, if applied to university youth, and the emergent political, intellectual, and cultural elites, may go far toward "sparking" the regeneration of Western cultural and spiritual values in Germany.

The second objective requires a broad set of means, ranging all the way from the improvement of the housing situation and employment conditions in order to make a satisfactory family life possible, to the rapid execution and termination of the program of denazification. These and similar measures, which will have the effect of stabilizing and normalizing the institutional routines of living, may give content to the present "formal" democracy of Western Germany, and thereby give Western policy strong roots in a most critical area.

The present book makes a contribution toward understanding the twofold nature of the German problem. Part I is concerned with the strength and composition of liberal and democratic tendencies in German history and with the extent of their survival in the anti-Nazi resistance. This part of the book represents an effort to correct the erroneous history of the war period which placed Germany entirely outside the pale of Western historical and politico-moral development. It is suggested here that this policy was based on an exaggeration of historical trends, and that it is now the task of policy-makers to discover and strengthen that part of the German heritage which inclines toward liberalism and democracy. Part II discusses the most significant phases of occupation policy—economic, governmental, political, cultural, and psychological—and their impact on the future of Germany. Each functional problem is placed in the context of the East-West struggle, and the various issues are evaluated in terms of their implications for the outcome.

A symposium always presents problems of consistency and coherence. The participants in this symposium in most cases had the advantage of having shared in common or related work during the war years, and of having discussed their general approach with one another as the project developed. While it is possible to speak, therefore, of a common approach to the German problem as underlying the various contributions, each writer has assumed responsibility only for his own section.

Those contributors now in government service wish to express their gratitude to the State Department for its clearance of their contributions. Needless to say, the opinions expressed are those of the writers. The authors of the chapters on the German resistance wish to record their appreciation to the many officials of the American, British, and French military governments in Germany for the courtesy and helpfulness shown them in their studies of the German resistance. Special thanks are due Professor Waldemar Gurian of Notre Dame University for his thoughtful reading and criticism of a part of the manuscript and Professor C. B. Robson of the University of North Carolina to whose original suggestion this book owes its inception and whose subsequent sponsorship brought the project to fruition.

Contents

I. THE HISTORIC POTENTIAL

II. OCCUPATION POLICY

I
THE HISTORIC POTENTIAL

Chap. 1 Freedom and Authoritarianism in German History

EUGENE N. ANDERSON

By a kind of inverted racialism, the German people are often branded as irretrievably authoritarian in government and politics and in the manifestations of social life. The father of the family and the labor leader, the social worker and the school teacher, all are accused of conforming to a pattern of authoritarianism set by the long domination of monarchism and militarism and of their servant, bureaucracy. The goose step is regarded as the normal manner of walking, thinking, and acting; and the sharp and rude precision of its jerky progress is found to be reflected in the gruff, staccato accents of the German language. The conclusion from this view follows illogically but inevitably: the Germans cannot be trusted to live peaceably with the rest of the world; they will succumb to the violent promises and deeds of another *Führer;* one must either reduce them to a harmless number or prevent the rise of another Hitler by assuming over them authoritarian power.

Since both prospects are repulsive to the Western world, it is essential that the premises on which such conclusions rest be reexamined. Are the German people congenitally authoritarian? Do elements of freedom find any support among them? The definitive answer cannot be found by turning to the study of the past alone; but as history supplies one of the few available sources of evidence, an analysis of German past experience with respect to freedom and authority should indicate the degree of permanence of National Socialist behavior and the dimensions of the German problem.

Taken as a whole, German historical tradition is rich enough to supply evidence in support of any thesis about the German people. It seems irrelevant and unnecessary for the purpose in hand, however, to explore any period prior to that which has exercised an immediate influence upon the present day. There are times in the history of every country when habits are formed, institutions are established, social classes and groups are fixed in relation to one another, legal systems and norms are created, and ideals are accepted which inaugurate a new period in the life of the country. These changes fundamentally condition the character of that period and incorporate into its living forms all that is relevant from earlier times. This period of history, with its particular institutions and ways, then endures until the course of time changes the foundations and evolves a new age.

In the case of Germany the present evidence indicates that the years between the unification of the country in the third quarter of the nineteenth century and the overthrow of Nazism may be called a historical period with a particular life of its own. It is the period of the rise and fall of the second German Reich, and its essential characteristics were developed during the unification of the country. That Nazism would actually be the climax of the period no one could foresee. Even though certain German nationalistic writers envisaged such a future occurrence, it would be attributing to Germany an omnipotence which neither it nor any other country ever possessed to assume that Nazism grew inevitably out of Bismarckian Germany. Since hindsight is not difficult, the historian can find many origins and a superficially convincing logical course for the degeneration of modern Germany into National Socialism. However, the interplay, particularly of international power politics, has been so sharp during the past three quarters of a century, not merely at Germany's instigation but at that of all the great Powers, and the course of economic life has been subject to such unexpected and violent depressions, that no one country can be credited with the full responsibility for its own history. One can at most state that, without being able to control the course of events in all its richness, Germany received through Bismarck's actions the social and political organization and ways out of which under favorable circumstances Nazism could develop. For Bismarck's work of national unification fixed the political, social, and institutional framework within which or against which German events have since then moved.

The three wars of German unification, in common with all other European wars after the French Revolution, affected both international and internal affairs. A unified Germany pushed her way authoritatively into the family of nations and assumed a position of power. At the same time a hierarchical relationship of social groups in Germany, in contrast to the free relationship in a democracy, became fixed for decades to come, and the governmental institutions of authoritarianism were firmly established. In 1914-18 it required the combined power of the rest of the world to undermine these dominant social groups and institutions, and even then the social groups escaped destruction. Able to revive and exploit the general despair of the economic crisis of 1930-31, these groups assisted National Socialism to power and without entirely identifying themselves with Nazism contributed elements essential for enabling it to wreck Germany and Europe and to menace the world.

When Bismarck was appointed Minister President of Prussia in 1862, he confronted a constitutional conflict which involved the future character of German government and society. In the Landtag the *Herrenhaus*, or upper house, being hereditary or appointed was safely reactionary; but the *Abgeordnetenhaus*, or second chamber, determined to compel the king to transform the constitution, which had been used as a front for reaction in the 1850's, into one of actual responsible government. The controversy crystallized over the king's demand for the training of his subjects in civil docility by lengthening the term of military service from two to three years. The dissolution of the lower house and the holding of new elections twice after 1859 had only strengthened the liberal opposition, and as a desperate last act the king had appointed Bismarck. King William feared the loss of his control over the army, a civil war, and the reduction of his own authority to the level of that of the British crown. He recognized that the outcome of the constitutional conflict threatened to shift social and political power from the upper classes, bulwarks of Hohenzollern Prussia, to the new liberal elements. Rather than acquiesce he considered even abdication. The King knew Bismarck's reputation as a rabid, reactionary Junker, so violent and headstrong that he might destroy the monarchy and the country; but as between surrender to liberalism and the possibility of retaining his power through Bismarck, he felt that he had no choice. He saw himself as a ruler obliged to do his duty, even if the process involved his destruction.

Since the 1860's marked the peak of liberalism and democracy in Germany, it is necessary to analyze the extent and vigor of these forces at the time. In Prussia the elections to the Landtag showed that the cities and towns supported the new political and social ideals and that the vocal elements in the rural areas did not lag far behind. The Prussian landowners, including even the stock Junkers, were divided. Many of them had been liberal for decades, ashamed of the incompetence of the bureaucracy in some fields and of its ruthless, inhuman efficiency in others. Already in 1848 they had joined the emerging capitalistic bourgeoisie and the middle classes in demanding constitutional government as the basic means for enabling a new order of society to develop. The economic and social forces of rising capitalistic industry and agriculture were cramped by the antiquated forms of the Prussian state and society. They saw unprecedented opportunities for material and spiritual development being curbed or withheld by the vestiges of mercantilism and an autocratic bureaucracy. As leaders in the economy and supporters of a new culture, they demanded freedom from petty and suspicious bureaucratic interference; they demanded freedom for creative action; they demanded political power by way of constitutional government to assure them that the government would respond to their wishes and needs; they demanded social recognition commensurate with their importance in the life of the country; above all they demanded national unification as a means of providing them with new areas of activity and power.

Similar conflicts were occurring in the rest of Germany. In a state like Baden the liberals had already won control. In other states the reactionary rulers and their few supporters set an example of tyranny of a mean, exasperating type well known in Germany in the nineteenth century and practiced vigorously by Bismarck. They threw people into jail without due process of law, curbed their actions and blocked their outlets in freedom of discussion; but they did not torture or kill. The liberals and democrats throughout Germany were organized in political parties, in social clubs, economic associations, and religious organizations. Some of the economic and religious organizations, and even one political association, the National Verein, extended more or less over the entire nation. They strove for the political and economic unification of the German people under a free, constitutional regime comparable to that in contemporary England. The period was full of their conferences, their discussions, and their verbal fights with the reactionary particularistic governments of the separate states.

In view of the overwhelming desire at this time on the part of the middle classes, and of their many supporters from the other classes, for a free government, the defeat of the movement for freedom by Bismarck in the crucial constitutional conflict may reveal certain weaknesses which likewise were in subsequent decades to prevent victory. The bourgeoisie and middle classes, like those groups in all countries after 1789, rejected the use of revolution. They had been drawn unwillingly into the revolution of 1848 and had disliked the experience. As property owners and producers these rational optimists placed faith in the efficacy of social evolution to bring them to power, a faith they shared with similar social groups in all countries. Failing in action, these liberals and democrats talked *in extenso*. Each had a solution to the problems of freedom and of national unification, and each ardently defended his solution, frequently to the exclusion of understanding another's. Although they held their conferences in beer halls, they were too gentlemanly to throw beer mugs, chairs, and tables at each other as the National Socialists, many of whom came from the same classes, later did. Instead, they found solace, not as during the Napoleonic period in transcendental philosophy, but in the concept of progress and in faith in the inevitable victory of middle class wealth, intelligence, and birthrate. They expected their sheer numbers to swamp the reactionary aristocrats and other opponents.

The liberals and democrats confronted the entrenched power of traditional rulers, courts, bureaucracies, and armies, skilled in the techniques of the police state and supported by a large section of the aristocracy and by many artisans. These traditional groups were all accustomed to the exercise of power from above and thought and acted in the ways of a well-ordered, hierarchical state and society. Law and institutions sanctioned the authoritarian character of this regime, and the more or less successful handling of life's problems over centuries added a moral justification. Although certain sections of the bureaucracy, such as the judiciary, veered toward liberalism, the administrative machinery of government continued to operate at the will of the ruler. After minor defections in 1848 and in spite of the presence of many liberal officers, the army remained loyal to the ruler and could on the whole be relied upon by him in case of social rebellion. The peasantry became largely inactive after it had achieved substantial material gains in 1848, and the proletariat did not yet count. In the small states the princely courts dominated economic and social life to such an extent as to make any opposition extremely difficult. The intellectuals were divided, but a few could always be found to justify by law, philosophy, and theology any act of any government and to supply it with the dignity and the odor of learning, or even the diatribe of the popular press.

The outcome of the conflict throughout Germany between the reactionaries on the one hand and the liberals and democrats on the other depended upon the course of events in Prussia. If Prussia, the largest state of them all, became liberal, the rulers of the medium-sized and petty states would face such an emboldened opposition that they would have to follow suit. The future social and political character of the German people depended upon the success or failure of the Prussian Minister President Bismarck. If he failed, Germany would align with the liberal peoples of the West; if he won, it would remain a stronghold of authoritarianism.

At the time of the constitutional conflict in Prussia, history had arrived at a point ripe for action. The person or force able boldly to grasp the opportunity with sufficient power could put his own forms of control upon the future Germany merely by conceding to the people some of their most urgent demands. Bismarck won the devotion of the German people by gaining national political and economic unity for them. At the same time he granted the legal freedom necessary for the second most important development in Germany during this century, the explosive growth of industrial capitalism. He supported its interests, together with those of capitalistic agriculture, with the power of the unified Reich. By these concessions to the bourgeoisie, the middle classes and their allies, Bismarck was able to preserve the power of the Hohenzollern dynasty in the new Reich and also the power of those lesser rulers whom he permitted to retain their thrones. He successfully transferred the Prussian Army and Prussian militarism to the new Reich, and he gained for them popularity, which had been steadily declining since the Napoleonic Wars. He created a position for himself in the government which the constitution termed responsible, but since it failed to say to whom or to what, he was able to play his responsibility to the Emperor against that to the Reichstag and in general to maintain a thoroughly authoritarian rôle for himself. The actual power of the Reichstag over the army and over the budget was so hedged about, either by constitutional restrictions or by political limitations, that the Emperor, Bismarck, and their supporters were able to gain their way. The authority of the Reichstag in these crucial matters could not be compared with that of the British parliament or even the French parliament of the Third Republic. While much more liberal than the government of Russia, the new Reich was nicely adjusted to Bismarck's authoritarian will.

The liberal and democratic opponents of Bismarck felt so enthusiastic about the actual achievement of national unification that on the whole, although at different rates of speed, they acquiesced in the defeat of their drive for constitutional and social power. Their nationalism undermined their devotion to freedom. One cannot say definitely that they preferred national unity under authoritarianism to freedom without it, for they never had the choice. Some of them, a rapidly declining few, held out against Bismarck and his successors in favor of a typical nineteenth-century liberalism, and consequently were doomed to dogmatic and ineffectual opposition. More of them joined the National Liberal party to fall increasingly under Bismarckian influence. They adhered to their liberal ideals in theory and supported either grudgingly or willingly most of Bismarck's demands. Others frankly became his followers. In all cases the social and political power of liberalism and democracy received a crushing defeat just at the period when it was gaining control in France with the establishment of the Third Republic and was expanding its basis in England by the reform bills of 1867 and 1884.

The brilliant and unexpected success of the policy of Blood and Iron crippled the moral supports of liberalism in Germany. The first war of unification, that against Denmark, only increased the wrath against Bismarck. But the quick and easy success of the war against Austria left the opponents breathless, while the outcome of the third one, that against a popular hereditary enemy notoriously opposed to German unification, transformed the German people into hero-worshippers. Might seemed to have proved to be right, deeds more important than words. A war which gained the longed-for national unity was glorious and gave Germany her rightful place among the power nations. Rationalism and liberal ideals receded before enthusiasm for action.

The fact that the liberals and democrats had bitterly fought Bismarck during his struggle to accomplish one of their own major objectives added to their humiliation and deprived them of the self-confidence necessary for the continued defense of freedom in internal affairs. They had dutifully paid their taxes and the conscripted subjects had docilely fought the king's wars, but their participation in victory had been forced. The Hohenzollern ruler, Bismarck, and the army, three forces of thorough authoritarianism, had accomplished what the liberals had talked about. The moral prestige of Blood and Iron supplanted that of freedom.

During the period of Bismarck's rule the German people received their basic training in political methods and morality. Given the character of the teacher, the training was primarily of an authoritarian kind even though it operated within the normal liberal institutions of a free press, popularly elected parliamentary bodies, and political parties. Bismarck knew how to manipulate these institutions so as to cripple their inherent tendencies for freedom and prevent them from acquiring a position of high prestige among the German people. With the aid of a large secret "Reptile Fund" he was able to bribe sections of the press, and his many public remarks of scorn for the press were echoed by the academic intellectuals. Sensitive about press criticism, Bismarck had a master's touch in spreading rumors, even falsehoods, and in using all the power of his position to keep the press in line. The evidence of his violation of the freedom of the press shows how successfully he prevented this fundamental instrument from becoming the democratic influence that it should have been.

Bismarck exercised a most pernicious influence upon the political parties. He wished to make them docile instruments of his personal authority. The introduction of universal manhood suffrage in the Reich elections, contrary to Bismarck's expectations, enhanced the prestige of the political parties; but by broadening the basis of the vote, it enabled Bismarck to throw the full weight of his position against stubborn parties through a direct appeal to the public. Bismarck used his unique power to weaken the parties, just as he did to weaken the press. He employed the methods of *Realpolitik* toward them in the same amoral way that he did toward any opponent, whether individual, party, or foreign country. When the National Liberals placed obstructions in his way, he succeeded in splitting their party. He did so by using them to fight the Social Democrats and the Catholic Center party, involving the liberals in such intolerant and brutal legislation that he wrecked what little moral power remained to them. They could not survive as an authentic liberal party while following his will in violating the fundamental principles of liberalism.

Political trading and maneuvering and the selfishness of *Interessenpolitik* became the dominant habit of political life. This method enabled the Chancellor, with the largest quantity of desired political favors at his disposal, to wield an influence unknown in British political life. He wished to school the parties, or even better the factions within each party, to come to the government as to a broker's shop to engage in a bargain over a special interest. They should concentrate on their own interests and leave to the Chancellor the responsibility for the national welfare. In the hands of a masterful tactician undeterred by moral scruples whenever the preservation of his personal power was at stake, the well-known autocratic technique of divide and rule succeeded brilliantly. The divine right of Bismarckian rule meant the degradation of the political parties. The second fundamental institution of a free people never overcame the characteristics or the reputation which Bismarck stamped upon it.

In the moral training of the German people in politics no events are more significant than those of Bismarck's conflicts with the Social Democrats and the Catholic church. They reveal the use of the full authority of the government against social and political groups which Bismarck feared might grow too powerful for him to control and manipulate.

In his persecution of the Social Democrats, Bismarck had the support of the upper classes on the usual grounds of the Marxian menace to property, morality, the new national unity. Whether legally sanctioned or illegally approved, the government's violations of the freedom of the press, of assembly, of the immunity of parliamentary members were so numerous and so ruthless that the Social Democrats lived precariously under arbitrary rule until Bismarck was overthrown. The most adored figure in the life of modern Germany thus gave the stamp of official approval to the most reactionary and authoritarian employer attitude toward the struggles of the proletariat for recognition. The official attitude and the social attitude of the upper classes toward the laborer in politics was set by a Junker statesman, a man more akin to the aristocrats of Russia than to the country gentlemen and the bourgeoisie of England or France.

For a combination of rationalistic and nationalistic reasons, enough liberals, especially in Prussia, backed Bismarck to enable him for several years to hound Catholic leaders as much as he did

Marxian ones. When he found that his attempt to coerce the church into a docile political instrument would not succeed, he began to retreat, while forcing as many concessions from the Catholic Centrist party as he could. But, as in the case of labor, by arousing popular mistrust of the Catholics during the first decades of the new Germany, he placed the stigma of a kind of second-class citizenship upon them.

The Chancellor lacked the respect for that sanctity of law which forms a third essential bulwark of a free people. His astuteness in interpreting the constitution or any particular law to suit his own momentary needs was so keen that it aroused admiration then and does so now. Inconsistency never troubled him. He might violate a law, then use the full influence of his office upon the courts to uphold his action. Since greatly increased opportunity for legal casuistry accompanied the vast expansion of legislation in the increasingly complex industrial society, Bismarck could with impunity encourage a practice which tended to weaken the moral foundations of law and promote arbitrariness.

Bismarck had certain personal habits of behavior in public life, habits also found among many of his aristocratic colleagues, which influenced the political behavior of the German people. These habits were antithetic to the ideals of bourgeois political behavior as manifested in countries like England and the Third French Republic. Whereas the bourgeois liberal ideal assumed a rational approach to a problem with a maximum effort to understand the other person's point of view and argument, Bismarck did not acknowledge any justice or reasonableness on the part of his opponent. He immediately transferred a political dispute into the sphere of a personal quarrel, and, making a caricature of his opponent's position, he accused his opponent of a personal attack. What began as a political discussion involving an honest difference of policies and aiming at an honorable and useful compromise soon became under the Chancellor's influence a heated dispute. Insignificant points quickly became crucial issues. A political debate took on the emotional quality of a menacing civil war. The opposition found itself accused of bad motives, insulted by extreme and even vicious language. It was always in the wrong; Bismarck was always in the right. If any blunder had been made, Bismarck threw the responsibility upon subordinates. He had a convenient memory and a flexible conscience; he could hate to vindictiveness, and even into the grave. The death of an honorable and distinguished opponent provided him with the occasion for one more public blast at the latter's character. Bismarck never understood the function of politics in modern society and never approved the sense of give-and-take, of compromise, of mutual respect, of representation of the many conflicting legitimate interests for which the function of a political body is to allow adequate scope. Bismarck transferred the political mores of a society based on caste distinctions, with the aristocracy at the top and always in the right, to the complex and fluid society of modern industrialism. He preserved and taught the German people political methods derived from the tough and ruthless ways of the Junker caste fighting in the political arena for its economic position and its social and political dominance. These methods derived from an *ancien régime* full of court intrigue, of duels and wars. Hence Bismarck's political behavior scarcely contributed to the education of the German people in the ways of free government. The Germans were to suffer for having been unified, ruled, and given their elementary political training by a Junker, even though he ranked as their greatest statesman.

The dismissal of Bismarck in 1890 occurred at a time when he was proposing to wreck the constitutional structure of the Reich set up two decades earlier by himself. Since he could no longer make it produce sufficiently humble obedience to his personal authority, he wished by a coup d'état to create a new constitution which would legalize the exercise of completely arbitrary power. It must be manifest that the hero of the German people was no longer *persona grata* to all elements. A few observers, even among conservatives, gauged accurately the effects of his political methods upon the Germans. One of them wrote in 1893 as follows:

You ask about Bismarck. . . . He is the most interesting figure one can imagine. I know no one more interesting; but this constant inclination to deceive people, this complete craftiness, is really repulsive to me; and when I wish to revive my spirits, I have to look to other heroes. To subordinate everything to expediency is in any case a terrible point of view, and with him everything is intermixed with so much of a personal nature and actually with nastiness, with the necessity for applause, with absolute faith in the justice of every one of his moods, of every fancy and of colossal rapacity. His genius manifest in every sentence enchants me again and again, and again and again destroys my doubts; but on calm reflection the doubts always return. One can never entirely trust him.*

The end of Bismarck's chancellorship, brought about not by the Reichstag but primarily by the Emperor, lifted the weight of this arbitrary personality from German government and society and released forces for freedom which had been struggling to emerge. Under his successors the institutions of parliamentary government, political parties, and a free press assumed increasing importance in national life. The German people vigorously participated in them and were learning to appreciate the ways of politics. If one contrasts their political naïveté in 1848 with their astuteness in 1914, the degree of their improvement is remarkable. In 1848 they did not know how to organize a political party; they knew nothing about party discipline and cohesiveness; their political leaders were all individualists; they did not know how to operate a representative assembly; they knew almost nothing about the need for a division of function within a party, about how to use committees in a party or in a representative assembly, about the value of letting certain ones speak for all on a particular subject; they knew nothing except in theory of the relation between the legislative and the executive organs of government. By 1914 they had learned the functioning of well-organized political parties and understood how to use parliamentary institutions, not merely in the Reich but in the separate states, for exerting such pressure upon the executive branch as to force its resignation. One cannot say that by the outbreak of World War I parliamentary responsibility had been achieved; but it did operate in some of the South German states, and in all German

---

*Erich Eyck, BISMARCK: LEBEN UND WERK, III, 626, quoting Theodor Fontane, Letter of 1893 (Zurich, 1941-44).

states and in the Reich the value of it had become manifest. The people at large had political means of expressing their wishes, they dared to use them, and they wished to enlarge their power.

It would be a mistake, however, to regard the improved use of politics and of representative governmental institutions as proof that all Germans were turning toward freedom. These institutions can also become means of defending vested interests of a conservative, authoritarian kind. The participants may learn nothing more about democratic ways from them than how to exploit them for undemocratic purposes. Whether they practiced real political freedom depended much upon economic and social interests and traditions and upon whether they knew how to live in freedom in nonpolitical respects.

In spite of certain authoritarian traits among the leaders and a large degree of docility and class consciousness among the followers, the Social Democratic party was buttressed by the free methods of trade unionism, adult education, cooperatives, and many other means. The German workers tried to practice freedom and equality in their economic organizations and in their social relations. They more nearly approached the American ideal of living democratically, not merely of governing democratically, than any other German group. They were more hostile to militarism, imperialism, and autocracy than any other elements, and they recognized that free government was essential for a free life.

The Catholic Centrist party shared much of the same democratic experience. Although the party included persons from all social classes and groups, it tended in general away from conservative control toward a somewhat democratic leadership chosen from the lower as well as the upper classes. The Catholics learned the ways of individual initiative, popular participation, responsible leadership through their trade unions, cooperatives, and especially through their many and varied social and religious organizations. Like the Social Democrats they knew how to reconcile and settle conflicts within their midst by reasonable means and a respect for divergent views. They produced masterly political leaders able to rely on an intelligent, disciplined, and alert party following; and while authoritarian elements continued to be far from negligible, the influence of political Catholicism lay on the whole in the direction of freedom.

At the other extreme from these two political and social elements stood the aristocrats and big landowners. Although forced to acquiesce in the existence of modern representative institutions of government, they had soon shown extraordinary political ability in utilizing the institutions for their own advantage. Confronted with the difficulties which large-scale agriculture suffered everywhere in the era of flourishing industrial capitalism, they used politics to supplement their declining economic force in the battle for the preservation of their position in German life. Political power afforded them the means of maintaining their dominant social and economic position. They needed tax favors, exorbitant tariffs on their products, rebates, and the like; and with the issue so vital, they fought political wars with Bismarckian vehemence. They were tough and ruthless, in many cases superb political tacticians, excellent intriguers, brilliant at exploiting court influence in their favor. They spoke and acted bluntly with the assurance that the court, army and, on the whole, the executive and the judiciary would support them. They were entrenched in the Prussian Landtag and government so firmly that nothing less than defeat in World War I dislodged them; and the power of Prussia was sufficient to block many acts of the Reich considered objectionable by them. They kept alive the Bismarckian methods of violent words and deeds, and by forcing the others to use their type of tactics they did more toward poisoning the political and social relations of the Germans than any other group.

Already by 1914 the bourgeoisie and the middle classes were showing strong signs of that political disintegration which was to continue until World War II. The upper bourgeoisie had, on the whole, come to be conservative in its political and social views and tended to align with the big agrarian and aristocratic elements. Intermarriage, common economic interests, common hostility toward the proletariat, fear of social conflicts, and a determination to retain their economic and social power with the aid of political influence kept them together with the aristocrats. In the big cities and in South Germany, however, the bourgeoisie was beginning to break away from this pattern of behavior in favor of genuine liberalism. It preferred responsible government not merely in the Reich but especially in Prussia, where a class system of voting kept reactionaries in power, and in a few southern states it was even willing to associate in a government with the Social Democrats. Many accepted social legislation much beyond the modicum of social insurance granted by Bismarck, and some rejected the Prussian practice of damning labor as unpatriotic and antisocial. The lower middle class sometimes aligned with these progressive elements, sometimes with the conservatives. It had not as yet degenerated into a state of chronic economic and political instability. But since the members of this class did not practice democracy in their social relations and were economically dependent upon the upper classes, they had almost no opportunity to develop the habits of a free people. They were relieved from some form of social, economic, or political pressure only in the polling booth with the secret ballot where the minimum of civic courage was required.

When the imperial court, the army, the government, the economic leaders, and the upper social groups all believe in and practice authoritarianism, not merely in politics and government but in social and economic affairs, one may well expect the schools and the intellectuals to reflect the same tendencies. Class distinctions dominated the educational system, with special types of schools for the lower classes and other types for the upper ones. The institutions of higher education trained loyal potential leaders in government and business, and entrance to these institutions became almost impossible for the poor. Patriotism and nationalism were standard intellectual fare to which imperialism was added; and both elementary school teachers and university professors had as a rule to be politically and socially conservative. Some called this attitude one of neutrality or indifference toward political party conflicts, a term which covered complete adulation of the Kaiser on the anniversary of his birthday and on every day condemnation of the Social Democrats and even in some areas of the Centrists. Scholarship tended to follow the authoritarian pattern in its methods and in its choice of content. Devotion to theory which justified things as they were kept pace with descriptive analyses of existing ways and institutions. Future bureaucrats were taught to accept things as they were. With rare exceptions like Max Weber, the number of original thinkers in the social sciences able and willing to criticize the existing order declined markedly, while the physical sciences developed brilliantly. The entire educational system rested on a closely controlled means of nationalistic conservative indoctrination through the primary schools, supplemented by training in docility during the years of compulsory service in the army.

The relation of the two churches toward the ruling system tended to be mixed. The Protestant church had been losing spiritual influence over the population for decades. The proletariat drifted almost entirely away from a church which openly supported the social ideals and practices of the upper classes, was even sometimes anti-Semitic, and failed to adjust to the needs of the developing world. Protestant pastors exerted themselves in chauvinistic organizations like the Pan-German League and blessed militarism for its teaching of obedience and physical cleanliness. The Catholic church proved to be much more aware of the existence of the proletariat and their problems. By developing clerics from all classes and serving the spiritual needs of all classes, it maintained a balance or understanding of the relationship between freedom and authoritarianism, preserved its influence in German society, and achieved the qualities and position which enabled it to become one of the bulwarks of the Weimar Republic.

If one belonged to good society before World War I, one was expected to conform to certain standards of behavior. Although the ruling emperor might be privately criticized, the Hohenzollern family had to be approved and some of its more militaristic members adored. Army officers enjoyed the highest social honor. Even in South Germany the snappy, hard-boiled elegance of the goose-stepping leaders came to be the quintessence of good form. Politics was considered as culturally and intellectually degrading and not as a topic of conversation in polite society, an attitude which tended to prevent the expansion of political interest and activity, especially among women and the middle classes. Sharp social distinctions had to be maintained toward the proletariat; the manner of speech differed from that of the proletariat, as did the character of social functions and even the selection of places to purchase goods and to enjoy oneself. The economic distinction might not be very great; the psychological difference was fundamental. The proletariat was expected to keep its place; the middle classes did not realize that by the same system they were kept in their places. In 1914 Germany remained a class society, with the upper elements— the monarchy, the military, and the bureaucracy—being under the authority of a few hundred families, interrelated by way of marriage, common membership on boards of directors, occupancy of top positions in the bureaucracy and the army, ownership of the press, and close connections with prominent educators and churchmen. The authoritarian regime regarded the future with confidence.

The upper classes nonetheless feared the outbreak of social conflicts. The Kaiser openly expressed his fear of the proletariat and ordered his troops to shoot any of his subjects who might have the temerity to attempt a rebellion. The upper classes failed to realize that with the rapid improvement in its standard of living the proletariat was seeking to find its place as a working class group in the existing order. While revolutionary in words, the proletariat was evolutionary in deeds, as was evidenced by its willingness to support the German war effort in 1914. It would have been satisfied, apparently, with the introduction of responsible parliamentary government, the formation of a free society like that in England or the United States, and the acceptance of the proletariat as respectable members. It sought to achieve the gains for Germany which the British, French, and Americans had made during the past century, and wished those reforms which are usually associated with the struggle of the bourgeoisie against the aristocracy.

Unfortunately for Germany, the ruling regime was determined to prevent this change toward democratization of society. It used the class struggle as a means of preserving its own authoritarian position in government and society. The bourgeoisie was caught in the class system into which it fitted so easily and which brought its members profits, the right to share political authority with the aristocracy, and protection against the dreaded menace of Social Democracy. The Bismarckian pattern of social and political control remained essentially unchanged, even though some defections in support of democracy occurred and some demands for an increased share of power came forward occasionally from the bourgeoisie.

The essential reason for the firm position of this authoritarian system prior to World War I could be seen in the results which the system had produced. All Germans felt pride in their unified, prosperous, and strong country. Most of them shared the belief that Germany and the Germans outranked in character and achievement any other European or indeed non-European people and that the present age in history received its dominant imprint from German culture. The contrast with the condition of Germany's neighbors —the low standard of living and backward governmental and political life of all peoples to the east and southeast, the apparent stagnation of French economy and population, the relative decline of Great Britain's economic and political position in the world— enhanced the pride of the late-comer in the society of great powers. The class character of German society fixed the pattern of thinking about the society of European nations. States and peoples were graded, and the Germans, although not yet accepting the view of the lunatic fringe of the nationalists about a super-man and super-folk, considered themselves to the the ablest, most vigorous, and most creative of them all.

International relations strengthened the hold of the authoritarian regime in Germany. They did so partly by virtue of wilful exploitation by the government. Bismarck and his successors on occasion inflated an international incident of no intrinsic significance into a major crisis for the sake of winning an election or rallying the public to their support. They could always utilize the prevalent nationalism in their favor; for the people of powerful Germany had adopted from Prussia the traditional belief that being in the center of Europe they were surrounded by enemies bent on their destruction. The Germans, newly unified, failed to perceive that what may have been true for Prussia did not apply to the strongest nation of the continent. Nonetheless, the popular belief benefited the conservatives by enabling them to point to the supposed menace of neighbor enemies as justification for the maintenance of militarism, an authoritarian government, and the social *status quo*. Any change, they argued in the time-honored fashion of their like, might provoke the enemies to attack and thereby endanger the existence of the country. The German people believed this danger real.

Further evidence of the health and efficiency of authoritarian Germany was presented by the astonishing capacity for carrying on a modern type of war. The nation seemed organized for war as much as for peace. Material prosperity, technical skill, physical health, and intellectual acumen were available to authorities who knew how to use them. The countries like Russia and Austria-Hungary that remained essentially under an *ancien régime* collapsed first. Democracies like France and Great Britain seemed ill-equipped and inefficiently organized for an emergency. Germany appeared to have the perfectly balanced society, one in which the vigorous elements of the *ancien régime* seemed blended with the best creations of bourgeois industrialism. The German leadership seemed the most efficient in its field of activity, the German industrialists, bureaucrats, laborers, soldiers, wives, and mothers in theirs; German institutions appeared to be adapted to the most productive and economical action of each group. Not even the Social Democrats could free themselves entirely from the prestige of this authoritarian ideal, and most of German society clung to it long after the reality had collapsed.

The effect of World War I upon the relative strength of freedom and authoritarianism in Germany cannot be summed up in a formula. The concentration of power incident upon the necessities of fighting set precedents in new institutions and habits for authoritarian rule which were essential as a basis for the rise of National Socialism. The war blended military and civilian methods and ideals to a degree not before experienced in German history and supplied the future Nazis with the pattern of a society organized exclusively for war. At the same time the growing aversion to the war aroused the proletariat and increasingly large elements of the middle classes and bourgeoisie to new recognition of the value of freedom from authoritarian control.

The postwar (1918-33) course of German history does not lend itself to adequate explanation in terms of class conflicts and material interests. The psychological effects of war, defeat, and revolution cut across class and occupational lines and left tensions which within a short time transformed the acceptance of freedom and democracy into a furious endeavor on the part of the old conservative forces and the lower middle class to destroy them. Groups picked up extreme ideals, of which German history had a copious variety, as a means of solving their problems; and the period is full of ists and isms, crisscrossing, merging, fighting, each with its own troubled history.

The Social Democrats, who supplied the force of the revolution, stopped with a transformation of government. Their leaders wished to establish a constitutional regime based on parliamentary control and the rule of law, and operating by way of political parties. They used these means to develop model instruments for handling labor-management relations and to transform the authoritarian state into a state concerned with the welfare of all its members. They established the conditions of intellectual and spiritual freedom, to which the response was immediate. The theatre, literature, and the arts flourished during the short life of the Weimar Republic as nowhere else in Europe. Educational reforms were vigorously discussed and experimental schools of a progressive type emerged. In spite of the recent war, the cultural ties with the rest of the world were closer than in any age since the time of Goethe. In internal organization and policy the Weimar Republic was endeavoring to align with Western democracies, and in its international relations it was striving to overcome German nationalism in favor of world cooperation and understanding. Democratic Catholics in the Centrist party and many of the middle classes and bourgeoisie supported this policy, and the world witnessed the extraordinary sight of political cooperation between Marxian Socialists and Catholic Centrists in the government of a democratic republic.

The Social Democrats and their new allies opposed a thorough social revolution with a fundamental change in the ownership of property and in the distribution of social power. Social Democrats in the revolutionary government used the old military leaders and forces to prevent the feeble attempts at the kind of revolution which, in theory, the workers had advocated for decades. The standards and ideals of the authoritarian groups had affected Socialist leaders like Ebert and Noske to the extent that they agreed on the necessity of preserving order. The war had not diminished the Social Democrats' faith in the essential reasonableness of man, and they apparently expected the former ruling elements suddenly to become converted to the same belief and to practice it. A democratic government thus established itself in a society which had little experience with democracy, which had suffered through four years of war and an accentuated form of authoritarian rule, and which was neither morally nor politically prepared for defeat. This society teemed with bitterness, inner conflicts, and fear. A majority was willing to accept democracy if it brought peace, full employment, and a high standard of living; that is, if it immediately established better living conditions than had obtained under the empire. The people, trained to look to others for leadership and to throw responsibility on them, expected a miracle to occur by the grace of the victorious and occupying Powers, with no more effort on their part than the formulation of a constitution and the erection of a new government. They did not know that they had to earn democracy; that they must practice democracy in every-day life, where it meant more than a formal structure of government and the secret ballot.

The Weimar Republic failed to teach all Germans that political parties, as well as all other organized groups, can live together in peace only by learning the ways of compromise, of respecting the views of others, of accepting defeat without recourse to violence. The Social Democrats and the Catholic Centrist party, and even certain middle class and bourgeois parties, had learned this elementary lesson; but the extreme groups on left and right, the Communists, the Nationalists, and all those elements rapidly turning to Nazism and similar organizations, never were willing to admit that their opponents might have some justice and truth on their side.

The course of developments during the Weimar Republic sadly disappointed almost everyone. When the miracle failed to appear, a large number of voters, especially from the lower middle classes, wandered from party to party, seeking a panacea, landing finally in National Socialism. The forces of conservatism and reaction revived and fought with their accustomed bitterness and ruthlessness to restore their control. Political freedom permitted them to do so. Economic interests re-established their affiliation with political groups. The Junkers and the big landowners remained as powerful economically as before and determined to regain through ardent nationalism their social and political dominance. In comparison with their prewar position they suffered under the handicap of having a Social Democratic laborer in place of the Kaiser and his court; but they soon found a thoroughly satisfactory substitute in Field Marshal von Hindenburg, president after 1925 of the German Republic. Loss of control by an authoritarian government and the lack of a disproportionate influence in the representative assemblies could not yet be overcome; but the bureaucracy, with the exception of a few departments, remained loyal to conservative ideals and never operated in a democratic way. Whenever a former army officer or other reactionary nationalist assassinated a democratic member of the Cabinet or political leader, or instigated a rebellion, the judges could be relied upon to free him entirely or impose a gentle sentence; after all, it would be said, he had killed from the finest patriotic motives. Most of the upper bourgeoisie, except for the Catholics, sided with the conservatives and financed the many patriotic groups bent on undermining or overthrowing the Weimar regime. The bourgeoisie disliked the so-called workers's republic, imposed, as most Germans believed, by the victorious Powers and alien to true Germanism. The numerous professional army officers, unemployed because of the Treaty of Versailles, provided invaluable men of action for these authoritarian groups and served efficiently as private and illegal adjuncts to the small professional army left to

Germany. The educational system continued to be organized mainly on a class basis, and teachers and professors remained on the whole as staunchly conservative and nationalistic as before the war.

The democratic forces had to contend not merely with these authoritarian powers. They confronted the problem common to every state, whether victor or vanquished, in the postwar period; namely, how to balance the necessity for large-scale governmental planning and action in order to cope with the numerous and unprecedented difficulties in economic and cultural life with the necessity for leaving an equally wide area for freedom of action on the part of individuals and private groups in order to allow the people the opportunity for training themselves in the ways of freedom and democracy. The Germans had to learn not to look to the state for guidance on all matters; they had to learn to rely on individual and private activities in civic affairs; they had to transform the bureaucracy into a servant, tolerant, at the least, of cordial relations with a respected and confident public; they had to overcome an awesome deference toward officialdom and to bring themselves to the point of taking the initiative or participating vigorously in affairs which they had formerly left to the government and bureaucracy. The problem acquired enhanced significance in Germany where statesmanship of rare quality would have been needed to prevent the powerful authoritarian elements from exploiting present needs for the revival and accentuation of traditional authoritarian forms of control as the sole means of salvation. The war, defeat, and revolution left vast difficulties on a national scale which an authoritarian government seemed most competent to handle. Every inducement, reasonable as well as emotional, seemed to lead the Germans, unaccustomed to self-government, to throw all their pressing burdens upon the state. Taxes were high while wages and salaries were low; the Weimar Republic was blamed. Social Security was expensive; the state was blamed. Foreign markets did not materialize; the state had failed to do its duty. Labor conflicts arose; if the state interfered it did not settle them properly or fairly, if it did not interfere, it should have. Credit was tight; the state should help out. Bankruptcy threatened; the state must save the firm. The schools must be left alone, the schools must be reformed; the state was blamed for doing one or the other. Newspapers published too much scandal; the state should forbid it. And so on and on. The times were full of uncertainty—as to economic conditions, markets, sources of raw materials, credit; as to social standards and social power; as to political control; as to governmental structure. It seems true that the majority of Germans disliked with more or less intensity the Weimar government and constitution and all that they stood for; but the opponents of Weimar could not go back to the old regime, and they did not know what kind of a new order they wanted. The realistic and immediate problems caused them to fight for control of the powerful machinery of government in order to use it for special interests. Those who thought that they had most to gain from reconquering the government, namely, the authoritarian groups, most loudly asserted their nationalism. The supporters of a democratic Germany had increasing difficulty in maintaining themselves.

The emotional currents of the Weimar period were rich and varied, with moral standards in flux. The war had brutalized many groups and individuals ready for any sadistic action. It had accustomed even the rest of society to acquiesce in legal arbitrariness and murder in times of stress, and, although most were appalled at the thought of another war and wished the lawlessness to stop, the odor of blood remained in the air. Almost all Germans believed that they had lost the war unjustly. Even more of them refused to accept the thesis of German guilt and regarded the Treaty of Versailles as a wicked imposition. When the inflation wiped out the savings of a lifetime, made some unjustly rich and others unjustly poor overnight, the economic order of life seemed shattered. The economic depression of 1930-31 completed the work of disillusionment. Germans came to believe that this was a world of hazard, of no fixed principles, a world in which the individual confronted overwhelming, arbitrary powers. Forces beyond one's control appeared too strong. The moral order seemed to have degenerated into moral chaos. The rule of law had given way to arbitrariness. Reason could not be trusted as a guide, for it had succumbed to the forces of blind and cruel chance. Intelligence offered no salvation. Compromise failed when others would not compromise; or if agreement was reached, some alien force or unpredictable economic crisis might nullify the result. Democracy meant, therefore, so it seemed, the continued shackling of Germany for the advantage of mean, selfish foreign Powers. Millions of Germans came to believe that the country could be saved only by repudiating the Weimar system and turning to a new messiah, a man of miracles, a leader, arbitrary and cruel, determined and ruthless, like the rest of the world. The problems of the Germans as individuals and as a people seemed insoluble without such a leader. Nationalism arose like a flame to help the Germans escape from freedom, to guide them into the hysteria of Nazism.

The Germans accepted National Socialism as a last act of desperation. A nation which appreciated its own excellent qualities and high abilities thought its existence menaced by chaos. It could not understand the reason for this plight and refused to acquiesce. Millions of Germans from all classes and occupations felt the crisis to be so acute that the Nazis were quickly transformed from a small group of crackpots into a mass party led by a messiah determined upon action to restore the vigor and the rightful glory of the German people. The ingredients of National Socialism were derived in sufficient strength from the German past to be acceptable as German. The *Führerprinzip* enjoyed the traditional prestige of centuries of absolute or strong monarchism, of Bismarckian authoritarianism, and of the traditions and habits of military and even bureaucratic command. It had been practiced, in an appropriate form, by Krupp, Stumn, and many other big industrialists. The new popular element in it was exalted as a sign of democratic equality and became immediately a powerful asset accepted even by the upper classes. The Germans also knew that in every crisis among every people the executive head becomes increasingly important as the instrument for quick and effective action. The relegation of parliament to an insignificant position seemed necessary and was fully approved by the millions of conservatives who had never liked representative government and by the middle classes and even many of the workers who cared less about it than about steady employment. Responsible representative government had had a short history, from 1919 to 1933, and had scarcely been crowned with success. The Germans were accustomed to a wide range of governmental authority, and in the crisis the individual wished the state to take even more responsibility away from him. The absence of tradition of private initiative and responsibility in civic affairs among most of the people and the dislike of politics and political parties as degrading influences led them to reject the potentialities of the Weimar Republic in favor of the wild promises of Nazism. They lacked democratic safeguards in the habits and standards of their private lives against the enticement of a seemingly easy way out of an unexpected and overwhelming crisis like that of the world economic depression. Certainly for some years until the destructive qualities of Nazism became apparent, few manifested any interest in defending moral principles against the nihilism of the National Socialist.

The qualities which German tradition regarded as the highest virtues became means of totalitarian domination. The Germans made a fetish of order, cleanliness, performance of duty, efficiency in craft or profession, concentration on the business in hand without interference in affairs about which they knew little, being obedient to officers and officials and to the law irrespective of the validity or morality of the order, ardent love of the nation and supreme loyalty to it. All peoples of our civilization have these traits in varying degrees, but in Western democracies they are balanced by a strong sense of civic responsibility and of individual worth as a citizen. In no other country than Germany did such a combination of qualities obtain on such a broad scale, qualities which in favorable circumstances could be exploited to the ruin of a people.

One important line of German political and social philosophy for at least a century and a half had been basically concerned with the problem of the relation of the individual and the state. Scholars and popular writers at all levels of intelligence had discussed the subject. It permeated the cheap pamphlet literature which Hitler read as an embittered, unemployed ex-soldier. At times of prosperity the rights of the individual might be emphasized; but at every period of crisis—the Napoleonic era, 1848, the 1860's, the Bismarckian era, World War I, the economic depression of 1930-31, the Nazi seizure of power—the belief in the subordination of the individual to the welfare of the nation-state became widespread. This exaggeration seems logical and understandable for a crisis situation where the individual finds no way to solve his problems alone and throws himself upon the mercy of the state. The view forms the core of nationalistic thought in every country, France, England, Italy, Russia, Germany, or any other. It is the peculiar fate of German history, however, that the idea, derived easily from a class society struggling to maintain hierarchy, suited nicely the needs of the upper classes, especially the monarchy and the aristocrats, in their effort to keep control over the rest of the population. Since they dominated, or believed that with a little more action they could restore their domination over the lower classes, they kept alive the ideal of the superior interests of the state over those of the individual.

When National Socialism arose, it adopted for its own purposes this rich tradition. For the first time in history a nation sought to organize and run itself according to the ideals of nationalism. The process of nationalism which characterized European history after the French Revolution thereby reached its culmination. As stated above, the National Socialists could have found most of their ideals in the nationalistic writings of any country; there is nothing peculiarly German in them. No other people, however, has attempted to realize these ideals, for in no other country has the combination of conditions, inherited and present, been comparable to that which gave National Socialism its opportunity. Only one further step is possible in the unfolding of nationalism and of authoritarianism. That step may be described as national bolshevism. Although one strong faction wished to go so far, the National Socialists were unable to force the German people into the final act of destruction of their social and institutional heritage.

It would be wrong to conclude that Nazism grew inevitably from the German past. This theory would imply a fatalism which is entirely out of place in any serious study of history. A careful

analysis of the events of 1932-33 shows that at that time a substantial majority of the German people favored an extraordinary
increase in governmental authority necessary to solve their problems but opposed National Socialism, that this majority was increasing, and that the recession of the economic crisis would have
entailed further losses of Nazi popular support. A relatively small
group of Junkers, industrialists, and militarists actually achieved
Hitler's appointment as Chancellor and utilized the senility of President von Hindenburg to accomplish its purpose. The group expected to control the Nazis and to exploit the Nazi power for its
own purposes; but the National Socialists proved too clever and too
ruthless for it, giving the next twelve years their own imprint. It
would also be wrong to equate the conservative authoritarianism
of the Hohenzollerns, Bismarck, the Junkers, the big industrialists,
and the army officers with National Socialist authoritarianism. The
conservatives believed in and practiced authoritarianism as a means
of preserving their social, economic, and political status, a status
quite different from that of Nazism. Their way of life included respect for at least some of the Christian virtues and for the qualities
of their own type of cultured personality. It implied a certain reasonableness and a disinclination on the whole to run desperate risks.
Perhaps one may counter by asserting that totalitarianism in all its
fulness and with its extreme ruthlessness lay dormant in these groups
and awaited the utilization of a Hitler. The growing evidence does
not bear out this accusation. Rather it points to a milder view that
these conservatives sympathized strongly with a popular totalitarian movement, the full import of which they did not understand,
that their nationalism and their craving for power induced them
to take a chance with Hitler, and that the authoritarian forms of
their own thinking and acting and of those of the German people
made possible the easy acceptance of National Socialism. The
obedience of the German conservatives and all other elements to the
Nazis through twelve years of hell does not prove the identity of all
the German people with National Socalism. It merely reveals how
politically irresponsible two generations of conservative authoritarianism had left a great nation and how susceptible the people were

to nationalistic and military success, how unable they were to distinguish between a form of authoritarianism in the old Christian tradition which might have helped to solve their problems without violating the ideals and standards of Western culture and the violent, sadistic ultra-nationalism of Nazi nihilism.

Few Germans seemed to regret the disappearance of freedom after 1933. The overwhelming majority of the population either joyfully accepted dictatorship or acquiesced in it. While history helps to explain this fact, it also offers the assurance that the Germans have not always approved authoritarianism, that they have not always been nationalistic, indeed, that a large percentage opposed vigorously the Hohenzollern authoritarianism and militarism and preferred the ideals of freedom. History shows that on several occasions the adherents to freedom were powerful enough almost to gain a decisive victory. Historical conditions differed markedly in Germany's development over the past century from those of Britain and France and produced the peculiar mixture of elements from the *ancien régime*, modern industrial capitalism, and mass social movements which reached its fullest authoritarian form in National Socialism. History offers the assurance that under new and favorable conditions the Germans have the elements of a liberal and even democratic tradition of sufficient strength to encourage and assist them in turning toward democracy. There is no historical reason to doubt that they are able and would be willing to learn the ways of living in social and political freedom; but it is equally clear that their experience since national unification does not offer them much positive guidance. Conservative authoritarianism provides no assurance against a resurgence of totalitarianism. The fate of the Weimar Republic demonstrates that democracy depends upon more than a free constitution and free political instruments; it must permeate likewise individual conduct and social relations. It is this conception of democracy that the Germans must for the first time and on a national scale learn how to practice.

Chap. 2 Resistance and Repression Under the Nazis

WOLFGANG H. KRAUS and GABRIEL A. ALMOND

Was there a German resistance? One is impressed with the frequency with which this topic is discussed in postwar German newspapers and periodicals and with the pathos and excitement of many of the polemics. Perhaps there is an element of health in this tendency on the part of many Germans to seek for something in the heritage of the past which was both German and hostile to National Socialism. History is one of the most important elements in prognosis, and prognosis in turn is one of the most important factors in the morale of the sick. A patient who is told that he has a bad heart but good lungs faces the future with more confidence than the one who learns that both organs are defective. A Germany burdened with the guilt of the last decade may find more courage to face a harsh future if it can find in itself some valid inclination to justice and peace which stood its ground against National Socialism. While the previous chapter attempted to evaluate the strength and qualities of the German democratic tradition in the fuller canvas of history, the present chapter is concerned with the fate of these tendencies under the Nazi terror.

CONTROL BY REPRESSION

Two main limiting factors stood in the way of the development of the anti-Nazi opposition into a coherent popular "counterrevolution." The first one was no doubt the political lethargy and the

33

traditional authoritarianism of the German masses. This impassivity was a complex phenomenon which can neither be satisfactorily explained by the simple popularized reference to the German national character nor to the socio-economic situation alone. It is more easily described than explained. A German Catholic writer has recently illuminated one significant facet in it when he wrote: ". . . everyone had learned in school and church that he might have to die a hero's death for his fatherland in a war, but to mount the barricades for freedom at home—for that nobody had ever found the decisive word. Fatherland and democracy had not become a living unity for the Christian citizen. Political education in the second republic must be clearly focused on the goal of such a living unity."[1] A combination of elements conspired to produce this condition: the political and social disorientation of the masses which became accentuated during the period of the depression, the skillfully exploited habit of obedience to "law and authority," which persisted even where law had become a mere façade for lawlessness and authority a caricature of itself, and the deep involvement of powerful interests in the continuity of the complex web of government in an industrial society.

The second barrier preventing the development of a popular counterrevolution against the Nazis was the extraordinary apparatus of control and repression which confronted those Germans who retained their freedom of thought and were determined to act in accordance with their convictions. It took the dictatorship about five years to build up this apparatus to its highest and most ruthless effectiveness. By 1938 the machinery of control had become completely comprehensive and penetrating. Its objective was, first, to condition, and next, to direct and manipulate the attitudes of all members of society to such an extent that nonconformity would require unusually vigorous, and thus more easily detected, conviction and practical effort. At this point a machinery of repression came into play, the basic principle of which was that every person or group whose antecedents or attitudes did not fully coincide with the established pattern must be regarded as an actually or potentially dangerous enemy of the rulers.

The mechanics and policies of the principal conditioning and manipulating agencies of the Nazis, education and propaganda, have frequently been described. The repressive system, more especially in its political police and intelligence phases, had by its very nature operated so much more under the cloak of secrecy that only now are we beginning to obtain a full-scale view of its operations. This apparatus of police intelligence and repression, supplemented by that of the thoroughly coordinated criminal courts and, ultimately, by the entire party machinery, was carefully designed to meet the challenge of any kind of dissent. The scope and character of the German resistance to National Socialism can therefore be most adequately understood if it is related not only to the functioning of these controls but also to their effect on the German public mind.

By the time the war broke out, the entire German political police machinery had been concentrated in one vast agency, the National Security Office (*Reichssicherheitshauptamt*, abbreviated as RSHA), which operated under Himmler's supervision in the Ministry of the Interior. The Gestapo on the one hand, and the Security Service (*Sicherheitsdienst*, SD) on the other, had become solidly entrenched as its mainstays. This was the culmination of a considerable development in the course of which National Socialism had progressively "coordinated" and centralized the hitherto parallel and relatively independent state and the local police forces in Germany in order to weld them into an effective tool of the dictatorship.[2]

Since 1936, after some jockeying for power against Goering, Himmler, already then the head of the Elite Guard (SS), had emerged as the chief of all German police. In this capacity he rearranged all governmental police services (on the national, state, and local levels) under two major divisions, the Regular Police or *Ordnungspolizei* (ORPO) and the Security Police or *Sicherheitspolizei* (SIPO). The Security Police comprised the established Criminal Police or Detective Force, *Kriminalpolizei* (KRIPO), and the Secret State Police, *Geheime Staatspolizei*, (GESTAPO). As the head of the SS, Himmler had also at his disposal the separate Security Service (SD) of the SS, a special Party spying machinery which had been developed into an efficient tool under the management of Reinhard Heydrich who was later to emerge into notoriety. When in 1936 Himmler had reached the top he had already made his SD chief, Heydrich, the head of the SIPO. But only on September 27, 1939, after the outbreak of the war, were SD and SIPO officially linked when these government and Party police agencies were coordinated within the National Security Office.

Regional control over all police services in each army corps area was vested in Himmler's representatives, the so-called "Superior SS and Police Leaders," whose operations became especially important with the outbreak of the war.

Within this large-scale organization it was the Gestapo, the Security Service, and the increasingly indoctrinated and "politicized" Detective Force (*Kriminalpolizei*) which, sometimes designated as the "State Protective Corps," constituted the prime buttress of power. While the influence of the SD over the other two services appears to have grown steadily, a real fusion or integration of Party and government political police apparatus does not appear to have been completed.

If one bears in mind considerable overlapping and the constant tendency, especially of the SD, to expand powers and activities, this State Protective Corps operated under a certain rough division of labor.

The SD, operating out of Office III[3] of the RSHA, was, within the borders of the Reich, primarily an elaborate and comprehensive intelligence and spy service. In the occupied areas, where it functioned in special units known as *Einsatzstaebe*, it was also a murder organization frequently charged with the brutal and unvarnished "liquidation" of prisoners and conquered populations as the evidence of the Nuremberg trial has shockingly brought into the open. Within the Reich, it developed from the spy organization of a revolutionary partly ruthlessly battling its way to power into an intelligence agency whose ultimate ambition it apparently was to guide, in the manner of an organized elite, the policies and administration of the Nazi state at war. Even after its joining with the RSHA the SD had retained its character as a party agency which served both Party and government. Documentary evidence shows that, certainly as late as 1937 and 1938 and possibly later, regional SD offices, after having investigated the activities of the several "internal enemy" groups, ranging from Free Masons to Socialists, Conservatives, and churches, on occasion not only supplied information to the rival Gestapo but also participated in police operations which were undertaken by that organization whose task was primarily "executive."

However, the compilation of general domestic intelligence and morale reports, which in the course of time became increasingly comprehensive and ambitious in scope, was the most important activity of the SD. These reports were initiated or, at least, regularized by an order of January 4, 1937 and, shortly thereafter, had become bi-weekly and quarterly reports. The original order described their objective as the furnishing of "information for the Reich Leader SS, the Government and the Party leadership on the political situation in the Reich and the morale of the people." From the outset no efforts were spared to make these reports as authentic and comprehensive as possible. The older Gestapo intelligence reports were regarded as inferior because they had been essentially simple progress reports. In 1940, Dr. Werner Best, the principal SS lawyer, summarized the SD's objective as the thorough exploration "of the background and activities of the great ideological archenemies of National Socialism and the German people, in order to facilitate a determined and effective effort for the annihilation of these enemies." By 1942, before a gathering of the Baden SD, its chief was far more inclusive in describing the purposes of his organization. First, he claimed, it was

. . . to support, advise and guide the government. In this connection I should mention that during the last meeting of the National Defense Council the problems posed by the SD were completely in the forefront and were described by Goering as excellently solved.

The second task, which is at least as great, is the raising of the war potential through the guidance and observation of government measures and decrees and their reception, and by raising the spiritual burden of our fellow-citizens through the guidance media of press, film, radio, propaganda, theatre, etc. . . .

That it is extremely important to report the people's morale, perhaps daily or almost hourly during the war, is absolutely evident. The SD has the job to help prevent all the mistakes which during the war of 1914-18 happened in the various government agencies, and thus led to a morale defeat at the hands of the enemy. Often the government, as the people see it, looks incomprehensible, despite our work. I mention the Hess case. . . . Because of the great importance of our task it is a matter of course that our reporting has to be completely substantiated and in accordance with the facts. . . .

The morale reports of the SD achieved a surprising degree of candor, so much so that they would not only criticize occasional government measures in terms of the popular reaction but also, in quite specific terms, the acts and activities of men highly placed in Party or government. Thus, for instance, Goebbels' propaganda measures often came in for acrimonious dissection when the SD reported on the people's response. A similar candor manifested itself in the elaborate, and sometimes alarmist, recitals of oppositional activities (with a strong apprehension of church influence permeating most of them). Such accounts would be bolstered with all manner of evidence, such as extracts from conversations, speeches, or sermons; current anti-Nazi jokes; as well as surveys of undercurrents among the several social, political, and religious groupings of the community.

The SD field agencies, the principal gathering points of intelligence, consisted in the final stage of Regional Offices (SD-*Leitabschnitte*) and District Offices (SD-*Abschnitte*), in addition to the local Branch Offices (known as SD-*Hauptaussenstellen* or *Aussenstellen*, depending on their significance). The organization of the lower echelons roughly followed the model of Office III, naturally becoming quite simple and compact on the local level because of the severe restrictions on full-time personnel. For this was not a large organization in terms of its full-time staff. Ohlendorff, the head of Office III of RSHA, has stated that the central directing body in that agency never exceeded eighty to ninety persons and that, in the end, it had shrunk to thirty. SD personnel throughout the Reich amounted, according to a statement made in 1942, to nine thousand, one third of whom had at that time been assigned to duty in the

Eastern zones of occupation. What it lacked in numbers, the SD doubtless sought to supply in quality. Its directing group must have at least had more than its share of zealous Party "intellectuals," if one may judge from the quality of their internal memoranda controversies which have survived.

In addition, extensive use was made of confidential agents, so-called *Vertrauensmaenner* (undercover agents), who according to Ohlendorff were recruited from among "the best and most reliable persons in all localities and occupations, in order to win them over for reporting from their special sphere of experience." In a large urban center like Munich, for example, the SD had several hundred such operatives at its disposal. While the majority of such informants was taken on by local branches, it appears that also regional offices and Office III itself did not disdain the practice for the purpose of cross-checking results. Many of these men no doubt regarded themselves more as agents of some national Gallup poll[4] than as informers, since they were primarily expected (in the regime's latter years) to give their appraisals of common attitudes and morale in particular groups and localities. While they received no salaries, they apparently did receive compensation for expenses or special inducements and gratuities in order to maintain their morale. According to one regional police chief, Heydrich had once pointed out in a lecture that "the organization of V-men was based on the voluntary cooperation of persons who were convinced of the necessity of such an establishment."

In effect, this elaborate organization produced what unquestionably constituted both the most comprehensive and the most objective morale reports in Germany.[5] The local reports prepared twice a week on general morale and once a week on the various special phases of social activity (*Lebensgebiete*) filtered upwards through channels, were pruned, edited, consolidated and integrated at each level, and finally circulated as secret inside reports at regular intervals among top government and Party agencies under the title "Messages from the Reich" (*Meldungen aus dem Reich*). Such general reports were supplemented, from time to time, by special reports of which a particularly elaborate one, dealing with all phases of war morale, was ordered in detailed outline in February, 1942, when the seriousness of the war had begun to strike home.

The Gestapo was in charge of actual police operations of a broadly political character, with the accent on "measures to prevent activities inimical to the state." It had, in effect, sweeping authority for the arrest, detention, and liquidation of any and all whom it regarded as actual or potential enemies of the regime. This authority, it must be remembered, had been unrestrained by any legal controls since 1936. Office IV of the Berlin RSHA constituted Gestapo headquarters. Its subdivisions included Opposition and its Repression, Central Registry, Foreigners (mostly involving anti-Nazi movements), Counter Intelligence, Border Control, and Intelligence (designated as *Nachrichtendienst*, N), apparently initiated in 1942.[6] The Gestapo's field organization was in all essentials analogous to that of the SD for which it had actually served as a model. As the primary operating branch of the political police systems, the Gestapo boasted of a much larger personnel than the SD. According to Kaltenbrunner's testimony during the Nuremberg trial, Office IV was staffed with 3,000 officials in the higher and intermediate ranks in Berlin alone and a total of approximately 40,000 throughout Germany. This, of course, did not include the army of informers and stool pigeons which had been built up by the Gestapo in the course of years. Their number was apparently much larger than in the case of the SD, owing to the fact that the several divisions of the local Gestapo offices were in the habit of recruiting their informers separately. We are told, for instance, that the Intelligence division N in Hamburg had 500 and Bremen 150 to 200 V-men. It was evidently Gestapo policy to have as many informants as possible and to check up on their work by duplication of coverage.

Despite the strict discipline and intensive indoctrination in this political police organization, it did not escape the effects of the general popular demoralization which became especially noticeable in late 1943 and 1944. Certain rivalries and tensions between Gestapo and SD, which had always been covered up in the official re-

ports by an ostentatious emphasis on the closeness of their cooperation, began to play a more significant role under these circumstances—although not enough to give real comfort to the opposition. Internal repression had to be resorted to. In some places
Gestapo officials were called together each week during this period
and were treated to a recital of punitive measures recently taken
against Gestapo officers.

The Detective Force, operating out of Office V of the RSHA,
was charged with the remaining police work involving criminal
offenses. Its character, too, had been thoroughly transformed in
keeping with the policy of the regime. A growing emphasis on
"crime prevention" simply stood for the ruthless persecution of
"undesirable elements." Gestapo and Kripo received essentially the
same indoctrination, and there was a good deal of transferring from
one service to the other in addition to some officers holding positions simultaneously in both. In 1938, SS qualification became a
prerequisite for recruitment and many Detective Force members
were given SS rank, especially during the war years. Yet the force
retained a quota of the older policemen among whom there were
not a few who had never lost their regard for the standards of law
and common decency which they had acquired in an earlier regime.
It is apparent that, despite the close cooperation with the more
specifically political police agencies, the persistence of older non-
Nazi (and sometimes anti-Nazi) elements in the ranks of the Detective Force on occasion resulted in tensions and even in the sabotage of Gestapo or SD-initiated action.

One of the last chiefs of the Detective Force, Arthur Nebe, was
possibly a good example of such "deviations." Testimony during
the Nuremberg trial has shown that, despite his SS rank and his
continuous association with Nazi police work, he maintained connections with anti-Nazis from an early date.[7] He was finally involved in preparations for the attempt on Hitler of July 20, 1944.
Secret orders had gone out over his signature instructing the Kripo
to arrest Gestapo and SD officials.

Associated with these major police agencies were others of less
importance, some of which were barely known even in the Third

Reich itself. There was, for instance, the closely guarded "Research Office of the Air Ministry" which, as it seems, was nothing less than a special super-secret information service under Goering's control. It specialized in the wire-tapping control of the German telephone system in addition to a close surveillance of postal and telegraphic communications. Its Division V comprised the "State Security" section which operated in close connection with Gestapo, SD, and the Wehrmacht Counter-Intelligence. It had the special assignment to provide additional surveillance over persons who had been described as suspect by Gestapo, SD, or Counter-Intelligence. While it may have been intended primarily as a subsidiary for these other agencies, it is clear that Goering also availed himself of its services against his personal rivals, such as Goebbels.

Such police organizations constituted the hard core of the Nazis' control mechanism. It was reinforced by further protective layers, with the SS and the Party's own machinery of course as important control devices in their own right.

The traditional instruments of legal control also had been geared into the totalitarian machinery. The ordinary criminal courts, essentially deprived of genuine independence shortly after 1933, had been put under increasing pressure in the following years. Moreover, criminal cases involving major or political offenses were in large measure withdrawn from the jurisdiction of the ordinary criminal courts and placed into the hands of either the Special Courts (*Sondergerichte*), composed of handpicked judges and prosecutors, or of the so-called People's Tribunal (*Volksgericht*), a central circuit instrumentality of Party terror which handled the most important political crimes under the chairmanship of Freisler.

The fiction of judicial independence had long been maintained. Hitler's Reichstag speech of April 26, 1942, while it attested to the fact that even then there still were judges and other civil servants who did not quite understand their proper place in the Third Reich, effectively stripped away the last pretense:

I . . . expect the judiciary to get it into their heads that the nation does not exist for their sake, but that they exist for the nation. The world to which Germany belongs will not be allowed to perish just so that a formal conception of law may live. Germany must go on living no matter what conventional interpretation of the law may say to the contrary. From now on, I am going to intervene in these matters myself, and I shall remove from office any judge who manifestly does not know what the time demands. . . In times like these there are no self-sufficient elements among us, with old vested privileges. We are, all of us, but the humble servants of the people's interests.[8]

Contemporary SD morale reports show how the legal profession was quick to understand and also to resent its final strangulation. A characteristic report from Leipzig related that according to the opinion in legal circles "the Fuehrer's speech severely damaged the reputation of the administration of justice. Henceforth there would no longer be any just, but only repressive judges. . . ." To prove the decline of the judiciary in the public esteem, one worker is cited in the same report as saying: "The leader is quite right. The lawyers should all be shot or sent to the front."

When Dr. Thierack became the new Reich Minister of Justice in 1942, as successor of Guertner and Schlegelberger, it was no accident that he was the first bona fide Nazi to hold this position. Armed with virtually unlimited special powers he set about to make the administration of criminal justice an effective adjunct of the streamlined machinery of terror.[9] "Circular Letters" containing the Minister's instructions to judges and prosecutors, the ascendancy of the Gestapo in the prosecution's preparation of political cases, and the institution of special controls over the disposition of pending cases were conspicuous features of the final political "coordination" of German justice. Although there were some courageous men who silently attempted to stem the tide, there is no doubt that the growing pressure was effective enough in most cases. Dr. Rudolf Flach, President of the Bavarian District Court in Kempten, described some of his experiences in the following statement:

All cases of wartime trade violations, adultery of wives whose husbands were at the front, sexual relations with P.W's and all cases in which a Party member was involved, had to be reported to the higher authorities by the court with a statement of the sentence proposed. From above, instructions as to the proper sentence would be returned. I always passed these directives on to the judges with the flowery phrase; 'Reserving your own judicial discretion in the light of fresh evidence obtained in the oral proceedings.' In this fashion, a direct pressure on the judges was to be prevented, though some weak characters were of course influenced. Hitler's speech of April 26, 1942, in which he threatened the judges with general dismissal, and made the whole judiciary a prostitute of his propaganda, while ostensibly upholding its independence (?), struck like a bomb. I am happy to say that all the judges in my jurisdiction, even those who regarded National Socialism as a necessary evil, shook their heads and combined to oppose the new dispensation so that the whole effort came to nothing.(?)

Yet, he continues in the next sentence: "The Fuehrer's orders were only carried out to the extent that actual criminals were given harsher sentences than before. . . ."

We get at least a hint of Thierack's "new order" in practice from the Minister's own "progress report" of August, 1944 which reproduces some of the statistical evidence:

In accordance with the commission given to me by the Fuehrer to administer justice, to proceed in time of war with the severest means against traitors, saboteurs and other undesirable elements, those committing crimes of violence and antisocial habitual criminals . . . . the number of death sentences has increased continually since the outbreak of the war. The total figures for this period are stated below:

DEATH SENTENCES

1939	99
1940	926
1941	1391
1942	2660
1943	5336[10]

A breakdown of the figures for 1943 (which comprise both Germans and foreigners) showed that 1945 or 32 per cent of the total involved treason, while only 938 cases or 17 per cent were classified as dangerous criminals (thieves, swindlers, profiteers from blackout and war conditions) and 182 or 3 per cent as involving the looting of bombed houses.

Count Helmuth von Moltke, a bitter anti-Nazi who was doomed to fall a victim of the terror in the end himself, possessed good information as legal adviser to the High Command. In 1942 he wrote an English friend in a letter which was successfully smuggled out that "the number of Germans killed by legal process in November was 25 a day through the judgments of civil courts and at least 75 a day by judgments of the courts-martial; numbers running into hundreds are killed daily in concentration camps without any pretense of trial."[11] In the light of such figures Thierack's official statistics appear like a singularly self-effacing understatement.

It can be seen that certain factors were especially responsible for the effectiveness of the system as a whole. Little was left to chance. The control machinery eventually became as comprehensive as the activities of the community itself, so that little could slip through its meshes. The older theories of the police as an agency of safety and constructive prevention had been superseded by a new doctrine which exalted its role as political shock troop and advance guard of the embattled nation. The change had been initiated well before the outbreak of the war, but wartime regulations drastically advanced it from year to year.

As has been shown, the police organizations were not only manned with full-time personnel. They succeeded in enlisting large numbers of unpaid or partially remunerated "volunteer" informers of all kinds. Until fairly late, both Party members and even average non-Party folk could be used as "patriotic" agents who were in some cases probably convinced that they were doing their patriotic duty by offering their services, while in many more they expected substantial advantages in return. The ubiquity of the informer contaminated all fibers of the community and poisoned its human relations. "Can you imagine," wrote Count Moltke in 1942, "what it means to work as a group, when you cannot use the telephone, when you are unable to post letters, when you cannot tell the names of your closest friends to your other friends for fear that one of them might be caught and might divulge the names under pressure?"[12] He might have added: for fear that one of them might turn out to be a traitor or have one in his family.

Most importantly, this elaborate machinery of control and compulsion was surrounded by a fringe of terror and fear which was symbolized by the unholy triad of Gestapo, SS, and concentration camp. It must be remembered that until shortly before the war, certainly until the annexations of Austria and Czechoslovakia, the population of concentration camps consisted exclusively of Germans, both non-Jewish and Jewish, and largely identifiable as dissenters and oppositionists. The indiscriminate arrests of Jews began rather late—the earlier persecution took mostly different forms. Already in 1933, there were forty concentration camps. Their number steadily increased from then on. It has been estimated that the nine major camps alone housed, between 1933 and 1939, an average of 100,000 Germans. The turnover may be gathered from the fact that of the 22,000 inmates of Sachsenhausen in November, 1938, between 20 and 25 per cent were dead four months later.[13] Although only a small number knew in detail about the conditions in the concentration camps, rumors and half-knowledge provided powerful deterrents. Those who did emerge from those camps had their mouths most effectively sealed. They very rarely told of their experiences because they feared retaliation against themselves or their next-of-kin. A stark fear of the unknown or partly known, enhanced by the observable severity of official legal punishment, gripped the average man, increased the demonstrable power of the control agencies, and covered up possible gaps in their network.

It is quite clear that the Nazi authorities deliberately utilized the psychology of terror. At a Passau staff meeting for officials of the RSHA Office III, Division B (in charge of "Germanic" affairs, including Nordic occupied areas), SS Colonel von Loew explained in terms of "sweet reasonableness":

Fear is the cheapest, but also the least reliable method for securing allegiance which, in unavoidable military and political crises will fail soonest and turn into its opposite. . . If the method is not used in the right proportion the danger exists, especially with Germanic peoples, that despair and hatred against the oppressor will overcome fear and make the oppressed an uninhibited and fanatical active enemy. . . . . It is of course a perfectly proper method and should be more widely applied than heretofore. . . . Fear in the form of a shock effect may also serve to bridge over an especially critical span of time during which it prevents the intimidated population from rendering support to the enemy or attempting an open uprising. However, it must be remembered that every such shock remains effective only a limited time and then produces an even more violent reaction of bitterness and hatred. . . .[14]

What was here said with particular reference to occupied Europe had long been practiced in Germany.[15] A former denizen of the Third Reich has recently expressed the experience of the terror in a moving parable:

Imagine the experience of a man who, on a lonely trip suddenly hears at a distance calls for help and sounds of horror and pain. He approaches a lonely house, looks into a window and discovers that a terrible slaughter goes on inside. He is about to interfere, to call a stop, at least to scream. But the strangeness of the thing, where medieval torture takes the forms of a secret and terrible justice, paralyzes him, and this seizure makes him miss the moment of spontaneous assistance. The loneliness of the place, the superior force of the men conducting their awesome office impress him, a pressure which seems to stem from powers other than his own deathly fear paralyzes the spectator's limbs, a more than egoistic dread constricts his throat. And while thus far he had remained unseen, he is suddenly drawn into the dreadful event. A connection is established between inside and outside by a pair of eyes which does not let him go any more, which haunts him, staring glowering from an extinguished face. And now he succumbs to the terrible ban of the spirits which command eternal silence to those who unwittingly enter their realm. He receives clear warning: you are next. You, with everything you have wanted on earth, with everything that belongs to you and is dear to you. Here your living body will be tortured and made to dust, here you will be silenced forever before the faintest sound of your voice will reach a human ear.

And this eye witness, this lonely wanderer, does not break into the room now which is darkened by the dusk of evening and resounds with strange singing. He does not scream, he does not run for help—and, once returned to his peacefully lighted chamber, he tells: nothing.

The picture of this curiously inactive spectator arose in me when I tried to express in words something of the mythical character of the terror. I wanted to say something of the terrible meaninglessness of sacrifice which was expressed so often in these years in the rebellion against overpowering force. The reader should feel that this spectator went and tilled his acre, conducted his trade, wrote his books, and that he did all these things out of a burning desire to maintain a world which outside of himself had nearly gone under. And also that, next to the sheer fright, he felt something like a shudder of awe for this evil. . . ."[16]

Thus average men were cowed by the fear of a lawless authority which to them still remained authority. There was yet a further element. Those with the strength of will and conviction necessary to take upon themselves, and possibly their families and friends, the potential consequences of anti-Nazi activity not only faced the risk of cruel punishment. They also had to assume that their sacrifice, which was meant to further a cause in which they believed, might well remain unknown to all but a few. It was one of the most effective tricks of the machine to conceal the fate of all but a few chosen victims who were intended to serve as an example. Everything conspired to isolate the rebels from the rest of the community which, as long as possible, was clinging to the appearance of normalcy. "While at the time of the (Bismarckian) anti-Socialist legislation," one German Social Democrat has recently written, "popular sympathy was with those who were willing to make sacrifices for their political convictions, the populace gave applause or stood indifferently aside when we went to prison. The bitterest road after such an experience was the homecoming, from prison through the streets to one's home, past coffee houses, cabarets and other places of amusement from which the noises of merriment were penetrating. What did they know, they who lived happy-go-lucky lives, of the sacrifices exacted by the tyranny? They did not see and they did not want to see. Those who had suffered could nowhere rise and give testimony of these days. Their mouth had to be kept closed, often even with the closest relatives. . . ."[17]

Men were completely helpless in the totalitarian environment. They could not expect any remedial or restraining action through legal channels, except under the most unusual circumstances. Political police operations after all had long been explicitly exempted from court control. A few found a precarious haven with the army —a rival power. But nothing was secure in the end.[18]

It is abundantly clear that the propaganda machine was, in the last analysis, the final buttress of the machinery of repression itself. It had long dinned into the ear of the common man that, for better or worse, he was "in for it," because the world was bent on the destruction of Germany and the Germans; that whether he liked the Nazis or not, he was like a man in a leaky boat who, if he wanted to survive, had to row regardless of his feelings for some of his fellow-passengers. Once the war was well under way any German with a reasonable stake in life could be impressed with his vested interest in a German victory. It is quite evident that only the exceedingly strong in character and vision could hold out.

In his speech of November 8, 1943, Hitler bluntly told the underground opposition: "The State of today is so thoroughly organized that these elements cannot work at all. The conditions indispensable for their work do not exist."

Was it not true? Actually, the control machinery had certain weak spots, some of which have been pointed out before. This immense and complicated organization had somewhat outgrown the limits of its efficiency, especially under the impact of war. Anyone who has ploughed his way through some of the paper remnants of this vast bureaucracy will appreciate that it was beginning to burst at the seams. As in any other overgrown organization, this resulted in two major shortcomings: there was imperfect coordination among its parts (the several police cadres, the Party, the courts, and other government agencies); and, especially towards the end, there was a manifest shortage of skilled personnel, considering the scope of the customary operations. We have many perfectly reasonable statements from Gestapo and SD officers about the growing manpower shortage in their ranks. Even though they had done pretty well by exploiting the puppet regimes in subject Europe, the fact remained that they had to spread their own men very thin.

This lack of coordination was naturally enhanced by the rivalries and even conflicts among various control services of which we have already spoken. Basically they were often due to the natural and continuing conflict between old-line career officials, trained to use some measure of objectivity and certain standards of honor and justice, and the new men, often (although not always) less well trained and certainly disdainful of the old standards of conduct. Insiders and close observers could use their knowledge of such gaps and undertake action which was otherwise impossible.

Last and not least there was a growing disaffection in the masses of the population which, coupled with a considerable measure of physical disruption of the control services in the air raid period, began to affect the machine. It lessened the numbers and enthusiasm of informers while, at the same time, it tremendously increased the task of policing and controlling in a period of general manpower shortage.

Yet the effectiveness of repression remained impressive almost to the end. The machine continued to function despite its internal flaws and the overwhelming futility of the work. While it was the imperfections which made possible the survival of a considerable number of anti-Nazis, the deterrent effects continued, perhaps largely because of the paralyzing shock of the final waves of terror.

HISTORICAL BACKGROUND OF THE RESISTANCE

In the period immediately following the seizure of power, anti-Nazi and non-Nazi Germans—a majority of the population—tended to act on democratic assumptions. The Nazis had come to power on the basis of electoral successes growing out of the economic crisis, and they lacked a majority in the Reichstag. They appeared to be ruling over a shaky coalition which would fall of its own weight as soon as the pressure of internal economic problems and the resistance to German expansion and militarism by the great powers would make itself felt. Their tragic error, which they shared with considerable elements outside of Germany, grew out of failure to assess the nihilistic dynamism of the Nazis, the extent of the political and moral collapse in Germany, and the general demoralization and breakdown of international relations. Ignorant of their risks, and reckoning on greater outside support, many of these groups engaged in fairly large-scale activity. They maintained contact with other groups inside Germany and had effective ties with groups abroad. Publication and distribution of leaflets and pamphlets were on a comparatively large scale. The underground groups numbered in the thousands in most large German cities, and only one or two organizations were sufficiently aware of the risks to take the necessary protective measures.

In the period of 1933-35 the Nazi party and police apparatus swept these groups of anti-Nazis by the thousands into prisons and concentration camps where many of them remained until the end of the war. Those who returned and those not apprehended had to revise their general strategy and tactics in the light of the real political and international situation which bitter disappointments and personal tragedies forced them to recognize.

The supineness of the great powers in the face of the rearmament of the Rhineland, the Italian conquest of Abyssinia, the attack on the Spanish Republic, the seizure of Austria, and the Munich agreement discredited the anti-Nazis with the German masses and spread demoralization among the democratic and anti-Nazi groups. The Nazi war economy created an economic boom and turned the heads of the great bulk of Germans who were prepared to embrace any system which won them some degree of economic security.

The changes in expectations and tactics forced upon these isolated and decimated underground groups during this period of shock and demoralization were briefly as follows. Bureaucratic, industrial, and religious conservative opposition groups rested their hopes primarily on ties with the Wehrmacht opposition and hopes that the army would provide the necessary force to remove the Nazis. The left-wing groups and liberal pacifists viewed such ties and expectations with misgivings or positive rejection. Considerable elements in labor circles viewed the Wehrmacht and the German Nationalists as the other side of the Nazi penny. Labor elements were, of course, involved in the July 20 plot but this coalition was established after the outbreak of war.

In the absence of any hopeful prospects of overthrowing the Nazis by means of any mass labor movement or with the aid of outside democratic forces, the main goal of the left-wing opposition came to be that of preserving anti-Nazi left-wing nuclei for the time when the Nazis would be overthrown either by military defeat or internal military revolt. Anything but the most circumspect recruitment of new personnel into the opposition was viewed as suicidal. The opposition was deliberately broken up into the smallest possible units, and knowledge of the full extent of oppositional organization was restricted to the smallest possible leadership. This era of German resistance may be referred to as the period of defensive survival strategy, a period which lasted roughly until 1943.[19]

In a study prepared by Himmler's Security Headquarters of the anti-Nazi political leadership as of June, 1939, a number of interesting points are made. The statistical summaries were based on reports on the whereabouts and activities of 553 former leaders of the so-called "Systemzeit."[20] This selection of leaders included 192 so-called Marxist-Communist leaders, 82 liberal pacifists, 76 leaders of the religious communities, 73 leaders of the "Right opposition," 48 Austrian political leaders, and 82 scientists, artists, writers, and journalists. Of the total of 553 anti-Nazi leaders 349 (63 per cent) were still to be found in Germany. Two hundred forty-seven (45 per cent) were at large; the remainder were imprisoned. Himmler was informed by this research report that approximately 50 per cent of the former leaders of the Marxist-Communist parties were still in Germany and that they continued to be, along with those who had emigrated, ". . . irreconcilable opponents of National Socialism." Three-fourths of the left-wing leaders remaining in Germany were described as being at large receiving pensions or engaged in former or new occupations. The liberal and pacifist leaders remaining in Germany are described by the report as having ". . . discontinued their political activity without resistance in 1933." They are viewed as continuing some resistance on a small scale in science, literature, and business life and as "anti-German propagandists" in the emigration. The Catholic Centrist and Confessional church leaders mostly remained in Germany (83 per cent). About one-fifth of these leaders are described as still being active in Catholic anti-Nazi organizations and the "Bekenntnisfront." The right-wing groups are reported as continuing a ". . . strong inner opposition against National Socialism." Three-fourths of these were former leaders of the German Peoples party and the German Nationalists. Ninety-five per cent of these leaders remained inside of Germany and about half were still active in industry and agriculture or in the bureaucracy. A number of these right-wing leaders had joined forces with the Catholic and Confessional church opposition.

This summary report on oppositional activity restricted itself to research on the fate of the anti-Nazi elite. Needless to say, these persons were in many cases associated with groups of followers.

The Nazi-Soviet pact and the outbreak of the war affected all trends of the opposition, but particularly the left-wing and Wehrmacht elements. The German Communists were bewildered and demoralized by these developments and entered a period of quiescence which lasted until the attack on Russia. The Wehrmacht opposition suffered particularly from difficulties of communication due to the movement of army units to various parts of occupied Europe. Naturally the successes of German arms from 1939 until the winter of 1942 rendered the small-scale propaganda efforts of the oppositional groups even more futile.

A 1941 report of Himmler's Security Service Headquarters describes "Communist" activity after the outbreak of the Russian war as having undergone only an "insignificant" increase.[21] A general preventive Gestapo clean-up in the Reich, the Protectorate, and the General Government of Poland in the days immediately before and after the outbreak of war with Russia netted 270 so-called Communist leaders. The Gestapo always used the terms "Communist" and "Marxist" to cover in both Communists proper, Social Democrats, and smaller left-wing groups such as the Socialist Labor party. The report nevertheless pointed out that the number of leaflets and "wall-scribblings" and the extent of oral propaganda was several times greater in July, 1941 than in the preceding month. On the whole the Gestapo viewed this moderate increase in left-wing oppositional activity as of little significance although it reckoned on the possible later impact of left-wing labor sabotage in the factories.

It was during the year 1942 that the conviction began to spread among Germans that the war was lost. The first blow to expectations of victory was the entrance of the United States into the war. But the really damaging blow to German expectations was the de-

feat at Stalingrad which made it clear that a large-scale two-fror
war was inescapable. From the point of view of the remaining ant
Nazi organizations the German population became more receptiv
to defeatist propaganda. The size and number of anti-Nazi grouf
increased as did the number of arrests by the Gestapo.

Estimates of the quantitative scope and composition of the ant
Nazi resistance during the war period must unfortunately be base
upon bits and scraps of Gestapo statistics and reports which su;
vived the execution of the Nazi order to destroy all Party and polic
files when capture of an area was imminent. Supplementary source
of data are interrogations of Gestapo personnel and interview
with surviving anti-Nazis. No one of these sources is fully reliabl
and even taken together and balanced against one another man
significant questions remain unanswered. The Gestapo statistic
available present a number of problems. Differences in police effic
iency and zeal in the various areas, inconsistencies in the interpreta
tion of Gestapo statistical categories, the "padding" of reports fc
purposes of budget justification, all constitute sources of error. Th
claims of surviving anti-fascist leaders also present serious prot
lems. On the one hand there is the understandable pressure of mak
ing out the best possible case; and on the other the atomized cha;
acter of the opposition which made it impossible for any one plan
area, or group leader to speak with accuracy for more than his ow
unit. All of these sources of error must be kept in mind in evaluatin
the quantitative data which follow.

A comprehensive statistical record of oppositional and sut
versive activity is available only for the first six months of 1944.'
The figures mainly reflect the status of German morale befor
D-Day, although the figures for the month of June may reflect th
beginning of the final wave of defeatism and demoralization afte
the successful landings in France. Since the period covered wa
before the July 20 plot and the rapid reconquest of France it is pe;
haps reasonable to assume that similar statistics for the second hal
of 1944 would reflect a substantially higher rate of resistance. Th

Gestapo tables available are entitled "Consolidation of Arrests Reported by the Regional Offices of the Gestapo." The areas covered include the "Greater Reich," the Protectorate, and parts of Poland.[23] A considerable foreign population and territory is covered by these reports, including all of Czechoslovakia except Slovakia, considerable areas of Poland, all of Austria, Alsace-Lorraine, and Luxembourg.

The figures for April-June, 1944 (see Table I) are broken down into the categories of "Germans" and "Foreigners," a classification which makes possible a rough comparison of resistance by Germans and some of the conquered peoples. Since these statistics did not cover the major occupied areas the picture of foreign resistance, needless to say, is quite inadequate. The reports cover a German population of more than seventy millions and a foreign population of perhaps forty millions. This last figure includes the six to eight million foreign workers in Germany proper, the entire populations of Bohemia and Moravia, Austria, the Saar, Alsace-Lorraine, Luxembourg, and possibly half of Poland.

Types of arrests in the Gestapo statistics may be classified under "political" and "economic" headings; and for the purposes of this discussion the economic offenses may be disregarded. The first category of political offenses is called "Communism-Marxism." Although the figures for the last three months (April-June) separate "Communism" from "Marxism" a study of detailed daily reports from the Gestapo blotters for a number of regions indicates that such Gestapo distinctions were quite untrustworthy. Social Democrats were often listed under the category of "Communism." The second category "Reactionary Opposition" included liberal and conservative persons—army officers, industrialists, bureaucrats, members of the professions, and the middle classes—engaged in some form of opposition. Analysis of the Gestapo blotters shows that the activities of the groups which led to arrest ranged from group radio listening, political discussion, and dissemination of enemy propaganda to the less frequent formation of organizations with more ambitious political, and later military, goals. The composition, organization, and goals of some of these more aggressive political formations will be discussed in the following chapter. The third category of "Church movements" was made up primarily of members of religious sects (particularly the *Bibelforscher* or German Jehovah's Witnesses), Catholic and Evangelical clergymen, and lay religious leaders. The fourth category, "Resistance Movements," appears, after careful study, to refer to "national" resistance organizations made up primarily of foreigners in the occupied areas and slave labor in Germany proper. The final category of arrests is entitled "Individual Subversion." In the original Gestapo tables the term used is "Acts of Treachery" (*Heimtückeangelegenheiten*). These offenses included individual listening to enemy radio broadcasts and criticism or attacks on the regime or of individual Nazi leaders.

GERMAN VS. FOREIGN ARRESTS

It is of considerable interest that foreigners were responsible for more than 60 per cent of the total of political arrests, although Germans numbered almost two to one to foreigners in the areas covered. It is also of significance that the offenses of foreigners fell into the more serious categories of organized resistance far more frequently than those of Germans. Thus more than 45 per cent of the arrests of Germans were for acts of individual subversion, while only 17 per cent of the arrests of foreigners fell into this category. More than thirty-three hundred foreigners were arrested for Communist-Marxist activity, a quarter of the total of foreign arrests. Twenty per cent of the German arrests fell into this category. The extent of "Reactionary Opposition" was greater among Germans than among foreigners.

The relatively small number of persons arrested for religious resistance may be attributed at least in part to the greater caution of the Nazi authorities in dealing with the churches. The number of anti-Nazis among religious groups was probably much larger than these arrest figures indicate. The main weight of church repression during the war years fell against the relatively uninfluential sects; greater circumspection and more moderate repressive techniques were employed against the more popularly supported Catholic church and the oppositional wing of the Evangelical church.

Although the category of "Resistance Movements" primarily included foreigners, a proportionately considerable number of Germans were involved in these organizations (20 per cent). Careful internal analysis indicates that most (about 80 per cent) of these arrests took place outside of the boundaries of the old Reich, among the Germans in Czechoslovakia, Poland, Austria, France,

TABLE I

Gestapo Arrests of Germans and Foreigners in the Greater German Reich, the Protectorate, and Parts of Poland, April-June, 1944

	GERMAN			FOREIGN		
	Number	Per Cent of Category	Per Cent of German Arrests	Number	Per Cent of Category	Per Cent of Foreign Arrests
Communism-Marxism . . .	1724	34	20	3322	66	25
Reactionary Opposition . .	1014	56	12	805	44	6
Religious Resistance	287	66	3	162	34	1
Resistance Movements . .	1737	20	20	6803	80	51
Individual Subversion . .	3826	63	45	2250	37	17
TOTAL . . .	8588	39	100	13,342	61	100

Norway, and elsewhere.[24] There were a number of cases in which Germans and foreign workers formed joint organizations in the old Reich.[25]

Thus, Gestapo evidence clearly indicates a vastly greater degree of resistance among foreigners than among Germans. The approximately forty millions of foreigners covered in these figures were responsible for more than three-fifths of the total of political offenses. Eighty-three per cent of the foreign arrests were for organized resistance, while only 55 per cent of the German arrests were in this category. Correcting for the differences in the size of the populations involved, foreign arrests to German arrests were at a ratio of three to one. The ratio of foreign to German arrests for organized resistance was at least four to one.

The substantial difference in the degree of active resistance against the Nazis on the part of Germans and foreigners may be accounted for by a number of factors. Certainly the most important factor was the simple and inescapable truth that the great majority of the German population was pro-Nazi out of ideological motives as a consequence of cynical participation in Nazi spoliation or out of an unquestioning patriotism and gratification of national resentment. But the greater effectiveness of police controls among Germans as compared with the occupied areas and the nature of the moral choice confronting Germans as compared with the conquered peoples had some significance for the extent of anti-Nazi opposition. The Frenchman, Norwegian, Dane, Dutchman, Belgian, Pole, Czech, Jugoslav, and Greek could face the risk even of death with only private and personal conflicts of conscience. He gave his life for his nation in an underground national and humanitarian war against a ruthless tyranny. He acted bravely in a supporting moral environment. The German who actively opposed the Nazis on political, religious, or humanitarian grounds had to work his way through more damaging moral and intellectual conflicts and accept the possibly greater risk of death with a courage that had little support among his compatriots. This conflict between national feeling, personal courage, and moral and political conviction contributed to the greatly limited scope of German resistance just as it has contributed to the demoralization of the potentially democratic elements in the occupation period.

Regional Distribution of Arrests in Germany

Some impression of the extent of opposition and subversion in the old Reich may be gathered from an analysis of Table III which summarizes arrests by cause for representative regions for a three-month period. It is of considerable interest that the regional breakdown of arrests does not follow the known patterns of German politics. Thus the Berlin-Potsdam, Hamburg, and Hanover regions, which from other sources are known to have had active oppositional organizations, reported only a relatively small number of arrests, while Breslau, Chemnitz, Weimar, and Nuremberg reported proportionately large numbers of arrests, particularly in the left-wing categories. Differences in Gestapo activity and the effectiveness of underground techniques may be responsible for these deviations.

Study of the regional Gestapo blotters indicates that the groups arrested for these causes ranged from little groups of five to ten enemy radio listeners and political discussants to more aggressive plant cells and anti-Nazi committees of various kinds. Whenever an extraordinary number of arrests were reported for any particular region it is possible that anti-Nazi organizations of larger dimensions may have been involved. Extreme instances of arrests of large scope are the June figure for Weimar listing 150 arrests for Communism-Marxism, the May figure of 115 arrests for left-wing activity in Nuremberg, the May figure of fifty-eight Communist-Marxist arrests for Breslau, and the February figure of fifty-six for the same cause in Chemnitz.

It is likely that when a particular region showed a consistently high rate of arrests over a period of months a single organization whose ramifications took a longer period to uncover may have been involved, on the order of the Sindermann case in Dresden, the Kampmann case in the Ruhr, the NKFD affair in Leipzig, and the ADV in Bavaria. Thus in Breslau during April, May, and June a total of 139 persons were arrested for Communism-Marxism. In Chemnitz over the entire six-month period a total of 249 persons were arrested for Communism-Marxism. In Weimar 272 persons were arrested for Communist-Marxist activity over the five-month period from February to June. These statistics and other Gestapo sources indicate that in the period 1943-1945 perhaps several dozens of such large-scale left-wing anti-Nazi organizations were uncovered and broken up by the Gestapo.

SCOPE OF ANTI-NAZI ACTIVITIES AND ATTITUDES

Any precise quantitative estimate of the scope and composition of anti-Nazi opposition must unfortunately be limited to the second quarter of 1944 when Gestapo statistical reports distinguished between German and foreign arrests. These figures may serve as a basis for computing the arrest rate for the whole of 1944 if we accept the assumption that the number of arrests increased in the second half of 1944. The general deterioration of German morale and the July 20 affair which resulted in large-scale arrests among all political groups in Germany suggest the validity of this assumption. If we can assume a higher rate in the period July-December, 1944, and balance this against the known lower arrest rate in the first quarter of 1944, it is possibly a cautious procedure to derive

TABLE II

Political Arrests for Selected Gestapo Districts
April-June, 1944

	Communism-Marxism	Reactionary Opposition	Religious Resistance	Resistance Movements	Individual Subversion	TOTAL
Berlin-Potsdam . . .	97	52	69	43	188	449
Breslau	140	34	13	130	155	472
Chemnitz	115	12	6	111	26	318
Dortmund	7	15	20	41	17	100
Dresden	17	16	13	17	226	289
Düsseldorf	95	43	21	154	149	462
Frankfurt a/M . . .	38	49	6	3	127	223
Hamburg	49	16	3	1	157	226
Hanover	15	41	2	32	66	146
Karlsruhe	20	2	10	129	87	248
Kiel	29	19	0	37	129	214
Köln	93	39	0	569	164	865
Königsberg	11	35	2	113	38	199
Leipzig	101	0	6	0	48	155
Munich*	27*	36	2	44	34	143
Nuremberg	116	2	4	40	249	411
Stettin	35	3	8	98	51	195
Stuttgart	27	103	15	12	7	164
Weimar	203	9	21	0	109	342

*April figures for Munich destroyed by air raid.

estimated 1944 totals from a multiplication by four of the April-June figures. On the basis of such calculations we arrived at the estimated and rounded-off figures in Table III.

These roughly estimated figures suggest that perhaps some thirty or forty thousand Germans were arrested for offenses defined as political by the Gestapo during 1944. Roughly half of these offenses fell into the individual subversion category. More than 6500 were

TABLE III

Estimated Gestapo Arrests of Germans and Foreigners in the Greater German Reich, the Protectorate, and Parts of Poland for the Year 1944

	Germans	Foreigners
Communism-Marxism	6500	13,000
Reactionary Opposition	4000	3000
Religious Resistance	1000	600
Resistance Movements	6500	27,000
Individual Subversion	15,000	9000
TOTAL	33,000	52,600

participants in left-wing groups, around four thousand in middle-of-the-road and right-wing groups and approximately a thousand were from the religious resistance.

It is reasonable to assume that the number of German subversives and oppositionists was larger than the numbers arrested by the Gestapo for these causes. This is recognized in Gestapo reports, and confirmed by the survival of many anti-Nazi groups until the occupation period. Just how many there were will never be known. One can only say that their number and aggressiveness undoubtedly increased from 1942 on and reached a high point in the months and weeks immediately before occupation.

All of the figures given above relate to *acts* of resistance. Naturally the number of Germans and foreigners in the areas subject to Gestapo jurisdiction who were anti-Nazi in attitude if not in action was considerably larger.[26] It is impossible to say how much larger since there were no statistically valid studies of German attitudes under the Nazis. The Security Service provided a crude barometer of German opinion based on the morale reports of thousands of undercover morale reporters strategically placed among labor groups, schools, churches, chambers of commerce, industrial organizations, societies and clubs, Party organizations, and the like. Study of these reports indicates that in the eyes of the SD there was an increasing proportion of the population which gradually lost faith in victory during the war years, until in late 1944 the central consolidated reports (*Meldungen aus dem Reich*) began to speak of the majority of the population as defeatist in attitude. These reports also referred to a segment of the population which was anti-Nazi in conviction, but no statistical estimate is possible on the basis of these qualitative reports.

A post-occupation opinion survey conducted under the auspices of the War Department by the Strategic Bombing Survey gives us some idea of the extent to which Germans continued to be Nazi in attitude after their defeat.[27] The interviewers questioned a sample of several thousand Germans in the American, British, and French zones. They proceeded by breaking down the Nazi ideology into component dogmas (e.g. racialism, leadership principle, etc.) and determined the general attitude on the basis of scores for the whole set of critical items, a procedure more likely to elicit an honest response than a more direct approach. On the basis of this study it was suggested that well over half of the German population when questioned did not accept any of the Nazi doctrines. A very small percentage ranging from 4 to 5 per cent among workers to more than 14 per cent for professionals and executives and managers were "full Nazis" on the basis of adherence to all the essential doctrines. In between there was a group of between 25 to 30 per cent of the sample who expressed faith in some of the Nazi doctrines but not in others. There were substantially more Nazis among business men, professionals, farmers, and students than among the workers.

It is, of course, clear that belief in Nazi doctrines was at its lowest ebb in Germany immediately after the collapse when the survey was made. A similar study in the period 1939-41 would have undoubtedly shown vastly different figures since acceptance of Nazi ideas varied to a considerable extent with German military success. But what these figures suggest is that possibly a quite substantial proportion of the German population throughout the period of the war was not Nazi in conviction. Its war participation was based on fear of the terror, the need to make a living, and the emotional pressures of wartime. Within this considerable group of Germans there arose continually and in increasing number, as defeat became imminent, individuals and groups whose conscience and conviction required some type of overt action against the Nazis— whether this took the form of a slogan fearfully chalked on a wall at night, occasional meetings with persons of similar conviction for political discussions, or more dangerous actions such as providing refuge to one of the many "U-Boote" (Jewish and political fugitives from the Gestapo), the publication and distribution of leaflets, engaging in defeatist propaganda in the plants, or forming and training armed groups to prevent last-ditch resistance. Some idea of the general scope of this more aggressive and overt type of reaction has been given in the above discussion. A more detailed study of the social and political composition of the German resistance is made in the following chapter.

Chap. 3 The Social Composition of the German Resistance

GABRIEL A. ALMOND and WOLFGANG H. KRAUS

ALTHOUGH THE VARIOUS SOCIAL CLASSES and the political and religious groups of the German population contained oppositional
tendencies, only labor and the surviving left-wing organizations
had a genuine "grass roots" organization. The primarily middle-
class and conservative groups which participated in the attempted
coup of July 20, 1944, were conspiratorial organizations. Only in
exceptional cases did they engage in propaganda or recruitment
activities or attempt to create a mass basis. The labor opposition, on
the other hand, had nuclei all over Germany, and the spreading of
propaganda on a small scale, and later the recruitment of new members, were typical of their methods of operation.

LABOR RESISTANCE

While the left-wing groups had given up hope by 1937-38 of
being able to overthrow the Nazis from within (with the exception of those groups later involved in the July 20 affair) they were
still concerned to maintain cadres of opposition among the workers, and thereby preserve an apparatus capable of creating a mass
basis in the period of German defeat. This implied the need to preserve nuclei in factories and proletarian neighborhoods. Though
they had to operate on a limited basis and in secret, it was necessary
in order to fulfill their function of a counter-elite capable of tak-

ing over power in the period of collapse to show activity, to remind the workers that there were anti-Nazi political organizations. This was the primary significance of the wall-scribblings, the oral propaganda, and the less frequent leaflets of the labor opposition. As long as these signs of activity could be maintained, elements among the workers were aware of alternative policies and organizations. Without these consistent preparations the immediate seizure of the plant and factory organizations by the anti-fascist cells after the occupation would have been much more difficult. Similarly without such efforts it would have been impossible in the days of defeat to develop general mass organizations and programs which would attempt to give occupation policy a left orientation.

Within the labor opposition, power and activity generally gravitated toward the left as the Gestapo terror became more effective.[1] Although the Social Democratic party continued to have a greater mass potential among the workers than the Communists, in the actual resistance leadership was about equally divided among the Communists and Social Democrats. One or two left-wing militant splinter groups like the Socialist Labor party in Bremen and the Communist Oppositionists in Hamburg played a role far out of proportion to their actual support among the workers. Resistance in Germany and elsewhere was a task for militants. The Gestapo terror resulted in an internal selecting-out process of those unwilling to go the whole length of sacrificing comfort, security, family, property, and life itself. Within the Social Democratic party (SPD) the mass following and many of the old leaders became largely quiescent, and the SPD left-wing in most places was in the van of oppositional activity. This trend had considerable significance for oppositional organization since the SPD left-wing was more disposed to collaborate with the Communists than the former SPD leadership.

SIGNIFICANCE OF LABOR RESISTANCE

If the great objective of the German labor resistance groups was to preserve anti-Nazi elites for the period of defeat, then it must be said that these groups were successful. Almost without exception as

Allied troops captured the larger German cities they were met by delegations of left-wing anti-fascists, ready with programs, nominees for office in the local administration, and offers of aid in the process of denazification. Their underground organizations had provided the basis for a swift campaign of mass recruitment.[2]

Claims that the activities of the left-wing anti-fascist opposition contributed in any significant degree to Allied military victory must be viewed with considerable doubt. In this regard those groups involved in the July 20 affair may make the greater claims. This incident and the wave of arrests among military circles which followed, coming as it did after the Normandy invasion, further undermined the fighting effectiveness and morale of the Wehrmacht and hastened the collapse of the German fighting forces. The local left-wing organizations may perhaps take credit for having saved a few hundred lives in a number of areas by encouraging mutinies in *Volkssturm* formations and adding their pressure to efforts to prevent demoralized Nazi and military leaders from carrying on a futile last-ditch resistance. Needless to say, this judgment from the known facts is not in deprecation of the activities of these organizations which were carried on in disregard of prohibitive risks and with a heavy toll of casualties.

The success of the anti-Nazi resistance in preserving a corps of political leaders capable of giving German politics a new direction after the occupation cannot be doubted after study of the local leadership of the new political parties. In Hamburg, Georges, Schmedmann, Detlefs, Borchers and many others came from the active underground, the prisons, and the concentration camps. In Bremen, Wolters, Eihlers, Buckendal, Busch, Lücke, and Gotthardt had the same background. In Luebeck, Klamm and Öllrogge, Passarge, and others came from the Communist and Social Democratic resistance. The Leipzig underground produced the Communists and Communist sympathizers Rossberg, Plesse, and Hildegarde Heinze. Bernhard, Hesse, Öhlschlager, Otten, and Köhn came from the Halle Social Democratic opposition; Koenig and others from the Communist groups. From the Hanover resistance came the present Social Democratic leaders Schumacher, Deike,

Karl, and Beerman, and the Communists Winters and Augustin. Schwamb, Ritter, Steffan, and Pause of Frankfurt came from the Social Democratic and Communist underground. Freytag, Kalujek, and Boenwetter from the Mainz groups, Marschmeier of Wiesbaden, and Zinnkann of Darmstadt, all had been active in the Social Democratic resistance in the Main-Neckar district. A large proportion of the left-wing and trade union leaders in postwar Germany are concentration camp veterans.

To the Allied Military Government the existence of these organizations presented a number of problems. In most cases these groups (which acquired the generic name of "Antifa") had undertaken ambitious programs of organization and activity. They occupied the Party and Labor front local offices; erased Nazi slogans and changed street names; took over houses, clothing, and food from Nazis; and made space available to returning concentration camp victims. They also presented MG officials with lists of names of Nazis in government offices and made nominations of persons for the new local administration. They made rapid strides in recruiting members and supporters.

Under Allied regulations political activity was forbidden, so that all of this activity soon came to a halt. This order was, of course, differently interpreted by the various commanding officers. In Bremen the organizations were tolerated, but under control. In Leipzig they were disbanded and the leadership placed under oath to serve as informers for any activity carried on in violation of the order. In Halle the groups were given some encouragement, as was the case in Hanover. Thus while the Antifa movement had some revolutionary potentialities, these were effectively restricted under the most benign MG policy. Most of these organizations were reduced to the role of informers on the location of prominent Nazis and automatic arrest cases.

The enforcement of the SHAEF order was of some significance for the future political party development in Germany. For while the Antifas claimed to be representatives of the anti-Nazi population and wished to have a share of political power under the military government, they were in most cases under the control of the more militant left-wing groups. The NKFD groups of Munich, Leipzig, and the Ruhr, the KGF of Bremen, and the Anti-Fascist Committee of Hamburg although inclusive of labor elements in general were controlled by Communists, left-wing Social Democrats, or militant "splinter groups." Where these anti-fascist organizations existed there were strong pressures for the formation of a united workers party and disregard of the older party lines. The common experience in the resistance had created a common policy and friendly personal relations between Social Democrats, Communists, liberal members of the middle classes, and anti-Nazi Catholics and Protestants.[3]

Had these groups been given recognition and support the predominantly Communist "left" would have been strengthened in many areas. There are, of course, exceptions such as Luebeck, Hanover, and Halle where the older Social Democratic leadership stayed in the saddle and had not formed a united front with the Communists. But broadly speaking this would have been the trend. The effect of Allied policy, consequently, was to break the elan of the Antifas and place them under considerable restraint.

This gave more conservative groups a breathing spell. The unorganized middle-class and religious elements had an opportunity to group themselves and work out programs. The older Social Democratic leadership regained its equilibrium. Thus, when the prohibition against political activity was lifted some months later, the older party divisions had been re-established, and the left-wing mass organizations broken up into their constituent political elements. One might say, therefore, that in the British and American zones in the first months of occupation, a primarily Communist political wave was blocked in its full development and a conservative trend was encouraged. This, of course, resulted in considerable embitterment among Communists, who felt that they had been robbed of the fruits of the victory they had won at the cost of heavy casualties and great personal risks.

THE ORGANIZATION OF THE LABOR UNDERGROUND

In the early period of anti-Nazi resistance the parties maintained central committees and fairly effective-liaison between local organizations. There were several political trends in the early underground. There were, of course, the Communist[4] and Social Democratic[5] party organizations, having ties with groups of exiles and the national left-wing parties of neighboring countries. Within the Social Democratic party there was the group of left-wing militants which had assumed the name and slogan of "Neubeginnen." There were also the left-wing "splinter parties," among them the Socialist Labor party and the German branch of the ISK (*Internationaler Sozialistischer Kampfbund*), the latter a small organization of non-Marxist left-wing intellectuals. Both the former "free" trade unions and the Christian trade unions had central nuclei which maintained contacts with cells of sympathetic workers in many factories. A group of trade union leaders in Berlin, who were involved in the July 20 affair, maintained ties with local labor groups throughout the entire Nazi period. Jakob Kaiser headed up the surviving nuclei of the Christian Trade Unions; Wilhelm Leuschner and Julius Leber, the free trade unions; and Ernst Lemmers had ties with some of the former "liberal" (non-Socialist) trade unionists.[6]

The effect of Gestapo terror was to atomize these organizations. Liaison became difficult if not impossible. By the time of the outbreak of war there was only occasional contact between the central committees and the local organizations. The Social Democratic party group in Berlin could issue instructions through occasional liaison men able to get to Berlin on one pretext or another or through occasional tours in the provinces by members of the central groups. The Communists maintained connections with Moscow through agents among the Russian foreign workers, as well as through German Communist refugees sent in as agents from Switzerland and other bordering countries. In at least one case contact with Moscow was maintained through a secret radio station. This was done by the "Rote Kapelle" group led by Harro Schulze-Boysen and Arvid Harnack. The name Rote Kapelle was given the group in the espionage trial of 1942 which resulted in the execution of fifty of the participants. Schulze-Boysen was a Communist, but many of his associates were unaware of this and participated in his group because of general opposition to Nazism. The Rote Kapelle groups were spread all over Germany and in the occupied countries. Schulze-Boysen had a secret radio station in Berlin through which he sent political and military information to Moscow.[7]

In the latter years of the war, both from the Social Democratic and the Communist sides there were significant tendencies toward coordination. The group around Leuschner and Leber constituted the focus of Social Democratic activity. The Saefkow group constituted the Communist central organization. The Saefkow group had cells in thirty Berlin factories and had ties with similar labor cells in Hamburg, Leipzig, Dresden, Magdeburg, and other cities. Unfortunately the Gestapo had penetrated the Saefkow group, and when the Social Democrat Julius Leber met with the Communists to draw them into the July 20 plot, the Gestapo acted swiftly and arrested the negotiators. This had the effect of forcing the hands of the July 20 leaders who feared that the full scope of their plans would be revealed.[8]

In 1943 the Russians established the National Committee for Free Germany among German prisoners of war.[9] They also encouraged the development of civilian "Free Germany" Committees through radio propaganda and through the activities of agents sent across the borders. The earliest known civilian unit of the NKFD was formed in Leipzig. Other units were formed in Dresden, Munich, northwestern Germany, and the Rhineland. The activities of these NKFD units were coordinated by Moscow radio broadcasts.

Despite these efforts, left-wing anti-Nazi activity was primarily a local matter, and even within local areas for security reasons activity was on a highly decentralized basis. Consequently any survey of labor resistance in Germany in the later Nazi period begins and largely ends with the descriptions of the local organizations.[10] In this connection it is unnecessary to describe in detail the activities of the dozens of local labor resistance groups the existence of which has come to light since the occupation. The pattern followed was pretty much the same in the various regions. A description of the Hamburg movement is given as typical of the larger and more aggressive labor underground organizations.

HAMBURG
The left wing had always been strong in the Hanseatic cities and particularly in Hamburg, where a number of violent Communist uprisings had occurred after the First World War. The Hamburg labor resistance had three main components—the Social Democrats and former members of the Reichsbanner, the Communists, and an important group of Communist oppositionists who were affiliated with left-wing Social Democrats and members of the Socialist Labor party. The Communists functioned separately from the Anti-fascist Committee because of mutual ideological mistrust and because of fear on the part of the Anti-fascist Committee that the Communists were careless of security measures. A large-scale Gestapo roundup of Hamburg Communists in late 1944 destroyed the central organization so that it was impossible to locate survivors capable of telling the full story.

These groups consisted of aggregations of factory nuclei, other occupational units, former Reichsbanner men, cells in the Wehrmacht barracks in the area, and other groups based on neighborhood relationships and friendship. Between one thousand and two thousand persons were involved in the activities of these groups and organizations in the latter years of the war. And the main groups cited above had a consistent record of organized activity throughout the Nazi period.

Most of the Hamburg shipyards and larger factories had small left-wing cells. To cite one example, the Deutsche Werft, largest merchant shipyards in Germany, had an anti-fascist group from 1933 on. A leader of this group estimated the active anti-fascists in the shipyards in 1939 at approximately thirty-six men, each of whom was associated with a group of sympathizers. During the period 1939-41, activities were suspended because of the Nazi-Soviet pact, an event which bewildered and demoralized the left-wing workers. By 1942 the Communist group had been reactivated and began to draw to it an increasingly large number of sympathizers. In one division of the shipyards it was estimated that about 15 per cent sympathized with the opposition cell in the period after 1942. The group in the Deutsche Werft attempted to undermine

labor discipline through defeatist propaganda and was among the
few which claimed to have engaged in sabotage. One reported
sabotage technique involved cutting parts to old designs just at
the time of a change in pattern. It was possible to avoid discovery
by claiming ignorance of the pattern change. Torpedoes were occasionally sabotaged by theft of various parts. The preparation of
leaflets was too dangerous, but handwritten wall stickers were occasionally placed in the plant. Oral propaganda was carried on by
means of slogans which were casually dropped in the course of
conversations. Thus after 1943 the group used the following
slogans: "For a workman it does not matter whether the war
is won or lost. It is only the business of the employer." "Hitler
wanted total war. Now we have it and we all have to suffer." After
the Normandy invasion the oppositionists became more active and
formed a loose plant-wide organization.

Other plants in the Hamburg industrial and shipping area reported smaller oppositional nuclei. In general the survivors of these
groups made no exaggerated claims of aggressive activity. Their primary goal in the years of Nazi victory was to preserve an oppositional group which might be in a position to act in the event of
military setbacks and defeat. The year 1943 represented a turning
point when more ambitious organizations began to form and more
aggressive actions were undertaken.

The activities of a group of Social Democrats and former members of the Reichsbanner in Hamburg were reported by Bruno
Georges who had been designated as Police Chief by the British
Military Government. Georges was a former police captain who
had been discharged by the Nazis in 1933 because of his leading
position among the Hamburg Social Democrats. He had been a
leader of the Reichsbanner (a paramilitary Republican defense
group in the period before 1933). Georges was associated with a
group of some two hundred former Reichsbanner men who maintained an organized existence throughout the Nazi period. Georges
claimed there had been more of these Reichsbanner groups which
had acted separately for security reasons. They met together in
small social groups and discussed foreign broadcasts and the politi-

cal situation. They made efforts to secure arms, but without much success.

A combined anti-fascist organization was formed in Hamburg in November of 1938 through the initiative of two former trade unionists, Schmedmann and Detlefs. Schmedmann was a Social Democrat, a former official of the white collar worker trade union in Hamburg (*Zentralverband der Angestellten*). Detlefs was a former member of the right-wing Communist faction and had also been an official in the white collar union. Both men were veterans of concentration camps and prisons. But they had been free (except for short roundups during the war) since 1938 and had been able to conceal the activities of their organization. The group in 1938 consisted of sixty-one Communist oppositionists, Social Democrats, and former trade unionists. The main activities undertaken by it in the earlier years consisted of oral and leaflet propaganda and organizing aid for the families of imprisoned persons.

This group, later called the Anti-fascist Committee of Hamburg, began in 1943 to hide and feed Wehrmacht deserters, an activity which was confirmed through the interrogation of the chief of the *Abwehr* in the Hamburg military district. The Wehrmacht knew of the existence of this underground deserters' organization but had not been able to break it up. As many as thirty deserters at a time were hidden in the air raid ruins in Hamburg. Foodstuffs were contributed by sympathizing shopkeepers, civilian clothing was collected, and identity papers were forged. Meetings of the Anti-fascist Committee were guarded by armed men. According to Detlefs' claim, by the end of 1944 the group had accumulated a considerable supply of arms. Some of these weapons had been stolen from the military headquarters in Hamburg, a claim also confirmed by the Hamburg *Abwehr*.

At the beginning of 1945 the Anti-fascist Committee claimed an organization of seven hundred men, two hundred of whom were organized in armed "Hundertschaften" at Baumfeld and St. Pauli. It was also claimed that groups of mutinous soldiers had been formed in the Hindenburg, Mackensen, and Wentorf barracks. The plan of the Anti-fascist Committee was to force the Hamburg authorities to yield up the town without resistance. If the Gauleiter insisted on fighting in the town it was planned to drive into Hamburg from Winterhude, Baumfeld, St. Pauli, and the Blohm and Voss Works, and from the Mackensen, Hindenburg, and Wentorf barracks, and seize government and Party buildings and communications centers.

The first leaflets demanding peaceful surrender of the town were issued in February of 1945 urging the Hamburgers to shoot down all "Werewolves," and to turn their *Volkssturm* weapons against the Nazis. The later leaflets were called "Counter-orders" and were issued in a numbered series. A leaflet was posted in the *Gaensemarkt* with a signature purporting to be that of Burgermeister Vincenz Krogmann. This leaflet, an effort to create confusion among the Nazi authorities, bitterly attacked Himmler and Gauleiter Kaufmann for wanting to continue resistance. It claimed that the city government had taken over authority and that only the radio remained in SS control. The leaflet announced the dissolution of the *Volkssturm*, ordered no resistance to British troops, the placing of white flags on all public buildings, and authorized the people to fight against any Wehrmacht or SS units which resisted. The leaflet was discovered by SS troops and removed, but not before it had been seen by several thousand people.

In the days immediately preceding the occupation the people of Hamburg were urged to put out white flags and go into the streets and demonstrate. The group also issued a leaflet appealing to the honor of the Germans in Hamburg to prevent the murder of the inmates of the neighboring concentration camps. The leaflet states:

Almost all of us are responsible for these deeds of utter shame in the camps, not only the ones who gave the orders and those who carried them out. No one can say that he did not know what happened in these camps. All the officials and all the supporters of this Nazi-fascist system of terror and murder are co-responsible. Whoever out of cowardice does not protest these actions in spite of our declarations and those of the outside world bears a share of the guilt. These deeds, among others, weigh on the consciences of almost all of our people, filling them with horror and a dread anxiety for their fate. It is too late to undo these unspeakable actions.

It is not too late, however, to prevent the even more cruel murder of the remaining inmates now that the front is drawing closer. We appeal to your feeling of honor, to your shame, to whatever remains of manly courage in you to prevent the worst in these last hours, and to free the prisoners. Use all means of protest including the threatening of the prison guards, and the use of force. This appeal is also being given to others in your district. Discuss this question among yourselves, act immediately.

In the last critical days the Hamburg Anti-fascist Committee threatened an uprising of workers if the city were not peacefully surrendered. A deputation was sent to the Chamber of Commerce. These efforts and apparently successful subversive work among the *Volkssturm* contributed to the peaceful surrender of the city.

OTHER AREAS

The other Hanseatic cities, Bremen and Luebeck, also had active underground organizations. In Bremen the Communist-led group was called *Kampfgemeinschaft gegen den Faschismus;* in Luebeck there were separate Social Democratic and Communist groups. The latter organization in conjunction with a group of Russian workers and prisoners of war planned an uprising, the discovery of which led to the arrest and execution of many of its leaders. Units of the Moscow-sponsored National Committee for Free Germany in Leipzig, Dresden, and the Ruhr have already been referred to. The existence of regional movements in the Ruhr and southern Germany has been confirmed by Gestapo reports. The Ruhr group, most of the leaders of which were executed in 1943 and 1944, had cells in Düsseldorf, Duisburg, Wuppertal, Oberhausen, Krefeld, Solingen, and Hohscheid.

Cologne had several small groups of Communists and Social Democrats. Similar groups existed in Hanover. The Anti-Nazi People's Front of Munich had units in various parts of south Germany in 1942 and 1943. Frankfurt a/M had an Antifa consisting of more than a hundred. The Eisleben Antifa forced the *Volkssturm* commander to surrender the town. Wuppertal and Remscheid had small NKFD groups. An Augsburg organization took over the bridges and communication centers and enabled ninety American troops to take the town without a shot. Mainz, Darmstadt, Wiesbaden, and Offenbach had a number of trade union and Social Democratic cells.

Data on the Russian Zone is especially incomplete. The investigations of Leipzig and Halle were made before these territories were turned over to Russian occupation. Had systematic investigation been made in the Silesian, Saxon, Berlin, and Magdeburg industrial regions it is quite likely that activities of a scope and character comparable to the regional studies reported above would have come to light. The contemporary German press contains considerable evidence on other resistance organizations and activities. It will be a matter of years, however, before a reliable and comprehensive story will be available.

The evidence which has thus far come to light leaves little doubt as to the existence of a German labor resistance. It was an atomized resistance and on a far smaller scale than in the Nazi-occupied areas both with regard to numbers and aggressiveness. Nevertheless, when it is viewed in relation to the special impact of the terror in Germany its proportions become more understandable.

The few thousands of surviving left-wing resistance leaders who met the Allied armies as they overran Germany have since been absorbed into the re-established left-wing parties and trade unions. They have provided the left-wing movements of occupied Germany with a considerable proportion of their new leadership. It is an overaged leadership, its physical condition marred in many cases by the hardships and cruelties of concentration camp life. It tends to perpetuate the virtues and faults of the pre-Nazi left-wing parties and trade unions. Furthermore, these surviving anti-Nazis have made very limited progress in recruiting vigorous successors among German youth.

MODERATES AND CONSERVATIVES

The weight and significance of left-wing opposition to National Socialism is relatively clear. It is more difficult to make an adequate appraisal of the resistance attitudes and activities of other groups in Germany, ranging from the liberal center to the conservative right.

What was true in most of the countries of Nazi-occupied Europe, where the middle class resisters had the additional satisfaction of identifying their resistance to the forces of Nazism with the national defense effort, was also true for Germany itself. "It was certainly easier," Jakob Kaiser has observed, "to see through the pernicious system if one came from the tradition of the labor movement or the democratic traditions of emphatically leftist circles rather than from the right wing."[11] The "substantial classes" as such, with their larger stake in the stability and cohesion of the social-economic fabric, were in general slower in becoming active. They had not been, at the outset, as obvious targets of oppression as the workers or the entire left and all its organizations. Only gradually and to relatively small groups did the Nazi system reveal its true colors and become an unmistakable threat to traditional values and institutions, even in the eyes of some of the less political-minded and some of the original sympathizers.

It was especially after 1936 that such middle-class opposition became increasingly active, although hardly much more noticeable to the average citizen of the Third Reich.

Broadly speaking, this resistance began to crystallize among the following groups as their attitudes stiffened with the experiences of the totalitarian dictatorship.

There were "liberal" middle class groups whose views could be approximately identified with the pre-Nazi Democrats and Liberals. Their numerical insignificance was further enhanced by the emigration or withdrawal of many active leaders.[12] Yet they contributed some active and experienced individuals to the underground work.

Middle and upper class conservatives, many of whom had active religious connections, constituted a significant section. More and more of them went into the opposition as it became clear, even to some who had wilfully blinded themselves in the beginning, that the Nazis' much-touted concern for the German tradition was largely a propagandistic trick, a veneer to cover the destruction of the cultural heritage. It was not merely the growing anticipation of disaster which drove them away from this regime. The first and most startling shock, whose effect was never permitted to wear off, was the utterly callous destruction of law and justice by the new rulers.[13] As this process was accelerated during and after the middle thirties, it contributed to a more realistic understanding of the nature of National Socialism while injuring and threatening a number of material and immaterial interests which had heretofore been thought safe.

Significant among this group in many cases were persons connected with the bureaucratic machinery of the state, whose judgment or innate decency outweighed their opportunism.[14] Their experiences with Party infringements, corruption, and violence became sufficiently terrifying to overcome indifference and caution.

The general sentiments of such circles have been noted by Hassell in many entries in his diary, especially impressively in October, 1939:

Among informed people in Berlin I encountered the deepest depression. While the people at large are still jubilant over 'the brilliant move of the Russian pact,' the victories in Poland and the achievements of submarines and aircraft against England, a sense of inevitable doom is spreading among the informed. These feelings predominate: the conviction that the war cannot be won militarily; the understanding that we live in an extremely precarious economic condition; the awareness of being led by criminal adventurers; and the sense of the deep shame with which the conduct of war in Poland, partly through the brutal use of air power, partly through the terrible bestialities of the SS, especially against the Jews, have covered the German name.[15]

Such views began to permeate growing numbers of administrative officials in municipal, state and federal offices, judges and other members of the legal profession. There were other professional groups with corresponding experiences, among which teachers and other intellectuals should be singled out. Elements in trade, industry, and agriculture which developed antagonistic attitudes and gave[16] political expression to them were apparently much more rare and isolated.

THE CHURCHES

Religious groups were of singular importance. They could be found among clergy and laymen of both major churches which, in the case of the Catholic group, had often been associated with the pre-Hitler Center party and the Catholic trade unions. The testimony is strong, although one cannot simply conclude that either the Catholic or the Protestant churches had always been on the side of the angels.[17] There were timidity and hesitation as well as outright defection within the churches and, especially in the beginning, what protest there was had little enough political connotation. Yet they constituted the only "visible" opposition to the Nazi monolithic state. It was visible in the sense that the public was widely aware of a mounting cleavage between the Nazi state and the churches, especially in the case of the Catholic church. From the point of view of the dictatorship this dissent always had a political character. For in the totalitarian system any assertion of separate institutional goals and spiritual allegiances is in itself a grave political threat.

Since the role of the churches in Germany has been the subject of some controversy, the question should be frankly aired.[18] In the case of both churches there were strong factors making for a policy of collaboration or, at least, toleration. The Protestant church, predominantly Lutheran, had for centuries been indoctrinated with deference to secular authority and accustomed to live under its bureaucratic control. Its clergy had largely come to share the outlook and even the prejudices of the ruling classes and the secular bureaucracy, with both of which it had intimate connections. This outlook was socially and politically conservative, authoritarian, and nationalist in character.[19] By the same token, the laboring classes had become increasingly alienated from active participation in the church in the last two generations. Seen against such a background, the professed aims of National Socialism did not appear unduly alarming to large numbers among this clergy, nurtured as they had been in this tradition. They seemed positively edifying to the group which was to enter fully into the spirit of the Third Reich under the name of "German Christians."

The Catholic church, as in Mussolini's Italy, had all too early entered into an agreement for a *modus vivendi* with the rulers of the Third Reich, for which the Holy See's Concordat of July 20, 1933 was to provide the formal framework. In an address to the College of Cardinals, on June 2, 1945, the Pope has since pointed out that, in the spring of 1933, it was the Nazi government itself which had requested the Concordat. To decline it, the Pope emphasized, would have put the church at a disadvantage in any effort to secure the protection of the Catholic religion in Germany. That such a treaty-making, on the other hand, put German Catholicism under heavy practical obligations and, in the eyes of the world, generally strengthened the hands of the Hitler regime was an unavoidable consequence in the realm of totalitarian politics.

Long before Hitler's assumption of power some of the most trenchant attacks on Hitlerism had come from Catholic critics in Germany. Catholic church authorities, unlike their Protestant brethren, had outlawed membership in the Nazi party to their flock as irreconcilable with basic Catholic dogma. Yet, apart from the reasons stated by the Pope himself, the new policy was doubtless found palatable in view of Hitler's repeated assertions of respect for "positive Christianity," his boasted anti-Communism and his rejection of all liberalism. At least some ecclesiastic quarters may have seen in this the harbinger of a new "social conservatism" whose deplorable revolutionary crudities could be expected to wear off with the exercise of power. Officially a line of cautious cooperation, if not appeasement, was initiated. The German bishops lifted the earlier ban on Party membership, although a pastoral letter of June, 1933 heavily stressed the church's opposition to nationalism, excessive authoritarianism, imperialism, and excessive body worship.

It seems that this policy was on the whole maintained in the face of mounting provocation and persecution. Its breakdown was foreshadowed by the Papal Encyclical of March 14, 1937 ("With Burning Sorrow").[20] While it lasted, the disciplined effort at correctness was burdened by embarrassing displays of subservience on the part of certain dignitaries and publications. On the other hand, it never quite concealed the growing oppositional efforts with which visible and audible spokesmen like Cardinal Archbishop Faulhaber of Munich, Bishop Preysing of Berlin, and Bishop von Galen of Muenster were clearly linked. Underlying this situation was evidently an internal rift among German Catholic bishops not unlike the one within Protestant Confessionalism. The majority, led by Cardinal Bertram of Breslau, was reportedly opposed to open resistance. It was in favor of religious rather than political methods. Bishops Preysing of Berlin and Galen of Muenster, representing the more political wing of the episcopate, were said to be in a minority which also included Bishop Groeber of Freiburg who had unhappily once been known as "Brown Conrad" himself. The anonymous and clandestine anti-Nazi movement received increasingly firm support from some bishops, the lower clergy, and particularly from certain orders, among them the Jesuits.[21] Probably Bishop Galen's statement of July 20, 1941 was as clear an indication of the prevailing character of church resistance as can be found:

We Christians do not make a revolution. We shall continue faithfully to do our duty in obedience to God and out of love to our people and fatherland. Against the enemy at home there is but one weapon: to hold out with vigor, toughness and hardness. One must become hard and stay hard. We are, at this moment, not hammer but anvil. But watch sometime in the smithy, ask the smith and let him tell you: whatever is hammered out on the anvil is shaped not only by the hammer but also by the anvil. The anvil cannot and need not hit back: it must only be firm and hard. If it is sufficiently tough, firm and hard, the anvil usually lasts longer than the hammer. However violently the hammer may come down, the anvil stands in calm firmness and will long continue to shape what is newly hammered out in the smithy.[22]

Yet the very statement, made in a series of notable fighting sermons, for all its wording did not conceal the political intent.

Of the Protestant church Hitler's deputy Bormann stated in 1941 that the earlier policy of fostering a unified Protestant Reich church had been completely abandoned: ". . . since the Protestant Church is just as antagonistic towards us as the Catholic Church, any strengthening of it would merely be harmful for us. . . The interest of the Reich lies not in the overcoming, but in the maintenance and strengthening of ecclesiastic particularism."[23]

There were, however, both compromising with National Socialism and outright surrender to it among the weaker and the more nationalist elements of German Protestantism. Yet, with all the willingness to make adjustments on the part of numbers of clergymen and laity, the Protestant church remained basically an unassimilated body. "Somehow," the Swiss theologian Karl Barth has recently written, "everyone who wanted to exist as a serious Evangelical Christian, let alone minister, in this state was harassed or at least badgered, and had to protest and profess, even though he might have little insight or backbone."[24]

What conscious and deliberate resistance was offered beyond that stemmed, apart from some smaller sectarian groups, from that growing band known as the Confessional or Confessing church. They were the ones who, again in Barth's words, "declined to capitulate to certain demands of the system because they were irreconcilable with the Christian confession and therefore with their conscience." Their opposition made itself felt virtually from the beginning of the regime. They resisted the introduction of "Aryan" requirements and the "leadership" principle into the church, and equally the claims of the so-called German Christians in the Confessional Declaration of Barmen (May, 1934). In 1936 they addressed a declaration to Hitler which protested certain practices of the Nazi Reich, the falsification of plebiscites, the degrading of law and justice, and concentration camps. Nor should it be forgotten that Confessional, like Catholic circles, often enough sought to extend aid and encouragement to persecuted Jews.

Since it was basically religious-theological and thus nonpolitical in intent the resistance of these men was often limited and narrowly confined. Coupling the Lutheran doctrine of the separation of church and state with a strong belief in the other-worldliness of God and the church they were ready enough to repulse state influence, yet could often give too little positive guidance in worldly matters beyond that. In Karl Barth's opinion they have been wrongly blamed "that their objection was not sufficiently comprehensive since it was the system as such and not some of its demands which they should have resisted as irreconcilable with their confession and conscience. They fought for the freedom of the church and its Gospel; yet it was hidden from them that, at the same time, the freedom of the people and the justice of the land were in jeopardy. But there were only partial struggles of resistance at that time. . . . And even if the battle-ground of the Confessional Church was admittedly too narrow it must not be overlooked that it took up positions from the very first, that it fought and suffered seriously and maintained these positions to the bitter end."

In a secret directive of 1938 the Security Service acknowledged the significance of this resistance.[25] Commenting upon a split in the "Confessional Front" with regard to its attitude towards the state as such, the directive refers to a "radical" wing which rejects any interference of the state with the church, and a "moderate" wing which avoids such a sharp position. However, it continues: "The two groups have partly united again and reject, in joint manifestos from the pulpit and in resolutions, the orders of the government. The Confessional Front comprises by far the largest majority of Protestant theologians and also a majority of the believing church membership. Not unlike Catholicism, with which intimate associations of a personal and spiritual-religious character are maintained, Protestantism seeks to gain influence in the various social spheres . . ."

In actual fact, the moderates and the radicals were hardly reunited. With the approach of war, and possibly under renewed pressure, Bishop Marahrens of Hanover together with the Protestant Bishops of Wuerttemberg, Baden, and Bavaria signed, on May 31, 1939, a document which signified virtual capitulation to Nazi demands. Marahrens, in a pastoral letter in the fall of 1943, speaking in behalf of a recently established Church Council of Trustees, proclaimed that "we must everywhere call forth the insight that we are engaged in a war which demands our total concentration, free of all sentimentality." Bishop Wurm of Wuerttemberg, on the other hand, although he had signed the 1939 declaration which opened the church door to Nazi policy, soon became one of the public accusers of the government. In September, 1941, at a Stuttgart meeting, he spoke of "difficult inner tensions." At the beginning of the third war winter he declared: "Our people cannot be described as sufficiently united to fulfill the tasks which lie before them" because of the "threat to our fellowship through events in the ecclesiastic field and intrusions upon the rights of the church. . . . Where is that courage—the ornament of German manhood—if the only argument that counts is the Gestapo?"

In July, 1943, Bishop Wurm, as senior bishop of the Protestant church, was protesting to Hitler and the Cabinet members against the methods of the regime, the general lawlessness, the persecution of the church, and the atrocities in the occupied areas.[26]

The ultimate consequences of such steps were drawn by a group of Confessional clergy and laymen which had been meeting in Freiburg since 1938. It secretly circulated a pamphlet which thoroughly re-examined the traditional Christian and basic Lutheran doctrine of obedience to authority (Romans, 13) in the light of modern conditions.[27] It asserted the right and even the duty to resist and demanded that the church admonish a clearly ungodly secular authority. This was a doctrine which was yet to assume importance as a justification for concerted direct action against the totalitarian state. It is highly significant that as Confessional forces became actively engaged in resistance activities they sought and received moral support from leaders and agencies of the Protestant ecumenical movement abroad. The importance of these relations, even before they had assumed any practical political significance, was sensed, with the acute awareness sometimes springing from hatred, by an opponent like Alfred Rosenberg.[28] Such contacts played a notable role in the work, for instance, of the Freiburg group which at the suggestion of British church dignitaries elaborated a series of memoranda on the reorganization of German life on a religious foundation. They were to be submitted for discussion to a postwar World Congress of Churches.

Although no well-balanced account of religious resistance in Germany could be given here, the following aspects may be noted in conclusion:

1. Both the Catholic and, on the Protestant side, mainly the Confessional churches, encouraged and developed attitudes and practices of nonconformity with the Nazi regime which became increasingly outspoken as time went on.

2. Little of this amounted to a deliberate political resistance in the early years. Yet the progressive estrangement between church and state, coupled with a drawing together of activities on both sides of the religious camp, began to encourage positive political efforts, that is, attempts to resist and undermine the dictatorship both spiritually and practically.

3. It is clear that a good many of those who, on the political right and center, were engaged in resistance activities derived much of their conviction and support from such religious sources. Beyond that, many on the left who saw religious resistance in action gained a new respect for the religious forces. This worked both ways. Karl Barth has observed that ". . . many Protestant Christians had their sights also raised in these days because, in prisons and concentration camps, under the force of the common oppressor, it came to meetings among Confessional ministers and Christians on the one side, of Social Democrats and Communists, of Catholics and Witnesses of Jehovah on the other, which did not lead to conversions but, for the first time, to real mutual understanding and respect. . . ."[29]

This became a starting point for alliances and alignments within the resistance camp which continue to have effect in post-Nazi Germany. The alliance between Protestants and Catholics in the Christian Democratic Union, Germany's largest political party, was greatly influenced by the common sacrifices of the two religious groups in the resistance.

YOUTH

Cutting across all these categories, including that of the political left, was that part of the young generation which had either never succumbed to National Socialism or had succeeded in unshackling itself. Nobody can possibly belittle the effectiveness of Nazi indoctrination upon German youth. Among the young an aggressive and dynamic political creed will always be most easily accepted. There is little or no experience with which to oppose the propagandists' more flagrant distortions of reality. Yet the manifest differences of intelligence, character, and early environment among them affect the plasticity of the young in any political system. A realistic appraisal of the situation of youth under the Nazis would presumably show that the fanatical zealots among the young were a declining group.[30] The majority of the young were doubtless neither genuinely Nazi nor anti-Nazi but superficially indoctrinated conformists. Like their elders they were playing the game because it was the normal thing to do or because it was indispensable for the building of an existence. A third group, and doubtless numerically the weakest, was genuinely opposed to the regime.

Such opposition among German youth could arise principally from the following sources. First of all, a number of the young had become so overfed with Nazi indoctrination and impatient of regimentation in the Nazis' youth organizations that they began to rebel in one form or another. Much of this revulsion was essentially apolitical, as for instance in the case of the so-called "Edelweiss" and similar bands which sprang up amongst disgruntled Hitler Youth members. Theirs has been correctly described as primarily a "negative, unpolitical rebellion of adolescents against an adult society in which they find themselves intolerably restricted and regimented." There were boys and girls who struck out for themselves, often simply in order to taste forbidden amusements (jazz), symbols of a strange world in which libertinism was an avenue to liberty. There were others who were morally repelled by what they experienced in Nazi youth organizations and began to draw their own conclusions. One of them, brought up in a monastery school and later one of the insurgent Munich students of 1942, has graphically described his own experiences:

What I saw was not good. It was dirty and repulsive; revolting talk, no respect for anything, indescribable relations of 12 to 15 year olds with girls, and an un-understandable conceit. . . I felt all this was a great misfortune. Only one thing was left: to be silent and act like the rest—or—to depart. One could not refuse to join. There was no way out. I took poison. Unhappiness, hospital and long sickness and shame followed this step. . . . Soon—I now was 16 years old—I founded my own group of friends. We were seven. We met regularly in one of our homes and discussed our problems. Quite emotionally we despised all the aspects of National Socialism. . . .

The Nazis themselves noted such developments early. Many SD

morale reports dwell on undesirable trends among the young. In 1941, an official and confidential analysis devoted an entire chapter to the rise of cliques and groups among the young which it divided into criminal-asocial groups and political-oppositional cliques.[31]

Next, there were certain surviving elements of the German youth movement, some of which had never given in although the old youth movement organizations had of course been taken over lock, stock, and barrel by the Nazi authorities. New underground cells and groups sprang up which sought to carry on the tradition of the good life as the founders of the German youth movement had understood it.[32] Their frequently romantic names perpetuated the spirit of the old movement, even when they were innovations of these years. There were the new "Navajos" and the old "Nerothers," the "New Germans," "Storm Groupers" (*Sturmschaerler*), "Quickborners," "Pathfinders," "DZ 1/11 s," "Federated Selfdefenders,"[33] "Free Groupers," "Falcons," and many others. The claim that these groups were genuinely part of a resistance movement is open to question. Yet they doubtless, in many cases, helped to shape the attitudes and convictions of active resisters among the young who knew how to live and die for them. Men like Dr. Rossaint, a Catholic priest and active leader in the youth movement, Helmut Hirsch, the Boeckling group in Essen,[34] all of whom were tried and condemned in 1937,[35] became the predecessors of the rebellious Munich students of 1942.

Against all the odds of a thoroughly coordinated school system there was finally the influence of certain stubborn teachers and stubborn traditions which persisted here and there in the schools of the land. There were individual professors in universities who taught as much of the truth as they could, sometimes even in the fields in which indoctrination had been pushed hardest. There was also the far from negligible influence of churches and individual homes. In Catholic regions, like the Rhineland, home and church influences tended to prove a particularly strong counterweight to the Nazi school system. An SD morale report from Bielefeld, in pointing out the general growth of religious efforts to gain influence in the school system, mentioned as an especially disgraceful example the statement of a literature teacher to her class that the

Jews were God's chosen people and that their persecution could never be pleasing in the eye of God. The report found this "pro-Jewish rubbish" especially disturbing "as the children would be driven into a serious conflict of conscience, because of all the other propaganda. ..."[36]

That such influences carried over into the armed forces is entirely plausible.[37] How effective they actually became in the atmosphere of this war is another question. Such influences were not, of course, confined to Catholic regions. For instance, in 1940 SD reports emphasized that the students of a certain Bremen high school were generally displaying marked antagonism to Nazi standards and ideas. This was even found for certain boys whose parents were described as zealous Nazis. In this particular case, the blame was laid directly at the door of the school and its teachers. Occasionally, some of these youngsters would find themselves face to face with Nazi "justice." In pronouncing sentence upon a Munich group of fourteen youthful defendants in April, 1943, the People's Court began ominously to wonder aloud about at least one such deplorable school situation: "The People's Court notes that three students from the same high school class appear in this case and that several others, from the same school, have been mentioned. There must be something wrong there, and it must have to do with the spirit of the class for which the court cannot blame these boys altogether. One is ashamed that such a class exists in a German humanistic high school (Gymnasium)."[38]

One law professor in Leipzig, himself a man of conservative convictions, related how accessible students remained to the personal influence of an upright teacher. That the undercurrents continued to flow is illustrated by his account of how student audiences, after the fall pogroms of 1938 (which had been widely described by the official propaganda as "spontaneous popular manifestations"), would invariably greet with demonstrative laughter any use of the term "spontaneous" in the course of a classroom lecture. Nor was it an accident that a man like the Freiburg historian Gerhard Ritter, well understood to be out of sympathy with the system, attracted increasingly large student audiences during the war.

Most of these strains become evident in the best-known (or worst-concealed) incident of oppositional student action which flared up in Munich in 1942 and 1943 and cost the lives of a number of youths in retaliation. It originated within a group of soldier-students who were active before and even more after they had been through the debacle of Stalingrad. Ordered back to the university to resume their medical studies they did more than was assigned to them. Early religious training, membership in youth groups,[39] repelling experiences, and the influence of a university teacher[40] drove them to group action. A few of these young men became the center of a group which comprised even high-school students. They wrote and widely circulated in cities throughout Germany flaming appeals for resistance against Nazi oppression and the war. They agitated and even staged with reckless abandon a demonstration against certain Nazi officials. Two mass treason trials, conducted by the People's Court under Freisler's chairmanship in the spring of 1943, took the lives of Hans and Sophie Scholl, a brother and sister, Christoph Probst, Alexander Schmorell, Wilhelm Graf, and Dr. Kurt Huber, while a large number were sentenced to the penitentiary.[41] In sentencing the second group, Freisler expostulated about one leaflet as using "the heroic struggle of Stalingrad to abuse the leader as military charlatan," as indulging "in cowardly defeatism and urging resistance to National Socialism and dishonorable surrender." "We do not," said Freisler on that occasion, "relapse into the error of the Weimar Republic which regarded such traitors as acting from honorable conviction and punished them by honorable confinement. The times are gone when everyone could run around with his own political 'faith'! For us, there is but one measure, that of National Socialism. This we apply to all!"[42]

While it was possibly only a relative handful of young men and women who followed the path of active, physical resistance, much which remained on a purely intellectual and spiritual plane has doubtless also served in the preservation of some healthy substance in a sick body-politic. It is too early and will perhaps remain altogether impossible to give a just appraisal of such activities. In a few instances concrete evidence remains. There was, for example, the magazine *Action and Dream* which two Saarbruecken students launched in the spring of 1939 and circulated in typed copies among a widening group of friends. By deliberately shunning political and current questions, they possibly lessened its significance and certainly their vulnerability. The fostering of unhampered creative effort was their aim. The sheet was published more regularly in 1943 when one of the editors was hospitalized. Between April, 1943 and March, 1945 there were twenty-two issues, of about thirty pages each, which went out to a few hundred friends and sympathizers, mostly in the armed forces.[43]

Why was it, one may ask, that there was not more, or more conspicuous, action by members of the German youth who had been under these similar influences? Why was it that among the substantial number of non-Nazis so relatively few become active resisters during the war in which they were caught? It must not be forgotten, of course, that the rigidly enforced secrecy in these matters is still effective today. We still lack a true picture of the political undercurrents in the German armed forces during the war. Until now, only individual cases have come to light.[44] Yet the answer lies somewhat deeper. There was a basic dilemma which youthful opponents of Hitlerism shared with other phases of the German resistance. One German veteran, a former American prisoner of war, has sought to express it:

It was a war of terror against liberty, you are right. But it was also a war of one nation against another. . . . There is an old national war, something that has always existed, and something else, something immoral, thoroughly rotten, which fights against the new common spirit of peoples. But how can the young people in Germany distinguish? A young Frenchman, a Pole did not have to distinguish. For him, the national enemy and the evil were simply identical. But the German? . . . The German had to decide that he had to commit treason. He did not have Hitler before his rifle if he decided on the right way—but the many small fellows who believed that they had to support a national war. All of them, his fellow countrymen, would have become his enemies. Of course, he would then have known that he had become a traitor from patriotism. But the decision is hard, perhaps too hard. . . .[45]

THE ARMY

In all probability the "converted civilians" of the German armed forces on the whole shared, at the beginning of the war, the attitudes and the outlook of the corresponding civilian age groups. Whatever changes occurred were largely due to the length and character of their war experiences and the influence of superior officers. One might expect that the members of the regular officer corps, unlike the mass of ordinary uniformed civilians, would display an impressive cohesiveness and a more definite pattern of political behavior. While this used to be true for the older Prussian and German Army, the Nazis had, since 1933, succeeded in effecting decisive changes.[46]

The army had facilitated Hitler's climb to power and accepted the new regime with considerable complacency. The reasons were not far to seek. The army leadership had never become fully reconciled to the Weimar Republic and, more importantly, it had no doubt that the Nazis in their aggressive nationalism would provide for an enlarged and modernized fighting force. On the part of the army leadership, this was a disdainfully entered, mutually useful arrangement with political parvenus, made on the understanding that in its own sphere the army would be left alone.[47]

Even then there were men like Generals Beck, von Hammerstein, and some others whose antagonism to the Nazis was barely concealed and who, in some instances, had connections with civilian opposition circles. They stayed on partly in deference to what they falsely assumed to be overriding interests of the army as a whole, partly because most of them in the beginning seem to have shared the easy optimism of civilian conservatives that it would be simple to get the Nazis again under control when their usefulness was gone.[48] As time went on, that small group of generals began to get worried. One well-informed observer has summarized the picture:

The knowledge of an incredible responsibility weighs heavily upon these men. They feel that no, ever so drastic, order can relieve them of it. Fundamentally, it is only a trifling number of (top-ranking?) officers who align themselves ideologically with the brown terror. The majority remains internally and externally "neutral." They simply belong to that human flotsam that drifts wherever there is an easy life, security and an unexpectedly good career. These all too many in goldbraided uniform, from which they derive protection and self-assurance, simply drift unthinkingly through their laborious days—more politely, they are completely absorbed in their work. However, in such savage times, aloofness from the world and detachment are misplaced. By their excessive passivity towards everything that occurs around them they willy-nilly, consciously or unconsciously, become privileged participants in the brown revolutionary history.[49]

The Nazis, on their part, could never have assumed power nor could they have completed the strait jacket with which they shackled German life in the first five years had the army offered serious resistance. As in the case of other essentially conservative forces, groups of officers began to recognize National Socialism as a threat to themselves and to their country as it became progressively stronger and ceased to respect the autonomy of the military in their own domain. The bloody repression of the so-called Roehm coup of June 30, 1934 (more correctly a Himmler coup) had served to avert Roehm's design to inject the S.A. into the army. This temporary victory was bought dearly enough. The price was the army's moral surrender to Hitler's claim that the arbitrary violence of that purge had anything to do with justice. With Hindenburg's death and Hitler's prompt assumption of formal authority as chief of state, the army leadership was taken by surprise. On August 2, 1934, it allowed the noose of unconditional obedience to be slipped over its head by taking an oath of loyalty to Hitler in person.[50] Given the system as it was and the prevailing conveniently technical conception of loyalty, this turned out to be a significant step in the army's progressive abdication.

Thus, as time went on, the very expansion of the army, which had been an objective of the military leadership, hastened its undoing. It meant a breaking-up of the old cadres with the large influx of junior officers, often slated for rapid advancement, men who had gone through the Nazi youth organizations and whose convictions had been properly conditioned in the process. As a group they could no longer be fully assimilated into the traditional officer corps, with its specific loyalties. To the extent that they were still in control on the eve of the war, the leaders of the old army no longer commanded an officer corps which identified itself whole-heartedly with the established military hierarchy and its traditional conservatism. "What this or that general might think, did not mat-ter," the Army Chief of Staff was reported as saying on the eve of the war. "The attitude of the junior officer corps was decisive for any enterprise resembling a coup d'etat, because they were in closest contact with the average trooper and thus with the mass of the people."[51] Hassell commented on the reverse of the medal when he exclaimed, in January, 1940, "Prussian discipline no longer has a firm hold where it is indispensable, namely among the enlisted men and the officer corps; but on the highest [army] level, where obedience should be supplemented by personal judgment and poli-tical responsibility, it is rendered more slavishly and contrary to better insight. The generals who want to overthrow a government refuse to act without its orders."[52] The initially secret establish-ment of an independent air force under Goering, which was merely coordinated since 1934 with the army and navy under the Minister of War, incidentally served the further strengthening of National Socialism in the armed forces.

At the same time, Hitler and his henchmen took further measures to neutralize the generals—as far as they were still thought to re-quire it. Their mounting opportunism was reinforced and spread by a clever system of corruption by money, splendid gifts, and special favors. Old Marshal von Mackensen, of First World War fame, read a declaration which rationalized the murders of Gen-erals Schleicher and Bredow to a General Staff Association meet-ing after June 20, 1934 and was rewarded with an estate.[53] Gen-eral von Kluge accepted a 250,000 mark check on his birthday, and Guderian a large estate in formerly Polish territory. Brauchitsch wanted a divorce which his wife refused to grant. He asked Hitler's intervention, who obligingly "suggested" the advisability of a di-vorce to the lady, thus enabling his general to marry another woman who was described as "150 per cent Nazi."

As is now known, Hitler's plans for aggression had been formu-lated by 1937. Absolute control of an army whose leadership was rightly regarded as partly very lukewarm had become essential. The Blomberg-Fritsch crisis, which burst into the open in February, 1938, was the decisive turning point. It terminated the period of "uneasy equilibrium between the reactionary, but also conservative forces which had contributed to put Hitler and National Socialism into the saddle, and the party led by Hitler."[54] The sudden retirement on February 3, 1938 of General von Blomberg, the Minister of War, and General von Fritsch, the army's Commander in Chief, along with a brace of moderate commanding generals, was the climax of one of the more sordid and picaresque plays for power which had up to that time been staged behind the scenes of the Third Reich. Goering, with Himmler the main wire-puller in this case, had long aspired to Blomberg's succession. When the occasion presented itself, he apparently enlisted the willing cooperation of the Chief of all German Police who was only too pleased to further a promising operation against the citadels of the rival military authority. The occasion arose with the blunder of the spineless Blomberg who asked and accepted highly compromising favors from Goering which would enable him to marry a young woman with a shady past.[55] At the same time, an old Gestapo file was conveniently fished out and presented to Hitler which falsely proved that Fritsch, as Commander in Chief the obvious candidate for Blomberg's succession, had been involved in homosexual activities. After much manoeuvring, Blomberg and Fritsch were "allowed" to retire,[56] but Goering did not succeed in his ambition. Hitler instead scrapped the War Ministry, practically assumed supreme military authority himself, and designated Keitel, a nonentity, as his own deputy to head the newly emerging High Command of the Armed Forces.[57] General von Brauchitsch became the successor of Fritsch.[58]

The crisis had run its full course when General Beck, the ablest and most widely respected military leader, resigned a few months later. The resignation was intended as an act of protest against the emasculation of the army leadership, as an alert against the imminence of war, and as a warning to all remaining military men with backbone to cease further surrender. Beck had already made himself suspect by speaking bluntly in behalf of Fritsch, whom he had mistakenly regarded as a "strong man"[59] who would eventually take the requisite action. In March while German troops entered Austria, Beck sent a memorandum to Hitler in which he declared that the continuation of a policy of conquest would unavoidably lead to a German and European catastrophe. This message was never answered.[60] He resigned after Hitler had revealed his intention of attacking Czechoslovakia in an address to the commanding generals in June, 1938. His resignation, which Hitler reportedly first refused to accept, was deprived of much of its practical significance at home and abroad because the government managed to keep it secret until the end of the Sudeten crisis. According to one account, the dissenting Chief of Staff was told by Hitler on that occasion: "The armed forces are an instrument of policy. I shall give them their assignment when the moment has come. The army has to carry out its task and not to debate whether it has been rightly or wrongly ordered."

Beck replied that he could not assume responsibility for orders of which he disapproved.[61]

Whatever forces of opposition to the Nazis existed among the military leadership on the eve of the war had thus been profoundly weakened. Opportunism had eaten deeply into the moral fibre of many potential allies. An apolitical discipline or lack of backbone, coupled with the cynical aggressiveness of the other side, had largely destroyed its earlier independence of action. Key men among the leaders, notably Beck, had lost, and others were going to lose, much of their effectiveness because they were no longer in authority. On the other hand, there was more and more prodding from civilian groups with "the right connections." There also was a slowly growing distrust in the political, let alone military, rationality of the "leader"—which, however, too easily succumbed to successes won by "intuition." Last but not least, Military Intelligence, under Admiral Canaris, had re-entered the political field and would, in future, lend invaluable support to the "right-minded." In 1935, its jurisdiction had, with Blomberg's approval, been strictly confined to military intelligence in a technical sense. Since it had been caught wholly unprepared by the Fritsch-Blomberg affair, it was not going to have any further jurisdictional qualms in the face of Gestapo and SD operations. With his chief's tacit approval, Colonel (later General) Hans Oster, a resolute anti-Nazi, was henceforth to maintain a careful watch on domestic events.[62]

The foregoing does not claim to be an exhaustive discussion. These elements may, however, be considered as the main sources of opposition among those who cannot be identified with labor or the Left in general. Their groupings and alignments must not be thought of as so many separate compartments. Rather they constituted a series of concentric or overlapping circles.

THE 20TH JULY: REVOLT THROUGH CHANNELS

All of the oppositional tendencies described above—the army, the bureaucracy, the Catholic and Protestant clergy, the aristocracy, industry and the professions, and labor—were represented in one way or another in the attempted coup of July 20, 1944. The Social Democrats and trade union leaders had been involved in the preparations for a long period; the Communists were brought in at the last moment through the ill-fated negotiations of Leber and Reichwein with the Communists Saefkow and Jakob. It would be a serious error to claim, however, that the coup had the unequivocal support of all the larger groups which contributed to the events. There were resistances to the idea of an army coup in at least two of the oppositional centers. Many of the local Social Democratic leaders distrusted the Wehrmacht and felt that a genuinely democratic Germany could only grow out of unconditional defeat. Some of the members of the Kreisau Circle took a similar view, fearful of the rise of a new "stab-in-the-back" legend and convinced that only thorough-going defeat could lead to a reconstruction of the German spirit. The last group mainly limited its activities to planning a postwar program until the eve of the July 20 attempt when some of its members joined the plotters.

The central figures in the Kreisau group (so named because they met on the von Moltke Kreisau estate) were the young Counts Helmut von Moltke and Yorck von Wartenburg. Both bore famous

German names, were men of considerable experience and broad culture and of deep religious feeling and conviction. The trade unions and Social Democrats were represented in the Kreisau Circle by Carlo Mierendorff, Theo Haubach, Adolf Reichwein, and Julius Leber. The Catholic clergy was represented by the Jesuits Roesch and Delp; the Protestant, by Eugen Gerstenmaier and Harald Poelchau. The professions and bureaucracy were represented at Kreisau by Theodor Steltzer, Paulus van Husen, Horst von Einsiedel, Hans Lukaschek, Hans Peters, and Adam von Trott zu Solz.

Allen Dulles claims that the Kreisau Circle provided the ideology of the July 20 movement.[63] This is perhaps an exaggeration since the Kreisau leaders were not representative of the movement as a whole. There is little doubt, however, that their point of view influenced one segment of the coalition which shared in the responsibility for the effort to overturn the Hitler regime from within.

The postwar program of the Kreisau group was strongly influenced by Christian ethics.[64] They favored a form of Christian socialism involving the nationalization of heavy industry, banks, and insurance. They proposed to change the status of labor by giving it a share with management in the control of industry. In the political sphere they proposed federalism and decentralization, including the breakup of Prussia and the formation of regional governing units of between three to five millions in population. The local and regional parliaments would be chosen by popular election, but the Reichstag was to be selected indirectly by the local and regional assemblies. They did not feel that Germany would be ready for full popular democracy. Originally elementary education was to be left largely in the hands of the churches. But the labor leaders of the Kreisau circle rejected these last points of view. They were representative of the position of the members of the clergy in the group and such men as von Wartenburg, von Moltke, Steltzer, and the like. The Kreisau group favored a European federation in which Germany would play the role of an equal. The German Army was to be abolished. The spirit of these Kreisau proposals is best represented today in the left wing of the CDU through such survivors of the plot as Jakob Kaiser.

The Kreisau group overlapped with the active proponents of the July 20 plot through Julius Leber, Adolf Reichwein, and Theodor Steltzer. Count Fritz von der Schulenberg, cousin of the former Ambassador to Russia, was in contact with the Kreisau circle and the July 20 conspirators. Von Stauffenberg had ties with Kreisau, but was not an actual member of the group. Most of the Kreisau Circle were executed after the failure of the July 20 attempt without regard to their participation in it.[65]

Those directly involved in the plot may be divided into the civilian and military sectors.[66] The civilian sector in turn had labor and upper class components. Some of the labor participants who were also involved in the Kreisau group have been mentioned. But by far the most important left-wing figure was Wilhelm Leuschner, former Social Democratic Minister of Interior of Hesse and the successor of Theodor Leipart as head of the free German trade union movement. In the negotiations over the composition of the government to be established after the successful execution of the plot, Leuschner was the candidate of the left for the office of Chancellor. But the more conservative Goerdeler was preferred, and Leuschner was to be made Vice-Chancellor. The Social Democrats (and apparently Goerdeler himself) expected that Leuschner would take over the Chancellorship as soon as popular forces in Germany could make themselves felt. The left wing of the plot viewed the July 20 coalition as a temporary matter designed to rid Germany of the Hitler regime. They hoped to take over the reins and carry out a Social Democratic policy. In addition to Leber, Haubach, Reichwein, and Dahrendorf, the Social Democratic leadership included Ludwig Schwamb and Hermann Maass.

The Christian trade unions were represented by Jakob Kaiser, former leader of the Catholic unions in the Rhineland, Heinrich Koerner, Franz Leuninger, Bernhard Letterhaus, and Nikolaus Gross. The political program of this segment of the July 20 coalition was quite similar to the Christian socialist position of the Kreisau circle. This represented a development of the earlier conservative, anticapitalist program of the pre-Nazi Christian trade unions.[67] But in contact with the Social Democrats, and under the stress of the Nazi and war experiences, the older conservatism and nationalism of these elements had been moderated if not eliminated.

The conservative group of the civilian sector was divided into two tendencies—that organized around the person of Goerdeler,[68] and that of Popitz, the Prussian Minister of Finance. Goerdeler was a former member of the German Nationalist party. Although he opposed the Hugenberg policy of collaboration with the Nazis, he served as German Price Commissar under Hitler from 1933-36. He resigned as Oberbuergermeister of Leipzig in 1936 in protest over the removal of the status of the German Jewish composer Mendelssohn. From this point on Goerdeler devoted himself to oppositional activity. Starting from the extreme nationalism and monarcho-conservatism of the *Deutschnationalen*, by 1942-43 he had come to advocate a decentralized and disarmed Germany, participating in a European and World Union, with European and international police forces. Germany was to be a loose federation which would include Austria and the Sudetenland and would have a share in the administration of the European colonies. In economic policy Goerdeler was a liberal, favoring customs unions and free trade. He collaborated with the Socialists in the plot and appears to have come around to the democratic view with regard to the solution of political questions in the future Germany. Goerdeler favored what he called "a democracy of the ten commandments," and pleaded for unity of Catholics and Protestants in the reform of Germany.

Most of Goerdeler's immediate associates were conservative industrialists or members of the bureaucracy. The firm of Bosch in Stuttgart gave him financial support, as did a number of aristocratic landowners. His conservative bureaucratic associates included Eugen Bolz, former President of Wuerttemberg; Werner von der Schulenberg, former Ambassador to Russia; Erwin Planck, pre-1933 State Secretary of the German Chancellory; Fritz Elsas, former Deputy-Burgermeister of Berlin; and many others.

The policy of the Goerdeler group might in general be described as a reformed conservative nationalism. They were ready to accommodate themselves to some measure of democracy and a regime of international law and organization. While they were conservative in economic policy they were ready to submit to the ballot box in contests with socialists. This development from the earlier Nationalist position was a consequence of the revulsion from Nazi policies as well as from the collaborative work of Goerdeler and his group with the trade union leaders of the July 20 coalition.

The Popitz[69] circle was distinguished from the Goerdeler group through its closer collaboration with the Nazis and its unequivocal conservatism and nationalism. Popitz served in Hitler's cabinet as Prussian Minister of Finance. In 1937 he was awarded the Golden Party Badge by Hitler. His opposition to the Nazis grew out of fear that Nazi foreign policy would lead to a German catastrophe. He favored a separate peace with the West. At first he thought this could be accomplished by substituting Goering for Hitler. Later he thought that Himmler and the SS might first take power and then be pushed aside by the Wehrmacht. Through an associate, Dr. Langbehn, Popitz sounded out Himmler with regard to these possibilities. Popitz felt that the complete removal of the Nazis would lead to internal chaos. It was mainly on these issues that his ties with Goerdeler were first strained and finally broken. Popitz rejected any thought of the re-establishment of free trade unions or of democracy. Because of his break with Goerdeler he was not informed of the later developments in the July 20 plot. He was, nevertheless, tried and executed after its failure. Special precautions were taken to keep the trial secret in order to conceal Himmler's part in the negotiations with Popitz.

The military sector of the July 20 coalition consisted of elements in the *Abwehr* (military intelligence) and in the army proper. The head of the *Abwehr*, Admiral Canaris, had no active part in the plot itself. He had been, during the Weimar Republic, a member of the "Black Reichswehr." He was rewarded for his militarist and nationalist record by appointment as chief of military intelligence in 1935. Convinced that war would lead to Germany's defeat, he began to resist National Socialist measures and gave protection to convinced anti-Nazis within his organization.

The real head of the July 20 group in the *Abwehr* was General Oster who was in close contact with the military and civilian leaders of the conspiracy. Oster maintained contacts in neutral countries and in general provided the plot with an intelligence service. Associated with Oster in this work were the Colonels Georg Hansen, von Freytag-Loringhofen, Rudolf Marogna-Redwitz, and many others. Freytag-Loringhofen procured the explosives used in the attempted assassination, Marogna-Redwitz was head of the *Abwehr* in Vienna, and Schrader was Oster's representative in Hitler's headquarters. Oster's civilian associates included among others Hans Schoenfeld, Dietrich Bonhoeffer,[70] Hans and Otto John, and Dr. Joseph Mueller. Schoenfeld, Bonhoeffer, and Otto John had contacts with the British. Otto John was in touch with Sir Samuel Hoare, the British Ambassador to Spain; and Joseph Mueller with the Vatican. In 1943 the SD was able to implicate the *Abwehr* in illegal currency transactions designed to enable Jews to escape from Germany, and a number of other illegal actions. This led to the consolidation of the *Abwehr* with the SD. Bonhoeffer was arrested, Oster placed under house arrest, and Canaris removed from office. All three of the above were executed after July 20.

The top Wehrmacht leaders of the plot were Field Marshal von Witzleben, the Generals Beck, Hoeppner, Olbricht, von Tresckow, and Colonel von Stauffenberg. These and many other of the army officers involved were convinced anti-Nazis. With the exception of von Stauffenberg the Wehrmacht oppositional leaders might be described as "Christian conservatives." Their anti-Nazism was not a product of liberal democratic conviction, but developed out of a combination of ethical and expediential considerations. Von Stauffenberg was the main advocate in the "military sector" of a Russian orientation. It was mainly at his insistence (and without the support of the other conspirators) that Leber and Reichwein made approaches to the Communists. He favored Leuschner rather than Goerdeler as Chancellor and almost split with the Goerdeler group when this was refused.

Outside of the high army officers who were anti-Nazi and prepared for action on the basis of religious and traditional conviction, there were many who collaborated simply for reasons of expediency, out of the feeling that the war was lost and that it was necessary to get on the anti-Nazi bandwagon. General Rommel was the outstanding example of this element among the plotters. The Berlin police chief Count von Helldorf, a Nazi of long standing, and Arthur Nebe, Chief of the Reich Criminal Police, also fell into the rather numerous category of July 20 participants who were mainly moved by expediential considerations.

The plotters, thus, were a rather representative German political group. With the exception of the Communists all elements of the left, center, and right of German politics were involved, but in unequal proportions. In the projected cabinet for the new government after the overthrow of the Nazis the Socialists were to have the Vice-Chancellorship and the Ministries of Interior and Information. The other ministries were to be held by Catholics and conservative civilian and military men. The larger number of the participants in the plot were men of a conservative military or bureaucratic mentality. They had, however, undergone some change in views particularly with regard to nationalism as a consequence of their experiences in opposition to the Nazis. In general the views of the conservative nationalists among the plotters became more liberal and internationalist as the German military situation deteriorated. This was at least in part an accomodation to the plotters' estimates of their bargaining position vis-à-vis the Allies.[71]

The plan of the July 20 group and the fatal events which led to its failure are now well known. The bomb left in Hitler's headquarters failed to take full effect since the meeting had taken place in a wooden structure rather than in the concrete bunker ordinarily used. General Fellgiebel, chief of communications in the high command, failed to destroy the communications leading to Hitler's headquarters which made it possible for Goebbels to establish contact and confirm the fact that Hitler was still alive. If the bomb had taken effect it is on the whole likely that everything would have gone according to plan. If the bomb had failed to have its effect but the destruction of communications had isolated Hitler for a period of time, the plotters might have had more critical hours to bring in troops, take the Nazis into custody and in general consolidate their position, at least in Berlin. These two failures sealed the doom of the particular plan which the plotters had contrived.

What is of especial interest in the evaluation of the July 20 affair is that the plotters had only one plan and no alternatives to turn to in the event any single step miscarried. The death of Hitler was essential in order to set aside the army oath to the Fuhrer, and gain the support of the military leaders who were on the fence. The steps which were to follow this event were legal-bureaucratic steps, "through channels." The sealed orders directing the first steps to be taken after the assassination were in the hands of the army commanders awaiting the transmission of the code word "Walküre." The troops of the Home Army under the command of participants in the plot were to march on Berlin, take over government offices, and round up the SS and Gestapo. The various field commanders were to take similar steps throughout Germany and in the occupied countries. Field Marshal von Kluge, Commander of the German armies of the west, General Rommel, the Belgian and French military governors—Generals von Falkenhausen and von Stulpnagel— all had given their support to the plot. Here was a group of men with formidable power and excellent staff training.

Could they have failed to anticipate the possibility that von Stauffenberg's effort might fail and that the Gestapo would take swift and integral measures against the Wehrmacht? Consideration of such possibilities might have led to the recognition that once the first step in the conspiracy was taken the fate of the entire effort was committed, and the lives of all the participants were at stake.

It is not immediately apparent why the plotters failed to make provision for the eventuality of an unsuccessful assassination attempt. The picture we get of the atmosphere of the *Bendlerstrasse* was of a kind of nightmarish paralysis. During the last fatal hours they sat awaiting the movement of Home Army units on Berlin. They had not even made certain of the loyalty of the commanders of these critical troop units; and it was their own Berlin Guard Battalion commander, Major Remer, who turned his unit against the plotters after Goebbels had convinced him that Hitler was still alive.

Among the factors which may account for these significant failures in planning and execution, perhaps three should be singled out for comment: first, the military bureaucratic mentality of the key plotters; second, the demoralization of the plotters; third, the simple and terrible anxiety of men who had taken their lives in their hands.

The July 20 conspirators were in the vast majority of cases members of the German military, governmental, and trade union bureaucracies. History has perhaps never known a more deeply ingrained bureaucratic tradition than the German. The Germans themselves coined the phrase which aptly depicts the implicit obedience to established authority characteristic of members of the German bureaucracy—"Kadavergehorsam." [72] The key figures in the plot had in almost all cases grown up in this tradition, and, even in the planning of a revolt, order was the all important consideration. When Gisevius in early July proposed to General Beck that Goerdeler fly to von Kluge on the western front and ask him to attack the Nazis and lead his armies back to Germany, Beck rejected the proposal. He was opposed to civil war. [73] And this was in July, 1944, with the Allies in France, the Russians on the offensive, and the air war on Germany in full swing!

Another aspect of this military bureaucratic mentality was the place which the assassination of Hitler played in the plans. The primary importance attached to the assassination was that it would relieve the army of its oath, and make resistance to the Nazis possible. Again the importance of an oath to a man who had led his people into catastrophic defeat and who had violated all standards of human decency, to say nothing of oaths! And yet the oath played a most significant role and at the most critical points. General Fromm refused to go along with the plotters when it appeared that there was doubt of Hitler's death. He considered his oath as still binding, submitted to arrest at the hands of General Olbricht, and later in the day turned tables on the conspirators, court-martialled some of them, and ordered their immediate execution. This did not save General Fromm from later torture and execution himself. The commanders on the western front took the indicated steps after the transmission of the code word. They arrested members of the SS and other high Nazis in France. But the moment von Kluge learned of the miscarriage of the assassination attempt, he ordered the release of the Nazis and issued an order of the day affirming his loyalty to Hitler.[74] Only the grossest self-deception could have led him to the belief that this action would save his uniform and life.

Some of the younger men fought against this inertia of the top echelon among the plotters. But they were hampered in their efforts by the paralysis of the "elders" of the plot, who could not, even in the face of an overwhelming national tragedy, break themselves free from traditional influences and bureaucratic red tape—not even if their lives depended on it.

As a consequence of this rigid through-channels mentality, precious time was lost and opportunities were missed. The plotters literally did not have a single trustworthy military unit to defend the *Bendlerstrasse* building and to arrest Goebbels and other Nazi leaders in Berlin. This is not to argue that the existence of an emergency plan and of such an indoctrinated military force would have insured the success of the plot. At best it might have resulted in a swift seizure of Berlin, and the raising of the flag of mutiny which might have brought about civil war and a quicker Nazi collapse. At worst the plotters would have fallen in action and not at the hands of firing squads in the *Bendlerstrasse* courtyard or, after torture and humiliating trials, at the hands of Nazi hangmen.

Aside from these bureaucratic inhibitions against spontaneity and unequivocal action, there was the simple fact of demoralization. The plotters were isolated; their attempts to establish effective contact with the Allied governments had failed. They had been on the point of acting many times in the past, and all of their attempts had miscarried or been postponed. Most of them were waging internal struggles against a kind of fatal resignation. Thus General Hoeppner had only half his heart in the action. When he heard that the assassination attempt had failed, he wanted to pull out. General Fellgiebel perhaps also suffered a loss of nerve at the last moment when he failed to cut Hitler's communications with the outside world. This isolated, conspiratorial atmosphere, full of doubts and misgivings, was hardly conducive to careful planning and swift and unequivocal execution.

It is unnecessary to elaborate at any length on the role played by anxiety among the participants in a conspiracy in which the stake was life itself. Von Stauffenberg, the pivot of the entire action, apparently showed symptoms of simple and understandable funk in the last weeks and days before the event. Had these been independent-minded men, capable of spontaneous action, and with a high morale, fear might have taken on less significant proportions. Among conspirators habituated to authority and whose hope had been drained by many failures, fear may have been just the factor leading to critical errors of judgment and failures of will and resolution.

This is not in deprecation of the courage of the central figures of July 20. Most of them were men of conviction and not mere band-wagon anti-Nazis. But in a plot against a resourceful, ruthless foe, they had made no provision for spontaneity, for last-ditch resistance. Because of this they not only hazarded the success of the plot by making it turn entirely on a single event; they failed even to realize the full exemplary value which might have been attained had they fallen in action.

The July 20 affair is of importance not only from the point of view of historical interpretation. It plays quite a significant role in postwar German development. A number of the key political leaders of postwar Germany are survivors of the plot. Jakob Kaiser, former leader of the Christian Democratic Union in the Russian Zone; Joseph Mueller, leader of the Christian Social Union of Bavaria; and Theodor Steltzer, former Minister President of Schleswig-Holstein, are among the most prominent surviving July 20 figures. There are a number of others in the ranks of the Social Democrats and the Liberals. The failure of the plot was of the greatest significance from a negative point of view. In the wave of terror which followed it hundreds of the already pitifully small, surviving, non-Nazi elite lost their lives, thereby accentuating the crisis of postwar leadership in Germany.

The affair was also of importance as laying the basis for postwar political alliances. The Protestant-Catholic merger in the Christian Democratic Union was influenced by the common sacrifices of the resistance. Similarly the shared sacrifices of the Socialists and the religious sector of the plot made a contribution to the postwar mutual tolerance and, to some extent, friendly relations between the moderate left and some parts of the Christian Democratic movement.

Perhaps the most important function of the July 20 affair is its use in propaganda and education as historic proof of the existence of "the other Germany." In the reorientation and democratization of Germany, the July 20 affair has already assumed mythic proportions, a development which is, on the whole, advantageous. In answer to the propaganda doctrine of "collective guilt" for Nazi barbarism which has the effect of accentuating despair and inducing nationalist resentment, the myth of the German resistance (in which July 20 has the function of dramatic climax) bears the promise of self-regeneration. If, in the process of rendering the tragic events of the plot usable for popular education, some facts are left out and historic human beings apotheosized, this is the common cost of myth-making. In this regard the Germans have done no more than the peoples of the former occupied countries, who have also not hesitated to add a little and substract a little in order to create a picture of resistance to an oppressor more in conformity to aspirations than to actual achievement.

The intensification of conflict between East and West has had important consequences for the German "resistance tradition." On the one hand the left (including the Communists and some of the Socialists) deprecate the July 20 incident as a simple Wehrmacht coup, lacking in genuine conviction. According to this view the success of the affair would have represented the triumph of militarism and reaction. The only valid anti-Nazi resistance is alleged to have been the many local Antifas in which the extreme left played a most significant role. On the other hand conservatives and moderate circles minimize the Antifas as having been Communist fronts set up to assure Communist domination in the postwar period. As we have seen, there is a kernel of truth in both allegations, but the real facts have been distorted to suit polemical purposes. Germany has two resistance myths today, corresponding roughly with the deep political and zonal split in that country.

II
OCCUPATION POLICY

Chap. 4 Germany's Economic Situation and Prospects

FRED H. SANDERSON*

WITH THE COLLAPSE OF THE NAZI REGIME, the economic life of Germany had come to an almost complete stop. Between four and six million Germans had been killed or permanently disabled; approximately as many again had become prisoners of war. Altogether about twenty-five million had lost their homes and property or were facing expulsion. All major cities had suffered severe damage from air raids. Most of the important highway and railroad bridges had been blown up by the retreating Germans in a futile last-minute attempt to stem the tide. In Western Germany, less than 10 per cent of the railway track mileage remained in operation. The Rhine and most canals were closed to traffic. Industry and coal mines were at a standstill. The roads were crowded with more than five million foreign workers and Allied prisoners of war and an approximately equal number of German air-raid evacuees, disbanded troops, and refugees from the East. National and regional administrations had ceased to function, and local police forces lacked the strength and authority necessary to maintain public order. This was the legacy which Hitler left to the German people.

THE BIG-THREE BLUEPRINT

When Allied Military Government stepped into this economic vacuum, its objectives were narrowly defined. It was "to assure

*The opinions expressed in this article are those of the author and are not necessarily shared by the Department of State.

the production of goods and services required to prevent starvation or such disease and unrest as would endanger" the occupying forces, including "repairs to and restoration of essential transportation services and public utilities; emergency repair and construction of the minimum shelter required for the civilian population," and measures "necessary to prevent or restrain inflation of a character or dimension which would definitely endanger accomplishment of the objectives of the occupation." Beyond this, no steps were to be taken "(a) looking toward the economic rehabilitation of Germany, or (b) designed to maintain or strengthen the German economy."[1] In addition, Military Government was to implement the Allied policies of military, political, and industrial disarmament which had emerged by that time.

The Big-Three blueprint for dealing with defeated Germany "during the period of Allied control" was sketched at Yalta (February 1, 1945) and filled out by the Potsdam Agreement (August 2, 1945) and the first Level of Industry Agreement (April 1, 1946). The *Yalta Agreement* called for the temporary partitioning of Germany into four zones of occupation, but at the same time provided for a central control commission in Berlin to coordinate Allied policies in the several zones. The *Potsdam Agreement* was very specific, however, in depriving the zonal boundaries of any economic significance by stipulating that "Germany shall be treated as a single economic unit." To this end common policies were to be established in regard to production, transportation and communications, wages, prices, rationing, foreign trade, currency, banking, taxation, and reparations, and five German central agencies were to be set up to administer these policies. Essential commodities were to be distributed equitably between the several zones so as to produce a balanced economy throughout Germany and reduce the need for imports. The proceeds of exports from current production and stocks were to be available in the first place for payment for such imports.

The area of Germany east of the Oder and Neisse rivers, with a prewar population of about ten million Germans, was exempted from these provisions. Most of this area was claimed by the provisional Polish Government, with the support of the Soviet Government, as compensation for the eastern areas which Poland had ceded to Russia. The Soviet Union itself claimed northern East Prussia, including the city of Königsberg, with a prewar population of about 1,500,000. At Potsdam the Western Allies agreed to place these areas under Polish and Russian administration, respectively, subject to final territorial settlements in the peace treaties. The Western powers also assented to the transfer to Germany of all Germans from Poland as well as from Czechoslovakia and Hungary. The Soviet and Polish governments interpreted this agreement as permitting the expulsion of some five million Germans then remaining in the area of Germany east of the Oder and Neisse and in the former Free City of Danzig.

The payment of "reparations in kind" (which constituted the core of Soviet demands at Yalta) was coupled with the concept of "industrial disarmament" (stressed particularly by the Americans). Reparations were to be exacted in the form of industrial plant and equipment rather than from current output. In this fashion, the industries which are the basis of modern warfare (metallurgy, machine tools, heavy engineering, heavy chemicals, synthetic gasoline, synthetic ammonia, aviation, ship-building, etc.) would be either totally removed or severely curtailed. "Excessive concentrations of economic power" (cartels, syndicates, trusts) in the remaining industries were to be broken up. This, it was held, would prevent Germany from "ever becoming again a threat to the peace of the world."

The original agreement on the German level of industry (whose full title was "Plan for Reparations and the Level of Post-War German Economy") provided for the total dismantling not only of the armament industries but also of such industries as aircraft, construction of seagoing ships, synthetic gasoline and oil, synthetic rubber, synthetic ammonia, roller bearings, heavy machine tools of certain types, heavy tractors, primary aluminum, magnesium, beryllium, vanadium, radio-active materials, hydrogen peroxide of above 50 per cent strength, specific war chemicals and gases, and radio transmitting equipment. (Facilities for the production of synthetic gasoline and oil, synthetic ammonia, synthetic rubber, and roller bearings were to be retained temporarily until the necessary imports were available and could be paid for). The production of crude steel was to be reduced to 5,800,000 tons a year, or 30 per cent of the production in 1936, and the steel production capacity to 7,500,000 tons a year. Other industries were to be reduced to the following percentages of the prewar level:[2]

Basic chemicals	40	per cent
Other chemicals	70	" "
Pharmaceuticals	80	" "
Synthetic fibers	50	" "
Machine tools	11	" "
Heavy engineering	31	" "
Other mechanical engineering	50	" "
Electro-engineering	50	" "
of which: heavy electro-engineering	30	" "
Passenger automobiles	16	" "
Trucks	67	" "
Motorcycles	7	" "
Agricultural tractors	72	" "
Optical and precision instruments	70	" "
Cement	68	" "
Electric power	60	" "

The Level of Industry Plan was the result of a hurried compromise[3] between three conflicting objectives of Allied economic policy toward Germany: (1) industrial disarmament; (2) maximum reparations; (3) the maintenance, without external assistance, of a tolerable standard of living and the provision of sufficient economic incentives to create an environment conducive to the development of a democratic and peaceful way of life in Germany. Soon after its publication, however, many observers came to feel that the plan gave too much weight to the first objective at the expense of the second and third. In limiting reparations to removals of industrial plants, it greatly reduced the total amount of reparations compared with those which could be obtained from current output if the "surplus" equipment were left in place. In Germany, it would have reduced the level of industrial production to about 50 to 55 per cent,

he total supply of goods (including agricultural products) to about
o per cent, and the standard of living (goods and services) to about
wo-thirds of the 1938 level. Such a standard of living would be
pproximately equal to the "European average," as stipulated in the
'otsdam Agreement—it would be well below that customary in
Northern and Western Europe of which Germany was an integral
art, but still somewhat above the standards prevailing in Southern
nd Eastern Europe.

Critics of the plan questioned the wisdom of programming for
Germany a standard of living below the level of the 1932 depression
vhich, more than any other factor, had been responsible for the
lissatisfaction and unrest which swept Hitler into power. They
vere disturbed by prospects of mass unemployment resulting from
he total or partial dismantling of Germany's most important in-
lustries. These fears found support in an official American estimate
hat in spite of an assumed 11 per cent increase in agricultural employment per hectare, the Level of Industry Plan would leave Germany with 3.8 to 4.2 million unemployed.[4] It was considered, there-
ore, that the plan would tend to weaken the democratic forces
within Germany. In particular, it would unjustly single out for
punishment German industrial labor which, unlike the politically
mmature and nationalistic peasantry and urban middle class, had
been the principal and most consistent democratic element in Ger-
nan political life.

Even as a security measure, it was felt, the plan would tend to
defeat its own purpose. While temporarily depriving Germany of
he ability to wage war, it would promote a desire for revenge. In
he long run, deindustrialization was held to be unenforceable and
unnecessary. "It is true . . . that armed strength depends on industrial potential. However, it does not follow that armed strength can
be effectively and permanently reduced by eliminating industries. . . . Left to themselves, the Germans could restore their capital
plant in a very few years and the new plant would be considerably
more modern and potentially more dangerous. . . . Real security
must be sought in other directions . . . the wiser and more effective
course is to deny to any German government . . . the right to an

army or to any arms or munitions whatever, and to police th prohibition."[5]

In spite of the impression created by some of the language in th Level of Industry Agreement, the "prohibitions" and "restrictions imposed on the German economy were never intended to be perm nent. The agreement, like the Potsdam Declaration on which it based, applies to the period of occupation exclusively. In most case it is even more specific in that it concerns one year (1949) only. is a formula for reparations removals and not a program for th economy which must be followed over any period of time. Th plan does not provide long-term controls over the German wa potential; such controls will be determined only in the final peac settlement. This view was already expressed in Secretary Byrne statement of December 11, 1945 and was later reiterated in h Stuttgart speech—after the completion of the reparations progran "the German people were not to be denied the right to use suc savings, as they might be able to accumulate by hard work an frugal living, to build up their industries for peaceful purposes."

The East-West Deadlock

Although the foundation had been laid for a unified Allie economic policy toward Germany, the Allied Control Council– to which France had been added after Potsdam as a fourth occupy ing power—remained deadlocked over the application of th policy. Conflicting interpretations of the Potsdam Agreement an the steps which the several occupying powers have taken towar its revision have made it appear certain that it will never be full implemented in its original form.

Ostensibly at the source of the conflict are differences of th four powers over three principal issues, all predominantly economi These are: (1) the treatment of Germany as an economic uni (2) reparations; and (3) the emergence of one of the occupyin powers as owner and operator of a giant industrial combine withi Germany. Difficulties also arose over the French demands for th separation from Germany of the Saar, Ruhr, and Rhineland area Institutional problems, including the degree and form of economi

entralization to be permitted to the Germans and the role of public
nd private ownership in the future German state, also gave rise to
ifferences and recriminations. But it soon became apparent that
ehind these economic questions lay conflicting political aims; and
hile disagreements among the three Western powers tended to
iminish, three protracted meetings of the Council of Foreign
linisters[7] failed to bridge the widening gap between the Western
nd Soviet positions.

The principal difficulty arose over the treatment of Germany
s an economic unit, required by the Potsdam Declaration. The
rench, who did not sign the Potsdam Agreement, at first refused
) cooperate in setting up central economic agencies under German
dministrators until French claims for German coal deliveries and
hose related to the Saar, Ruhr, and Rhineland were satisfied. At
loscow the French indicated, however, that they would agree to
he economic unification of Germany without awaiting the deter-
nination of the future status of the Ruhr and Rhineland, but in-
isted on the immediate incorporation of the Saar into the French
conomy.

The Soviet Government, while repeatedly reaffirming its support
f the Potsdam Agreement, made economic unification contingent
pon the acceptance by the Western powers of a number of con-
litions, some of which appeared to be not only additional to but in
ffect inconsistent with those agreed upon at Potsdam. In partic-
llar, the Russians refused to proceed with economic unification
ntil the other Allies recognized the Soviet demand for substantial
eparations from Germany's current production over a number of
ears, a claim which was originally presented at Yalta but rejected
t Potsdam in favor of reparations in the form of capital removals.

Even if these French and Russian demands had been satisfied,
here remained some doubt whether "economic unification" meant
he same thing to each of the four controlling powers. All four
owers agreed that economic unification should include: (1) the set-
ing up of central agencies to administer economic affairs through-
ut Germany; (2) the sharing of indigenous resources among the
ccupation zones; (3) a common export-import plan; (4) the

allocation of commodities in short supply on the basis of unifor
ration scales; (5) an agreement defining and limiting occupatic
costs; (6) a nation-wide financial and monetary reform. Sovi
statements indicated, however, that Russia intended to retain for i
zonal commander the right to suspend measures taken by the Ge
man central departments whenever he deemed such measures to i
inconsistent with the fulfilment of German obligations to the Allie
the security of the occupation forces, or any other Allied policie
The French, on their part, considered the transfer of central exec
tive authority to Germans to be premature and preferred to reta
the direction of the economic departments in Allied hands. Both tl
French and the Russians indicated their reluctance to share tl
burden of financing the German deficit until Germany becom
self-supporting.

Obviously, German central agencies whose operations are sul
ject to unilateral interference by each zonal commander would i
futile. Real economic unity can be achieved only if these agenci
receive full governmental authority over all four zones subject,
course, to the directives of the Allied Control Council acting as
whole. This was pointed out clearly by Secretary Marshall at tl
London meeting of the Council of Foreign Ministers:

> Any German Government called upon to administer a German
> divided as it is today by the policies of the occupying powers would i
> a sham and a delusion. It is useless to debate the desirability of a centr
> German Government unless the Allies are prepared to create the con
> ditions under which such a government can function . . . [it is] cruel
> misleading . . . to pretend that the mere setting up of a central Germa
> Government would result in healing the division of Germany.
>
> The United States wants a real government and not a facade. Th
> government should reflect the free will of the German people ar
> should be permitted to administer Germany without outside interferen
> except for such necessary security measures as the Allies may jointl
> decide to impose.[9]

While the Control Council remained stalemated over the impl
mentation of the economic unification clauses of the Potsdam Agre
ment, both the Soviets and the French embarked on a policy

unilateral exploitation of their zones, with exports and requisitions exceeding imports. At the same time, the British and American zones, which are more deficient in food and had suffered greater destruction and disorganization than the Soviet Zone and whose import and export programs took greater account of the minimum needs of their population, accumulated a deficit at the rate of more than four hundred million dollars per annum, mostly for the importation of essential foodstuffs.

Although the Potsdam Agreement did not specifically exclude reparations out of current production, it was quite explicit on this point: exports from the Soviet and French zones, as those from the other zones, were to be pooled in order to pay for essential imports into Germany before they would become available for any other purpose. Consequently, the unilateral appropriation by any occupying power of export surpluses from its zone constituted a violation of the Potsdam Agreement.

In the American view, moreover, reparations from current output were precluded in any event by the Level of Industry Agreement by which Germany would retain only such productive capacity as was then considered necessary to maintain a standard of living (including exports to pay for essential imports) equal to the European average. The opposition of the United States to any further restriction of the German standard of living, after the completion of the reparations removals as stipulated by the Level of Industry Agreement, was first announced by Secretary of State Byrnes on December 12, 1945. In his Stuttgart address (September 6, 1946), Mr. Byrnes stated the position of the United States Government as follows:

In fixing the level of industry, no allowance was made for reparations from current production. Reparations from current production would be wholly incompatible with the level of industry now established under the Potsdam Agreement.

Obviously, higher levels of industry would have to be fixed if reparations from current production were contemplated. The levels of industry fixed are only sufficient to enable the German people to become self-supporting and to maintain living standards approximating the average European living conditions . . . the United States will not agree to the taking from Germany of greater reparations than was provided by the Potsdam Agreement.

This view is not shared by the Soviet Government. Only three months had elapsed since the conclusion of the Level of Industry Agreement when Mr. Molotov served notice of the Soviet Union's desire for its revision or supplementation. He considered that in fact "no plan for reparations has been drawn up"[10] and revived the original Soviet claim for reparations to the amount of $10,000,000,000 which was raised at Yalta but subsequently dropped in favor of the Potsdam plan.[11] He also indicated that Russian troops would continue to occupy their present zone until reparations to this amount have been exacted. Mr. Byrnes replied that the United States would stand by the Potsdam Agreement and added that the value of the taxable property in the area east of the Oder-Neisse alone which was separated from Germany amounts to more than $10,000,000,000.[12]

In Moscow, Mr. Marshall, Mr. Bevin, and Mr. Molotov agreed on the desirability of a substantial revision of the German level of industry. "The people of Europe lack the elementary necessities of life," Secretary Marshall stated. "A reasonable increase in the level of industry in Germany will help in time produce more goods. With a four-power treaty, which we have proposed, guaranteeing the continued demilitarization of Germany, a reasonable increase in the level of industry should not endanger European security, but should contribute materially to European recovery. The United States is opposed to policies which will continue Germany as a congested slum or an economic poorhouse in the center of Europe. At the same time we recognize Germany must pay reparations to countries who suffered from its aggression."[13] The Secretary therefore suggested that the Level of Industry Plan be reviewed to allow for increases of population and losses of territory and to eliminate "internal inconsistencies in the plan such as, for example, the shortage of power to meet planned requirements, the inadequacy of planned provisions for certain basic chemicals, some fertilizers, and possibly steel."

In London, Mr. Bidault joined the other three foreign ministers in an agreement to revise the Level of Industry Plan on the basis of a level of steel production of 11,500,000 ingot tons annually.

No agreement was reached, however, on the Soviet demands for reparations out of current production. A minor concession to the Soviet point of view was made by Secretary Marshall at the Moscow session of the Council of Foreign Ministers, but his offer to consider reparations from current output was "limited to compensation for the plants which were destined for removal but which are no longer available by reason of an increase in the level of industry . . ." and provided such compensation does "not increase the cost of occupation, retard the repayment of Allied advances to Germany," or "prevent the equitable distribution of coal and other raw materials. . . ."[14] The Secretary later amplified this statement by saying that this compensation might include the value of the non-removable parts of the plants which would otherwise have been dismantled.[15] The Russians insisted, however, that Germany deliver $10,000,000,000 worth of reparations to the Soviet Union over a period of twenty years, the bulk of which would be in the form of deliveries out of current production.[16] They stated that they considered the acceptance of reparations from current production as an absolute condition of Soviet acceptance of the principle of economic unity.

In London, Secretary Marshall restated the United States position and explained some of the reasons for it:

I have already stated that the United States Government considers that the questions of reparations were finally settled at Potsdam. We will not agree to the program of reparations from current production which under existing conditions could only be met in one of two ways. The first would be that the United States would pay for such reparations. This the United States will not do. The only other method of obtaining reparations from current production from Germany at the present time and for the foreseeable future would be to depress the German standard of living to such a point that Germany would become not only a center of unrest in the heart of Europe but that this would indefinitely, if not permanently, retard the rehabilitation of German peacetime economy and hence the recovery of Europe.

I wish it to be clearly understood that the United States is not prepared to agree to any program of reparations from current production as a price for the unification of Germany.[17]

Taking issue with this statement, Mr. Molotov considered that the reparations demanded by the Soviet Union would not impose an excessive burden on the German economy once the level of industrial production had increased "to at least 70 per cent of the 1938 level. . . . In this case the allocation of 10 per cent for current reparation deliveries will leave the Germans with 60 per cent of production instead of the present 35 per cent . . . and yet efforts should be made to achieve a level of German industry even higher than 70 per cent of the 1938 level. . . . It is only a matter of clearing the way and of making it possible for German industry just to make a start . . . then it will be easy to solve the problem of allocating a part of industrial production for reparations deliveries and at the same time to meet more fully the needs of the German people. . . ." This remark was interpreted by some as hinting at a possible Soviet concession by which reparations deliveries would be deferred until Germany becomes self-sustaining. This interpretation is difficult to credit, however, if it is considered that Mr. Molotov's remark was buried in the midst of a lengthy statement which was so abusive of the Western powers that it provoked Mr. Bevin to say it did not inspire respect for the dignity of the Soviet Government.

Opposition in Great Britain and the United States to reparations from current output is not only motivated by the belief that they would tend to increase the German deficit or delay the repayment of American and British expenditures on behalf of Germany. Perhaps even more important are political considerations: the fear that the exaction of reparations deliveries would lead to "long drawn-out wrangling among the victorious Allies,"[18] and that it would make "Germany into a slave state working for Russia."[19]

In view of the present unsettled conditions in Germany, it has been the policy of the United States and the United Kingdom to oppose foreign acquisitions of ownership interests in the German economy, including investments by their own citizens, regardless of whether they are transfers of existing property or new investments in the form of foreign exchange or capital goods. The only exceptions are replacements of lost property, and bona fide gifts and legacies.[20]

The reasons for restricting the transfer of existing property are compelling. The lifting of these controls at this time would open the door to carpetbagging and might well lead to the alienation of most of Germany's tangible assets as a result of political or economic pressure. It would thus tend to jeopardize Germany's economic and political independence and the achievement of a self-sustaining German economy.

The prohibition of *new* investments, on the other hand, can hardly be justified on the ground that they would tend to weaken the German economy. New investments in the form of foreign exchange or goods would, on the contrary, greatly assist in Germany's economic recovery. It can be assumed, therefore, that the opposition of the American and British governments to new foreign investments was intended primarily to prevent friction among the Allies and to reassure the Russians that the United States would not use its superior economic resources in order to establish its own economic supremacy in Germany.

The Russians, in their zone, followed a completely different policy. After dismantling and removing equipment from more than one thousand plants, they seized and transferred to Soviet ownership an additional 220 of the zone's largest industrial establishments, accounting for about one-third of the zone's remaining industrial capacity. These plants were organized in a giant Soviet Combine, enjoying extraterritorial rights and producing reparations for Soviet account. "This has resulted in a type of monopolistic strangle hold over the economic and political life of eastern Germany which makes that region little more than a dependent province of the Soviet Union."[21] While it is likely that many of these plants were subject to dismantling in accordance with the Level of Industry Agreement, the latter does not give an option to the Soviet Union to acquire these plants *in situ*, there to be operated for their benefit.

At Moscow, the Soviet delegation conceded that foreign-owned properties in Germany should be subject to German law and should not enjoy special privileges. It also agreed that in the future, Control Council approval should be required for all acquisitions of German property by foreign governments or nationals, but refused to submit its own previous acquisitions of German plants to Allied review.

The French demand for the separation from Germany of the Ruhr, the Rhineland, and the Saar was formally presented by the French delegation to the Council of Foreign Ministers' Conference in Paris, on April 25, 1946. The French memorandum proposed (1) the incorporation of the Saar into the French customs and monetary system and the transfer of the Saar coal mines to the French government; (2) political and economic autonomy for the German territories situated on the left bank of the Rhine; (3) political and economic separation of the Ruhr area from Germany and transfer of ownership and management of its heavy industry to international public corporations. The memorandum also envisaged the permanent military occupation of the Saar and Rhineland by the forces of adjacent Allied countries.

The separation of the Saar from Germany and its integration into the French currency and customs system was accomplished in 1947 by a series of measures which received American and British *de facto* recognition pending final settlement in the peace treaty. The Soviet Government denounced the French steps as unilateral acts in violation of the Potsdam Agreement.

The United States is opposed to the political and economic separation of the Ruhr from Germany because it would make it extremely difficult for the rest of Germany to develop a self-sustaining economy. Secretary Marshall also stated at Moscow that such Allied controls as may be imposed after the end of the occupation "should not interfere with German responsibility for the management and operation of Germany's resources" or deprive Germany of "responsibility not only for the production but the marketing of her own industries."[22] He suggested, however, that the United States would be willing to consider placing the Ruhr—as well as other great industrial centers such as Upper Silesia which serve more than one country—under some form of international supervision, perhaps similar to that exercised by federal regulatory agencies in the United States. This supervision should be guided by the principles of (1) equitable distribution of essential commodities in short supply, and (2) access to essential commodities on a nondiscriminatory basis. Therefore, he declared, "It is only if the Germans take action contrary to the just interests of other countries that the attention of an international agency may have to be called to the question."

The Soviet Government also opposed the political and economic separation of the Ruhr valley from Germany, but endorsed the principle of international control under the condition that the Soviet Union would participate in it.

In subsequent tripartite discussions, the French abandoned their demand for territorial separation of the Rhineland and Ruhr. In June, 1948 a conference of representatives of the United States, the United Kingdom, France, and the "Benelux" countries unanimously recommended the establishment of an international authority for the control of the Ruhr in which these countries and Germany would participate. The international authority would be responsible for the allocation of coal, coke, and steel from the Ruhr as between German consumption and export and would prevent discriminatory practices in the marketing of such exports.

Although economic issues remained in the foreground in the Council of Foreign Ministers and eventually became the ostensible cause of the breakdown of its negotiations, the underlying political differences played a role which was hardly less important. The economic unification of Germany was intended to be a first step toward political unification. Neither economic nor political unity could be achieved without the transfer of governmental functions to German agencies, leading up to free nation-wide elections for a constituent assembly and a government responsible to the German people. This in turn requires freedom of assembly and of information in all zones, and the free movement of persons, ideas, and goods throughout Germany. It presupposes the noninterference by zonal commanders with the processes of government except at the direction of the four-power Control Council. Soviet actions made it appear unlikely that these conditions would materialize even if it should have been possible to reach a paper agreement on economic unification.

The Council of Foreign Ministers failed, not because of any

vagueness or internal inconsistencies in the Potsdam Agreement, but because the general European settlement between West and East outlined at Yalta and Potsdam was no longer accepted by the Soviet Union. That settlement, while safeguarding the independence of European nations, recognized a new balance of power in Europe which would have given to the Soviet Union a measure of influence in the affairs of Western Europe, at the same time assuring to the peoples of Eastern Europe outside the U.S.S.R. democratic rights and access to the world-wide trade of ideas and goods. In spite of initial mistakes in approaching the German problem, this scheme included, as an objective, the emergence of a peaceful, democratic, united Germany, "neither pawn or partner" of the East or the West.

The breakdown of quadripartite negotiations has shown that the time for a permanent settlement has not yet come. The terms of the Yalta and Potsdam Agreements have been violated wherever Soviet influence extended. The failure of the Council of Foreign Ministers merely confirmed the split between East and West. The present competition for economic power and political influence does not necessarily mean that no settlement will ever be reached. But there can be no settlement until the situation in Western Europe, including Western Germany, is stabilized so definitely as to remove any possibility of Soviet penetration or conquest.

OBSTACLES TO ECONOMIC RECOVERY

While the Allied Control Council in Berlin remained stalemated over all major issues and the Council of Foreign Ministers tried in vain to resolve these differences, the occupying powers began to pursue independent policies in their zones, tending to create different administrative systems and conflicting vested interests which will render more difficult the ultimate unification of Germany. Zonal demarcation lines instead of merely delimiting areas of military commands became almost absolute economic barriers separating regions whose economic interdependence had developed in the course of centuries. Ordinarily, millions of tons of grain, potatoes, and sugar would cross zonal boundary lines in a general east-westerly direction. In turn, millions of tons of coal and steel would be shipped from the Ruhr toward the east and south. Presently interzonal trade was reduced to a trickle, precariously dependent on complicated barter agreements. Manufacturing industries in the American and Russian zones were practically cut off from their usual sources of coal and steel. Tire plants in the American Zone were unable to produce because they depended on synthetic rubber supplies from the British and Soviet zones. The I. G. Farben plant at Hoechst in the American Zone was unable to procure liquid ammonia needed for nitrogenous fertilizer production from its sister plant in Oppau, only fifty miles south of Hoechst in the French Zone, until additional coal needed for the operation of the plant was received from the Ruhr. Tractors in the Soviet Zone could not be operated because vital repair parts could not be obtained from factories located in the British Zone. Sugar which was relatively plentiful in some parts of the Soviet Zone was virtually unobtainable in the American Zone.

In an effort to overcome these difficulties, Mr. Byrnes, in a statement to the Council of Foreign Ministers on July 11, 1946, said he was instructing the American representative in the Allied Control Council to invite the representative of "any other occupying power or powers" to join him in an immediate economic merger of their zones. This offer was accepted by the British representative on behalf of his government on July 30, 1946. The French Government indicated that it would consider it only after the question of the Saar, Rhineland, and Ruhr was settled. Soviet sources denounced the move as a step toward the division of Germany. The economic merger of the U. S. and U. K. zones was implemented by the bizonal fusion agreement of December 2, 1946, which was revised and extended on December 17, 1947.

Negotiations for the fusion of the French Zone with the combined Anglo-American zones began in the spring of 1948. The ensuing months saw the lifting of all controls on interzonal traffic between the French Zone and the Bizonal Area, the merger of the monetary, banking, and credit organizations, and the amalgamation of the French Zone foreign trade agency ("Oficomex") with the Anglo-American Joint Export-Import Agency.

The zonal barriers to internal trade were, however, only one of many obstacles in the way of economic recovery. At first, the breakdown of transportation and communications and other public utilities caused a paralysis of the entire economy. Rail and water traffic had almost ceased when the fighting ended, as had postal, telegraph, and telephone services. Many cities were without gas and electric power. Later, as public utilities were gradually restored, such stocks of fuel and raw materials as still existed locally were used up, and further recovery was increasingly hampered by the shortage of food and of coal, steel, and other materials. With liberated areas commanding a higher priority on commodities in short supply, the relief afforded by imports was limited to essential foodstuffs.

Within Germany the difficulties in procuring raw materials, repair parts, and other goods were aggravated by the breakdown of the monetary economy and the consequent disruption of the customary channels of trade. The existence of large wartime savings and decreasing confidence in the stability of the Reichsmark reduced the incentive to work and to sell. Except for legal food rations, rent, and transportation, which could be obtained at prewar prices, there was little money could buy. The health and morale of workers was impaired by undernourishment, the lack of clothing, housing, heating fuel, transportation, and medical care. Unpleasant working conditions, fatigue, sickness, and the necessity to fix homes and to procure some extra food made for a high rate of absenteeism.

As a result of these almost unprecedented difficulties, economic recovery was extremely slow. By the middle of 1948, more than two years after the surrender, when industrial production in most countries of Northern and Western Europe had regained or exceeded the prewar level, German industry west of the Oder-Neisse was still operating at less than half of the 1938 rate. With the value of production and services about three-fourths of that in 1938, and with foreign contributions to the Western zones approximately offset by Soviet takings from the Eastern zone, the German net national product was probably less than two-thirds of the prewar figure. This smaller national income had to be divided among a population 16 per cent greater than in 1938, so that the individual standard of living was reduced to less than half of the prewar level.

DEVELOPMENTS IN THE WESTERN ZONES

This state of economic paralysis extended to all four zones of occupation. Such slight differences as existed between the zones in the first few months following the German surrender can largely be ascribed to differences in the degree of destruction in the wake of hostilities.

In the British and United States zones, which had suffered relatively more damage by air raids and invasion than the other zones, the first post-surrender effort was necessarily directed toward emergency repairs of railroads and highways, the removal of rubble from city streets, the clearing of waterways, the restoration of essential services including electric power, water, and sewage, and the maintenance of food distribution. Machines and factory buildings which were only slightly damaged were repaired. This essential but nonrevenue-producing task of rehabilitation was financed without much difficulty, even during the two or three months' bank holiday following the surrender, from large cash holdings accumulated by German concerns during the war.

The first phase of reconstruction was essentially completed by the end of 1945. Its tangible results were meager: industrial production had progressed from about 15 per cent of the 1938 level at the time of surrender to little more than 20 per cent at the turn of the year. In the following months, the pace of industrial recovery quickened and by November, 1946 the index stood at about 33 per cent. A sharp setback began in December when severe winter weather interfered with transportation and many industries were closed down because of a lack of fuel and power. The peak level of 1946 was not regained until May, 1947. In the following year, a further moderate advance carried the index to a new postwar high of 45 per cent in April, 1948. Progress was greatest in mining, gas, electric power, lumber, chemicals, electrical equipment, rubber goods, and glass, while iron and steel, machinery, and the light industries producing furniture, pots and pans, optical products, ceramics, textiles and clothing, footwear, soap, and paper were lagging.

The slowness of economic recovery in the Bizonal Area must be attributed primarily to five major factors: (1) lack of food; (2) lack of coal; (3) lack of transportation; (4) lack of economic incentive; and (5) what the London *Economist* called a "lack of government."

Food

Even before the war, the agricultural resources of the area which now constitutes the combined US/UK zones provided only about half of the 3000 calories per person per day required by its urban population. Since that time, the shortage of fertilizer and other factors curtailed agricultural production, while the population increased by 20 per cent owing primarily to the influx of some seven million refugees from the east. As a result, in spite of the wartime shift of a part of Germany's agricultural resources from livestock feeding to the production of crops for direct human consumption, its agricultural production now provides only about 1200 to 1500 calories per capita for its nonfarm population, and the balance of the requirements must be imported.

In the first few months following the end of hostilities, civilian food rations declined to as low as 600 to 900 calories per person per day in the larger cities, while food stocks remaining in surplus areas were rapidly dissipated through irregular distribution and looting. The lack of food entailed a dangerous deterioration in the health of the civilian population which manifested itself chiefly in marked losses in body weight, fatigue, hunger oedema and other symptoms of malnutrition, an increase in tuberculosis, an increase of up to 50 per cent in the general mortality rate, and an alarming rise in infant mortality. In certain districts of the worst hit cities, it was reported that one out of two newborn babies died in their first few months. However, the availability of potatoes and vegetables from the new harvest, emergency feeding programs, the liquidation of private food hoards, and a gradual increase in rations helped to prevent mass starvation. By the fall of 1945, the normal consumers ration, first in the British and then in the American Zone, approached the level of 1550 calories (plus supplementary allowances for heavy workers, pregnant and nursing mothers, and other special consumer categories) which was the maximum permitted by SHAEF Directive. Establishment of this ration, which together with non-rationed and black market food supplies resulted in an average food intake of about 1900 calories per person per day, was reflected in a slight improvement in the health and productivity of the population. This rate of consumption was made possible only by the issuance to the German civilian population of about 1,000,000 tons of grain from SHAEF stocks.

It soon became apparent, however, that because of the worldwide food shortage and priority claims of liberated areas, food imports sufficient to maintain this ration could not be effected. In spite of the importation of food equivalent in calories to three million tons of grain in the crop year 1946-47, and of more than five million tons in 1947-48, the target ration of 1550 calories was seldom distributed in full. Moreover, major food crises recurred in the winter and early spring of each year almost with clockwork regularity.[23] As a result, the ration call-up for normal consumers in the Ruhr and other deficit areas had to be reduced repeatedly to 1000 calories or less. These ration reductions led to the renewed appearance of hunger oedema and severe weight losses, reduced capacity to work, reduced resistance to disease, and social unrest. The qualitative composition of the diet also continued to be wholly unsatisfactory. In January, 1948 the nominal daily normal consumer's ration consisted of twelve and a half ounces of bread, ten ounces of potatoes, and one and a half ounces of cereals, but of only one-fifth of one ounce of fat, one-half ounce of meat, two-thirds of one ounce of fish, two-thirds of one ounce of sugar, less than one-tenth of one ounce of cheese, and one-tenth of a quart of skim milk. Persistent failures to meet even these inadequate rations led to food demonstrations and strikes culminating in a one-day walkout of several million workers.

In February, 1947 the Hoover Mission found over half of the children and adolescents and a considerable part of the "normal consumer" group, especially in the lower-income groups, in a "deplorable condition." At a time when nutritional conditions in Western Europe had recovered to almost the prewar normal level, these German groups were found to be "not only far below the other nations but disastrously so." The ensuing threat to public health was aggravated by "the worst housing situation that modern civilization has ever seen," with tens of millions being crowded into rubble and basements, at the rate of "three and four people to a 12 x 12 room." Practically no household coal was issued in spite of the severe winter.[24]

One of the factors which did much to aggravate the food and housing problems in the Western zones was the influx of refugees from the east. It is estimated that by the fall of 1945, between two and three million persons had already found refuge in the American and British zones. In addition, the military governors of the American and British zones agreed to receive almost four million Germans expelled from Czechoslovakia, Poland, Hungary, and Austria. Furthermore, about 750,000 non-repatriable foreigners remained in the Western zones. As a result, the population of the United States Zone increased from 15.6 millions before the war to 19.0 millions in the fall of 1947 in spite of war losses, the population of the British Zone from 20.7 millions to 23.5 millions.[25]

The acute food shortage could not fail to have a disastrous effect on labor productivity, in spite of attempts to minimize the damage by granting supplementary rations to increasing numbers of manual workers. As long as nonworker rations were kept at extremely low levels, workers naturally tended to share their supplementary rations with their families. Consequently, any significant increase in labor productivity depended to some extent on a general increase in German food consumption levels.

COAL

The close connection between economic recovery and food supply was particularly evident in the case of coal. Even before the war the German coal mines, as those in other countries, faced increasing difficulties in retaining and recruiting labor for this heavy, dangerous, and disagreeable work. During the war young German miners were drafted for military service and replaced by foreign "slave" labor. When the foreign workers left the mines, the total labor force in the Ruhr mines was reduced to about one-half its peacetime level, and those left were mostly over age.

In the following three years, Ruhr coal production was gradually brought up from a low of less than 10 per cent of the 1938 level at the time of the German surrender to successive highs of about 40 per cent in February, 1946, 50 per cent in March, 1947, and 65 per cent in March, 1948. This increase was brought about primarily by the recruitment of 150,000 additional underground workers who were induced to enter the coal mines by means of supplementary food rations and special allocations of other incentive goods. As a result, the underground labor force increased from 50 per cent of the prewar number in 1945 to 75 per cent in 1946, 100 per cent in September, 1947, and 110 per cent in September, 1948.

The output per man, on the other hand, after recovering from one-fifth to one-half of the prewar level in the first six months of the occupation, increased only slightly during the following three years reaching about 60 per cent in 1948. Even this slight increase in individual output since 1946 was due in large measure to a decline of absenteeism rather than increased productivity per man-shift. Low productivity is a problem which the Ruhr coal mines share with the rest of German industry, and most of its causes are common to all of German industry. These are:

1. An unfavorable age composition of the labor force. For the reasons which have been indicated, this problem is more acute in the coal industry than elsewhere. In the Ruhr, the percentage of underground miners over forty years old increased from 33 per cent in 1939 to 55 per cent in 1946; by mid-1948, however, it had declined to 46 per cent.

2. The large influx of inexperienced new recruits also presented a more serious problem in the mines than in most other industries.

3. In spite of the distribution of supplementary food rations, it was impossible to insulate the coal miners from the effects of the severe food shortage prevailing in the Ruhr. Although miners' ra-

tions, equivalent to 3500-4000 calories per capita per day, are adequate to meet the workers' individual food requirements, it is natural that they would share their rations with their dependents. It is estimated that during the period when the normal consumers' rations declined to 1000 calories per day, an average coal miner's family of five received rations averaging only 1600 calories per capita. Even if allowance is made for off-the-ration purchases, the family's total food consumption probably did not exceed 1900 calories per person, or two-thirds of their normal food requirements. It is not surprising, therefore, that in spite of the high miner's ration, coal miners did not receive enough food to sustain their ability to work. As a result, every reduction in general ration levels in the Ruhr was immediately reflected in a sharp, though temporary, drop in production.

4. Overcrowding and generally unhealthy living conditions also make for low productivity and a high rate of absenteeism. Coal miners who must live at considerable distances from the mine are forced to spend much time and energy in commuting to and from their place of work. This factor is equally applicable to other industries.

5. The poor condition of the mines, the deterioration of the equipment, and the interruptions in the shipments of mining supplies also contributed to reducing the output per man-shift; but because of the overriding priorities given to mines, this factor was probably less important than in other industries.

6. The partial breakdown of price and wage controls in the face of rigidly maintained controls over miners' wages impaired the role of money as an incentive to work. A coal miner could obtain food and other goods worth a multiple of his miner's wage by hiring himself out to a farmer, by doing some gardening, by raising chickens, or by engaging in black market deals. It is obvious that under these circumstances his willingness to work in a mine depended largely upon incentives other than his miner's wage. The most important of these incentives was his right to a preferential food ration which he obtained at legal prices. This food ration and the few other goods and services which were still available through legitimate channels

and at official prices could be paid for with the earnings of a few shifts. Since any additional money he might earn by mine work was practically worthless in relation to prevailing black market prices, his interest in working a full work week, and in working overtime, depended on additional incentives in kind. In the Ruhr, regularity of attendance was rewarded since January, 1947 by the distribution of limited quantities of food, liquor, tobacco, clothing, and household goods which were made available according to a point system. But since the number of points received by each miner was not tied sufficiently to increased output, the point scheme was more successful in attracting new recruits and in reducing absenteeism than in stimulating production per man.

During the second half of 1947, this incentive plan was supplemented by the distribution of food packages to underground workers as a reward for reaching specified mine production targets. At the same time, part of the foreign exchange proceeds from coal exports (calculated as a percentage of output, with the percentage increasing with rising output) was set aside for the importation of incentive goods for the miners. The introduction of this supplementary scheme led to an immediate improvement of coal production and at the same time made an important contribution toward overcoming the apathy and the feeling of general uncertainty and hopelessness which permeated the entire German economy.[26] It soon became obvious, however, that the privileged position of the coal miners could not be maintained indefinitely without causing resentment and discouragement among less favored groups of workers. A gradual improvement of the living standard of the rest of the population was therefore an essential prerequisite for further economic progress.

Coal is the basis of industry. Just as the striking postwar economic revival of Germany's neighbors was made possible by an even more rapid recovery in their coal supply, so was the industrial stagnation in Germany a consequence of its lack of coal. At the time when most countries of Western Europe were regaining or exceeding their prewar coal consumption, the bizonal area disposed of only one-half to two-thirds of its prewar coal supplies.

Bizonia's coal shortage was aggravated to only a minor extent by coal exports to other areas. Moreover, in order to aid the economic recovery of the bizonal area, coal exports to other countries were actually cut from 17 per cent of total production[27] in 1946 to 12 per cent in 1947 (as compared with 11 per cent in 1938). Less than 3 per cent of the bizonal coal production went to the French and Soviet zones. Not coal exports but the near stagnation of coal production during most of this period must, therefore, be considered together with the food shortage as the most important single cause of the slowness of industrial recovery in the bizonal area.

Since the overhead energy requirements of a highly urbanized economy—for railroads, public utilities, etc.—cannot be reduced below a certain minimum level, the main impact of Western Germany's coal shortage fell on industry, and particularly on those basic industries which consume large amounts of coal per unit of output, such as steel, cement, bricks, etc. These materials, however, are essential to the reconstruction of Germany's ravaged cities and to the rehabilitation of its transportation system. In the face of an unprecedented demand for steel not only in Germany but throughout Europe, Ruhr steel production in 1947 did not exceed 2.7 million tons, or less than 16 per cent of that in 1938.

TRANSPORTATION

The lack of steel in turn was felt most acutely by the German transportation system which had suffered much heavier war damage than industry in general. Although at the beginning of 1947 the railroads in the bizonal area had about 60 per cent of their pre-war number of serviceable locomotives and 75 per cent of the freight cars, this equipment proved to be insufficient to cope with even the greatly reduced traffic of that area. The principal reasons for the area's transportation difficulties were in the general disorganization of the railroad system; the destruction of terminal facilities, switches, bridges, and track; the necessity of roundabout routing to avoid zonal boundaries; and the lack of a monetary incentive to speed up the movement of freight cars, factors which all contributed to increase the average length of haul and the turnaround time of railroad cars.

During the first half of 1947, the condition of the rolling stock deteriorated further as the pool of cars requiring only light repairs was gradually exhausted and cars requiring thorough overhauling had to be laid up indefinitely for lack of repair facilities and materials; consequently, railroad cars were becoming unserviceable faster than they could be repaired. In addition, a large number of cars which crossed the borders to neighboring countries and the Soviet Zone in the normal course of business failed to return. As a result of these conditions, the number of freight cars in operation fell from 280,000 in January, 1946 to 240,000 in January, 1947, and 200,000 in June, 1947. Although a slight improvement occurred in the following year, the railroads were unable to move the increased coal output and during the winter of 1947-48, about one million tons of coal which were badly needed by German industries as well as those of neighboring countries had to be dumped at the mines.

LACK OF ECONOMIC INCENTIVES

Economic recovery was also increasingly hampered by the ineffectiveness of monetary incentives which was the result of the financial chaos inherited from the Nazi war economy. Between 1935 and 1945, the Reich debt (excluding obligations for the compensation of war damage) increased from RM 15,000,000,000 to RM 400,000,000,000; the currency in circulation increased more than tenfold from RM 5,000,000,000 to 50,000,000,000; bank deposits increased from RM 30,000,000,000 to RM 150,000,000,000. Altogether, it is estimated that the total of all unduplicated claims against real assets more than doubled, from about RM 350,000,-000,000 in 1935 to more than RM 700,000,000,000 at the time of the German surrender.

In 1935, the total of monetary claims and equities was approximately matched by the total value of the national wealth. By 1946, the value of Germany's real wealth had declined by about one-third as a consequence of destruction, under-maintenance, territorial losses, and reparations removals. In other words, paper assets amounting to more than RM 700,000,000,000 were confronted by real assets amounting to about RM 250,000,000,000. (At the same time, Germany's real national income declined from RM 60,000,-000,000 to little more than half this amount.)

In an uncontrolled economy, this gap would be absorbed by a general rise in the price level. In order to avoid social unrest, however, the Nazi government used every means to prevent such a development. Although fewer goods were available for purchase, prices and wages were frozen approximately at their prewar levels, the black market was held down by the threat of severe penalties, and the ever-increasing amount of unspendable money accumulating in the hands of the German population was siphoned off in the form of bank deposits, social insurance premiums, etc., which in turn served as the basis of Germany's war finance.[28]

Except for minor modifications, the structure of official prices and wages was maintained even after the surrender;[29] but the relative scope of the legal market in which these prices prevailed diminished. Fewer and fewer of the goods produced were sold (and to some extent fewer services were rendered) through legal channels.[30] Black market prices reached levels from fifty times to several hundred times the legal price; a package of twenty American cigarettes, for instance, sold for RM 20 to 150; a pound of butter for RM 600 to 800 as compared with the legal price of RM 1.80. When a worker can earn a day's wage by selling just one cigarette, his willingness to work will, of course, largely depend on incentives other than his legal wage.

However, either the average German's reluctance to charge more than the legal price was so great or his confidence in the Reichsmark was shattered so completely that money was accepted only to a limited extent even in the black market. Instead, Germany reverted to a primitive barter economy. Thus a toy manufacturer might be unable to procure sheet metal unless he agreed in return to sell to the supplier toy trains and construction sets. A garment manufacturer might undertake to sell clothing to a cellulose manufacturer in exchange for cellulose needed by a third plant which supplied the garment manufacturer with synthetic fibers.[31]

"Suppressed inflation" in the extreme form which prevailed in Germany prior to currency reform reduces the productivity and efficiency of the German economy in several different ways.

1. Every individual barter transaction involves enormous complications and delays. This is due not so much to the fact that most barter deals must be conducted *sub rosa*—official regulations were openly flouted in correspondence and advertisements—as to the difficulty in finding a partner and in coming to terms with him. Frequently a person must make not one but several successive barter transactions before he gets what he wants in return for the commodity he has to offer. When the deals are closed, the merchandise must be shipped in small lots to many destinations, only to be reassigned if the consignee is not the ultimate user.

2. Manpower which would otherwise be available for more productive tasks is either diverted to this complicated system of trade by necessity or attracted to it by the large profits which it offers. As barter expands, more goods are diverted to this market from the legal market, thus increasing the necessity for barter and reducing the usefulness of money.

3. Economic resources are diverted from the production of essential but not readily exchangeable goods (such as grain, steel, basic chemicals) to less essential but more barterable articles (such as eggs, butter, manufactured luxury goods).

4. Lack of confidence in the stability of the currency leads to the replacement of bank savings and money hoards by hoards of goods. Badly needed raw materials and equipment are thus withdrawn from productive uses.

5. With money supplies ample, employers do not watch costs closely and tend to hoard workers.

6. Where barter is impossible, the incentive to work or to sell diminishes to the point where only the cost of food rations, rent, and transportation can be covered. Moreover, many persons of the middle and working classes were still able to meet their current expenses by drawing on their wartime savings.

CURRENCY REFORM IN THE WESTERN ZONES

Although the paralyzing effect of the monetary "overhang" on Western Germany's economy was generally recognized, plans for a separate financial reform for the West were shelved again and again for fear of deepening the rift between East and West and in the hope that somehow four-power agreement could be reached on a uniform program for all of Germany. It was only after protracted and frustrating negotiations had failed to secure Russian agreement to a plan which would assure effective central four-power control of monetary and fiscal policy in all four zones that the three Western powers decided that action could no longer be postponed.

After some consultation with German financial experts, a currency reform was put into effect in all three Western zones by a series of Military Government decrees published on and after June 20, 1948. The reform was deliberately confined to the conversion of Reichsmark holdings and claims into the new Deutsche mark. It made no provision for the equalization of losses among holders of monetary and real assets; this issue, which would raise difficult problems of social equity, was left for ultimate decision by the Germans themselves.

The over-all effect of the currency conversion was to reduce the aggregate of monetary claims, as well as the total money supply (cash and free bank deposits), to less than one-tenth. The reform wiped out all but 6.5 per cent of money holdings and bank balances of individuals and business enterprises, of which 6 per cent was released, and one-half per cent was blocked for long-term investment. All other private monetary claims, including outstanding loans, mortgages, private insurance claims, etc., were reduced to one-tenth. Social insurance payments were continued at the old rates. Financial institutions, whose assets were virtually eliminated through the cancellation of the public debt, were provided only with sufficient funds to cover the liabilities arising out of the reform and to provide them with working capital. In the initial stages of the reform, lending was limited to short-term credits on bills of exchange and promissory notes. After August 8, 1948, banks were authorized, within certain limits, to open book credits to private individuals and business concerns. Public bodies were also started with a virtually clean slate. Their credit balances were cancelled, but all public authorities were supplied with sufficient funds to meet normal expenses for two months and the railway and postal administrations received funds equal to normal expenses for one month. In addition, the *Länder* were authorized to issue some new debts in order to prevent the insolvency of financial institutions. The occupation powers were provided with DM 750,000,000.

Several other steps were taken simultaneously with the currency reform. Taxes which had been abnormally high, but so far had been paid in part out of accumulated savings or black-market proceeds, were reduced by between 30 and 40 per cent. Price and allocation controls were withdrawn from an important sector of the economy. By the end of 1948, only a few basic commodities and services, including coal, steel, liquid fuels, fertilizers, public utilities, basic foodstuffs, and dwelling space, remained under price and allocation control. Prices of all imported goods except those remaining under price control (mostly foodstuffs) were adjusted to world market levels at a conversion rate of 1 Deutsche mark = 30 U.S. cents. Special incentives in kind for workers in export industries and coal miners were eliminated, but the foreign exchange bonus for manufacturers engaged in export was temporarily retained.

The immediate effect of these measures on the Bizonal economy was highly encouraging. The reform with one stroke seemed to have restored the role of money as an incentive to work, to sell, and to save. Money was again accepted as a means of exchange, and barter practically disappeared. Commodity hoards accumulated prior to the reform were offered for sale. Industrial production rose sharply, from 43 per cent of the 1938 level in June, 1948 to 63 per cent in October. To be sure, part of the increase was purely statistical—goods produced for stocks or for the black and barter markets, which hitherto had not been fully reported, appeared in the statistics for the first time. But in most industries there were abundant signs of a real increase in productivity. Industries which so far had been lagging behind tended to catch up with the general recovery trend. Steel production increased from an annual rate of 4.25 million tons during the second quarter of 1948 to an annual rate of 6.2 million tons in the third quarter and an annual rate of 7.3 million tons in October. The production of machinery and of consumer goods also took a remarkable spurt. The increased efficiency of railroad operations was reflected in a sharp reduction of the turn-around time of freight cars compared with the same period a year before.

The mass unemployment which had been anticipated as a result of the reform did not materialize. The prompt absorption of commodity stocks by anxious buyers increased the velocity of circulation of money—each of the new marks may have done the work of two—and favored the rapid dispersal of purchasing power from the retail trade to wholesalers and manufacturers and from the consumer goods industries to those producing investment goods. The release to the coal mines of the DM equivalent of accumulated export arrears and similar *ad hoc* devices served to tide over those industries which were hit hardest by the reform. Fortified by its cushion of hoarded goods, the Bizonal economy easily withstood the first shock of financial stringency. There could be no doubt that the reform had marked a real turning point.

Not all of its effects were favorable, however. It soon became apparent that the reform carried a threat of maldistribution of incomes and resources which could not be overlooked.

The first and perhaps the most welcome effect of the reform on income distribution was to re-establish a more healthy relationship between farm incomes and city incomes. For the first time in many years, farmers were short of money and therefore anxious to sell produce at reasonable prices. Within the city, however, the main beneficiaries of the reform were those who had hoarded goods and now reaped spectacular profits from their sale. Fixed salary groups, who prior to currency reform were in the worst position because as a rule, unlike the manual workers, they were unable to sell part of their labor in the black and barter markets, benefited more from the reform than the workers. The real victims of the reform were all those without current earning potential—war widows and orphans, old and disabled people, welfare clients and pensioners who depended for their livelihood on legitimately acquired savings and public welfare payments, and the millions of dispossessed refugees who before the reform may have found some solace in the common sharing of misery and whose hopes for some immediate consideration through the "equalization of burdens" were disappointed. These people were the worst hit when prices began to rise immediately after the reform.

To be sure, price increases were to be anticipated if the level and structure of German prices were to be adjusted to the world market at a rate of exchange which is approximately equal to the prewar purchasing power parity rate.[32] By June, 1948, the index of wholesale prices in Germany had increased to more than 150 per cent of that in 1938; wholesale prices in the United States, however, had more than doubled. To adjust the German price level to the world market level, German prices would therefore have to rise by at least one-third. Furthermore, the *structure* of German prices had developed quite differently from that in the world market. In the United States, prices of agricultural products and industrial raw materials had increased much more than those of finished manufactured products; in Germany, price control had been least successful in the field of manufactured goods, particularly consumer goods, which had risen to as much as 250 to 300 per cent of the 1938 level. Consequently, the establishment of a 30 per cent rate would restore the prewar equilibrium only if prices of finished manufactured goods in Germany could be reduced in the face of substantial price increases for primary products.

The economic, political, and administrative difficulties inherent in such a course are obvious. To be sure, manufacturers were able to reduce their unit processing costs as a result of a more efficient utilization of their productive capacity; but in many industries— particularly textiles, leather goods, and electrical equipment—the resulting savings were not sufficient to enable them to compete in the world market unless the exchange rate was reduced. The devaluation of the Deutsche mark, in turn, would lead to further price increases within Germany.

An additional inflationary factor was introduced by the decontrol of specific "bottleneck" products. Tight controls over the total money supply could not prevent the heavy concentration of the available purchasing power on certain goods which had been in extremely short supply for many years, such as clothing, footwear, and household furnishings. As production could not be expanded immediately to meet this demand because of the lack of raw materials (the flow of ERP imports had not yet started), prices in these fields increased more than would otherwise have been necessary. The prices of certain foodstuffs released from price control (eggs, fruits) also rose sharply. Some experts claimed that prices of such scarce items could have been held in check if selective controls had been maintained until supplies became more plentiful.

The price increases in the free sector of the economy soon forced substantial upward adjustments in the prices of controlled items. By the end of 1948, the Bizonal Economic Council had approved price increases for coal, fertilizers, grain products, potatoes, meat, fish, oil seeds, and an increase in railroad freight rates. However, since most of these prices had long been kept at artificially low levels, these adjustments would probably have become necessary in any event. Rents were kept stable, while reductions were effected in railroad passenger fares and postal rates.

Except for a few bottleneck items, the price increases which occurred during the first six months following currency reform remained within the framework of the official policy objective, which was to adjust the German price structure to that prevailing in the world market. In fact, food prices were kept down deliberately, partly with a view to protecting low-income groups, partly in the expectation of a decline of world food prices. Nevertheless, the price increases which had taken place and the accompanying redistribution of incomes carried a threat of run-away inflation which it would be dangerous to ignore. Shortly after the currency reform, the workers' nominal take-home pay was approximately equal to the prewar level; the cost of living had increased by about 50 per cent; the resulting decline of real wages, by about one-third as compared with the prewar period, reflected the decline in productivity. In the following months, however, prices began to outrun payrolls in spite of the increased output. The conclusion was inevitable that the workers' share in the national product was being reduced; the shares of business and agriculture (the latter via the black market) increased. So far, the traditional discipline of the German working class and the moderation of its leadership had prevented widespread strikes; undoubtedly, the depletion of workers' savings and trade union treasuries also had a restraining influence. However, a number of incidents culminating in a riot at Stuttgart[33] and a one-day walkout of some eleven million workers[34] foreshadowed a period of increased social tension and the danger of a price-wage spiral.[35] Demands for increased welfare benefits and pensions also became more insistent.

The maldistribution of incomes led to the misdirection of production. Windfall profits were spent on expensive restaurant meals, high-quality furniture, electrical kitchen ranges, vacuum cleaners, luxury metal and leather goods, and even automobiles as long as they were available, while millions could not afford basic necessities. Collections of agricultural products declined as increasing quantities of meat, butter, etc. were diverted to the black market. The serving of coupon-free meals at higher prices became customary in most restaurants.[36]

There also was some misdirection of resources available for investment. The anticipation of further price increases and the fear of taxation for the equalization of burdens led to renewed hoarding of commodities. Building materials went into the construction of luxury shops while residential housing projects had to be postponed because low controlled rents repelled private investors and public funds were lacking. High interest rates—ranging up to 10 per cent—discouraged investment in long-rang industrial reconstruction projects. In spite of the provision of the currency law prohibiting deficit spending, public budgets continued to run in the red. In Swiss markets, the Deutsche mark was quoted at 7 U.S. cents, well below its current internal purchasing power, and it was falling. Obviously, there was considerable doubt regarding its future.

REPARATIONS

Reparations so far have not been an important factor in delaying recovery in the bizonal area. Originally, 1636 plants had been scheduled for removal in accordance with the first Level of Industry Plan. But as of January 1, 1947, only seventy-six plants had been actually allocated and dismantled or were in the process of being dismantled in accordance with the stipulation on "advance deliveries" of the Potsdam Agreement. In addition, some three hundred pure war plants had been destroyed or "neutralized" after removal from seventy of these plants of some 25,000 machine tools and other general purpose equipment convertible to peacetime purposes which were made available to the Inter-Allied Reparations Agency. In the British Zone, individual machine tools were also removed from a number of nonwar plants.

It soon became apparent, however, that several of the assumptions underlying the first Level of Industry Plan would not be fulfilled.

1. The population of Germany generally, and in the bizonal area in particular, turned out to be greater than assumed in the plan.

2. Experience revealed serious internal inconsistencies in the original plan. It was now becoming evident that the sharp cuts in production capacities in the metals, machinery, and chemical industries provided in the old plan would make it impossible to sustain even the low level of general industrial production at which the plan aimed.

3. The original plan failed to allow for the worsening of Germany's terms of trade in the world market. "World food and raw material prices have increased more rapidly than the price of manufactured goods since 1936 and the situation seems likely to continue. Consequently, the bizonal area must be prepared to exchange in foreign trade proportionately larger quantities of industrial products in return for necessary food and raw material imports."[37]

4. It was becoming apparent that the original plan in some cases had assumed unrealistically high levels of production for the nonreparations industries and had aimed at a higher volume of exports from these industries than other countries were likely to absorb.

5. Finally, it had become increasingly apparent that the drastic reductions provided for Germany's traditional export industries would prevent them from contributing their indispensable part to the economic rehabilitation of Europe.

There were growing indications, furthermore, that the prevailing uncertainties regarding the reparations plan were beginning to discourage the reopening of a large number of plants threatened by the prospect of eventual removal. It was imperative, therefore, to remove this uncertainty without delay.

The American and British military governments were therefore instructed to develop a revised reparations plan which was announced on August 29, 1947. The new Level of Industry Plan reduced the number of plants to be dismantled in the bizonal area from 1636 to 682. Three hundred and two of these plants were war plants; the balance consisted of 380 nonarmament plants, of which 224 were in the engineering industry, 92 in the iron and steel industry, 42 in the chemical industry, 11 in the nonferrous metals industry, and 11 in miscellaneous industries. No provision was made for removals from any of the industries which were prohibited under the original Level of Industry Agreement (such as aluminum, ball bearings, synthetic ammonia, synthetic rubber, and synthetic gasoline and oil) or for removals from the ship building industry. The Anglo-American authorities stated that a modification of these prohibitions was being considered, but that it should not be assumed that these industries would be exempted from reparations. In the meantime, the production of ball bearings, synthetic ammonia, synthetic rubber, and synthetic gasoline and oil for German needs was being continued in accordance with the first Level of Industry Agreement; a few months later, virgin aluminum was added to this list.

On the basis of the revised Level of Industry Plan, it was estimated that the bizonal area would retain sufficient industrial capacity to enable it to regain about 80 per cent of its general level of industrial production in 1938, as compared with 50 to 55 per cent under the old Level of Industry Plan. This production level would be approximately equal to that prevailing in 1936, a year that was not characterized by either boom or depressed conditions. Substantially the entire difference between the original and the revised plan was in metals, machinery, and chemical industries. These industries would be cut back to a level which would be about 55 to 60 per cent less than the wartime peak reached in 1944, but only

5 to 10 per cent less than that of 1936. The steel industry would be reduced to a capacity of 13 million tons of crude steel a year, as compared with a current rated capacity of 19.2 million tons, and a capacity of 7.5 million tons under the old Level of Industry Plan. It is estimated that this capacity would be sufficient for the production of about 10.7 million tons of crude steel yearly.

While the production targets implied in the revised Level of Industry Plan represent a considerable improvement over those contemplated in the original plan, it is important to realize that because of the influx of population the per capita level of industrial capacity will be only about 60 per cent of that in 1938, or 75 per cent of that in 1936.

In the meantime, the dismantling of plants continued. As of January 1, 1948, 80 plants had been dismantled and removed and 91 plants had been completely dismantled but not yet shipped. Dismantling was in process on 169 plants, but on most of these work had hardly begun. In the case of the remaining 342 plants, or half of the total number subject to removal under the new plan, dismantling had not yet started.

DENAZIFICATION

There is not much evidence that the economic recovery of the Western zones was seriously hampered by the program of denazification. By 1946, when responsibility for denazification was transferred to German tribunals, U. S. Military Government had removed or excluded approximately 207,000 active Nazis from public employment, 100,000 from important positions in private business, and 64,000 from other types of employment.[38] In Greater Hesse it is reported that 23 per cent of the leading personnel of business concerns with ten or more employees, 14 per cent of the technicians and foremen and 6 per cent of the white collar workers were dismissed; in addition, 11 per cent of the leading personnel, 5 per cent of the technicians, and 2 per cent of the office employees, while also affected by denazification, were temporarily retained. In large concerns with more than one hundred employees, 29 per cent of the leading personnel were removed.[39]

However, most of the persons found unemployable by Military Government, when later brought to trial before the German denazification tribunals set up under the Law for Liberation from National Socialism and Militarism, were either exonerated or classified as mere "followers" and had their employment restrictions removed. Altogether, as of September 1, 1948, when denazification was virtually completed, some 533,000 former Nazis had been charged under the German law as major offenders, offenders, or lesser offenders; of these only about 123,000 had been found guilty and barred from employment in responsible positions. In most of these cases, furthermore, these employment sanctions were limited to a short "probationary period"; only about 21,000 major offenders and offenders were held permanently ineligible to hold public office and excluded from other responsible positions for a period of five years or more. Moreover, appeals had reduced the number of major offenders and offenders to 18,000 and the number of lesser offenders to 85,000. Only 32,000 persons out of a total of more than three million chargeable cases remained to be tried; in addition, 43,000 appeals were still pending. Previously, on March 20, 1948, it had been announced that the employment restrictions imposed on professional men found to be lesser offenders would be lifted completely.[40]

In the British Zone, some 200,000 active Nazis were reported removed from public and private employment as of January 1, 1947, and about 100,000 had their applications for such employment rejected.

There is little to bear out the charge that denazification in the American Zone, which is often alleged to have been more precipitate and sweeping than in the other zones, interfered to any important extent with economic recovery. On the contrary, in many instances the morale of workers and employees was impaired where denazification was delayed for reasons of expediency.

CONTROL AND OWNERSHIP OF PROPERTY

In contrast with the Soviet Zone, the Anglo-American zones did not undergo any fundamental reorganization of their economic structure. Such minor changes in the control and ownership of property as have been initiated may be summarized under the headings of sequestration, deconcentration, socialization, and land reform.

As a result of the blocking of properties of Nazi organizations and leading Nazis, and of certain other assets, the occupying authorities found themselves custodians of a huge amount of wealth. In the U. S. Zone, as of the end of September, 1947, property valued at RM 12,400,000,000 was thus held under property control, of which RM 4,000,000,000 were properties of the Nazi party and of leading Nazis, RM 3,000,000,000 properties of the German state, RM 2,200,000,000 properties of foreign governments or nationals, RM 1,100,000,000 properties of the *I. G. Farbenindustrie* A. G. seized under an ACC law, and RM 1,000,000,000 properties which had been wrongfully acquired during the Hitler regime. In the British Zone, all coal mines, steel plants, and the I. G. Farben and Krupp combines as well as many other properties were sequestered.

The disposal of these properties raised a number of problems. So far as the property of residents and citizens of United Nations or neutral countries was concerned, all transfers were prohibited; but in other respects, control reverted to the former owners. Regarding property of Nazi organizations, the Allied Control Council decided that properties taken from the pre-Hitler trade unions and cooperatives and incorporated in the *Deutsche Arbeitsfront*, and properties of charitable and humanitarian organizations, should be returned to the former owners or their successor organizations; all other assets of Nazi organizations were to be transferred to the *Länder*. In regard to the *I. G. Farbenindustrie*, the Allied Control Council passed a law in November, 1945 by which it took legal title to all assets owned or controlled by the combine. However, a four-power committee charged with developing policies for their disposal was unable to reach agreement. After fruitless discussions in the spring and summer of 1948, the Bipartite Military Government of the Bizonal Area, proceeding independently, began to transfer all I. G. Farben assets to a Bizonal I. G. Farben Dispersal Panel operating under an Anglo-American Control Office. The coal mines of the Ruhr, which had been in British custody, first under British, and then under Anglo-American control, and the Ruhr steel mills, which had been transferred to a German Board of Trustees under British control, were finally placed under a uniform system of decentralized German trusteeship, operating under combined Anglo-American control (Military Government Law No. 75, November 10, 1948). With few exceptions, however, these measures represent interim solutions only, and the problem of eventual disposal of these properties remains unsolved.

Similar problems arose in connection with Allied policies aimed at eliminating excessive concentrations of economic power in Germany. Laws designed to break up cartels, combines, trusts, syndicates, and all concerns with more than 10,000 employees (but excluding public utilities) were promulgated in the U. S. and British zones in February, 1947, ostensibly as a measure of economic disarmament.

In spite of the broad implications of the law, it was implemented with considerable caution. Various steps were taken to decentralize the management and ownership structure of industries which had come under Allied trusteeship. In the case of I. G. Farben, the German Dispersal Panel was instructed to arrange for and supervise the breaking up of the former combine into a large number of separate and independent corporations, the issuance of new stocks to be sold to the public, and the compensation of I. G. Farben creditors and shareholders.

The Ruhr steel industry, which in the past had been organized in a closely knit cartel dominated by a few large combines led by the *Vereinigte Stahlwerke,* was similarly broken up into a number of separate units. The splitting up of the old steel empires need not result in important technical disadvantages; plants belonging to one combine were often scattered over considerable distances and did not necessarily complement each other. It soon became apparent, however, that the original British "segregation" scheme went too far; it created units too small to operate economically, and it tended to sever technically desirable relationships. The strict organizational separation of steel mills from their coal and coke supply, in particular, gave rise to widespread criticism because of the close technical integration, based on the interrelated use of gases, which exists between steel plants and adjacent coal mines and cokeries. Consequently, when the organization of the steel industry came up for review by the Combined Anglo-American authorities, it was agreed that some of the newly created units should be combined and that coal and coke production facilities and iron ore mines should be included wherever this appeared necessary in order to obtain units capable of competing in the world market. At the same time, Law No. 75 provided for the deconcentration of the trusteeship function, which was formerly performed by a central Board of Trustees for the entire steel industry.

Law No. 75 also provided for the reorganization of the coal industry along the same lines as in the steel industry, except that the company managements would remain subject to supervision by a German central management group, the *Deutsche Kohlen Bergbau Leitung,* which in turn would be responsible to the UK/US Coal Control Group. The DKBL was established late in 1947; Law No. 75 converted it into a corporation whose shares are held by Military Government.

Deconcentration proposals in industries not under trusteeship were limited to a few concerns in the chemical and equipment industry and in the wholesale coal and steel trade.

In the U. S. Zone, all assets and liabilities of the three leading German banks were placed under trustees appointed by the Land governments. At the same time, the entire German banking system which, like those of most other European countries, used to be highly centralized, was reorganized in the bizonal area after the model of the Federal Reserve System. No bank may open branches outside the *Land* in which it is licensed to operate. The functions of the Reichsbank were transferred to *Länder* banks and a central note-issuing bank owned collectively by all the *Länder* banks.

In March, 1948 statements by General Clay that the provisions of the deconcentration laws should be considered as discretionary rather than mandatory foreshadowed a considerable relaxation of the deconcentration policy where it comes into conflict with considerations of industrial efficiency.

Meanwhile, ownership of the bulk of the German properties subject to sequestration or deconcentration—including the heavy industries of the Ruhr—is in a state of suspense. If as is likely, the disposal of the properties involved is left to the *Länder* or some other German authority, the question will arise which of these properties are to be (a) returned to their former owners, (b) sold to private interests, (c) transferred to semi-public corporations, (d) transferred to Reich, Land, county, communal, or other forms of public ownership.

Public opinion in Western Germany is about equally divided on the issue of socialization. The Social Democrats and the small Communist party, which together represent somewhat less than half of the electorate, favor the transfer to public ownership and control of all large industrial plants. The Socialists are not firmly committed on the issue of Reich versus state ownership, but there are indications that they would prefer to see control over basic industries affecting the German economy as a whole—such as the heavy industries of the Ruhr—eventually vested in the future central government for Germany (or Western Germany); but for the present they would probably agree to the transfer of these industries to the *Länder* or to mixed, but predominantly public, corporations. However, even the Christian Democratic Union, which represents the bulk of the conservative vote, supports the transfer to public control of the basic (mining, iron and steel, and heavy chemicals) industries in the form of autonomous corporations managed by experts and owned and supervised jointly by regional and local authorities, the workers and employees, and private investors. It also favors government control of banking and insurance. This program represents a compromise between the corporative and paternalistic ideas of the conservative wing, and the Christian-socialist tendencies of the left wing of the party. Only the right-wing Liberal Democratic party, which represents about 10 per cent of the electorate, is opposed to public ownership of the basic industries, but for tactical reasons it usually supports the Christian-Democratic Union.

The present tendencies of the German parties make it appear

likely that the transfer of large-scale industries to public ownership or semi-public corporations would meet little opposition,
whereas their sale at this time to individuals would invite widespread criticism. As in other European countries, there is no parallel
in Germany to the American tradition of "trust-busting." Large-
scale enterprises, including trusts and combines and to some extent
cartels, are accepted by conservatives and socialists alike as an inevitable product of modern industrialism; the parties differ only on
the form and degree of public control to which they must be
subjected.

The policy of the United States regarding the disposal of seized
properties and large industrial enterprises is guided by the fundamental precepts of democracy. On December 17, 1946, Secretary
Byrnes stated to the press that the United States does not oppose
the socialization of German industry if the Germans themselves
wish to socialize their industries through democratic processes. The
State-War-Navy Directive of July 15, 1947 instructs the American
Commander in Germany to "refrain from interfering in the question
of public ownership of enterprises in Germany, except to insure
that any choice for or against public ownership is made freely
through the normal processes of democratic government."

In a speech before the *Länderrat* on September 9, 1947, General
Clay elaborated the American policy as follows:

Much has been said about the opposition of American Military Government to socialization in Germany, and much that has been said has
been distorted and inaccurate. I would not be frank with you if I did
not say to you that America believes in free enterprise.

We believe neither in monopolies nor in cartels in restraint of trade.
We are convinced that we have attained a high standard of living for
our people through a system of free enterprise. Nevertheless, as strongly
as my country believes in free enterprise, it believes even more strongly
in democracy.

It is not our purpose nor our desire to impose any economic structure
on the German people that the German people do not desire for themselves. We believe, nevertheless, that that desire can only be expressed
by the German people as a whole.

Within the field of state utilities and state enterprises which operate
within the bounds of a single state, that decision lies within that state.

However, where there are resources and industries that are essential to the economy of all Germany, that decision passes beyond the power of a single state to make. It then becomes a decision that can be made only when the political structure of Germany has been determined and when the German people within that political structure have had the right to express their views. It will be their opinion that makes the decision, and not the imposed dictates of Military Government.

The British Labor Government favors public ownership of Germany's basic industries as a safeguard against a new aggression and will "give active support to the German plan for their socialization." It is opposed to a return of these industries to the industrial magnates who financed Hitler and had been in two wars part and parcel of Germany's aggressive policy.[41]

In accordance with the policy announced by the United States, Military Government raised no objection against Article 41 of the new constitution of Greater Hesse providing for mandatory socialization of the mining and steel industries and of all public utilities in that state. This article, which was voted upon separately from the constitution, was approved by 63 per cent of the votes cast, a majority exceeding the combined vote of the Socialist and Communist parties (49 per cent) and almost as high as the vote in favor of the remainder of the constitution.

Previously the assembly of Hesse had voted unanimously to socialize the I. G. Farben plants in the *Land*. These properties were, however, excluded from Article 41, presumably because legal title was still vested in the four-power Control Council.

So far as the heavy industries of the Ruhr Basin are concerned, the American and British Military Governors have stated, in the announcement of Law No. 75, that the question of socialization of these industries "is properly within the competence of a representative freely elected German Government, the sovereignty of which may extend over the whole of Germany or may be confined to Western Germany only. Accordingly, the [Bipartite] Board will not take any action in regard to the coal and iron and steel industries in the Combined Area which will prejudice a decision by such future German government as to the pattern of ownership to be established for those industries."

It may thus be concluded that public ownership of basic industries is not considered by the Western Allies as a dangerous concentration of economic power as long as the management is open to public scrutiny and accountable to the elected representatives of the people.

Meanwhile, some steps have been taken to give labor a greater share in the management. Under the British segregation scheme for the steel industry, each of the newly established corporations was placed under a board of managers consisting of a business manager, a technical manager, and a personnel manager (the latter selected from the ranks of labor). Each Board of Managers was supervised by a Board of Directors consisting of four representatives of management, four representatives of labor, one representative of the public taken from the Right-of-Center parties, one representative from the Left-of-Center, and one neutral chairman. In the DKBL two out of seven directors are representatives of labor. Trade union demands for increased labor participation in the management of large-scale industries are supported by the Social Democratic party and an important group within the Christian-Democratic Union.

The concentration of large land holdings in a few hands was a serious problem only in the areas now under Russian and Polish administration. Liberal opinion in the American and British zones, with the support of the occupation authorities, nevertheless began to press for a land reform which would provide land for workers' garden plots, and for small farms to be cultivated by peasant refugees from the east.

As a result of this pressure, a "Bill for the Procurement of Land for Settlers" was submitted by the Council of States and enacted into law in the three states of the American Zone. It is a mild measure involving the cession, according to a sliding scale, of 10 to 90 per cent of the acreage of properties over one hundred hectares (250 acres) of arable land, with full indemnification to the owners. This bill represents a compromise between the stand-pattism of the land-owning interests which are strongly entrenched in the Christian Democratic party, and more far-reaching proposals of the Social Democratic party. Since less than 3 per cent of the agricultural land in the U. S. Zone is in holdings over one hundred hectares, it is estimated that the land levy will yield only about 75,000 hectares, to be delivered by 834 individuals, plus 75,000 hectares formerly owned by the German Army, and small amounts of confiscated land of leading Nazis and war criminals.

In the British Zone, where holdings over one hundred hectares account for more than one-tenth of the agricultural land, an ordinance was passed on September 4, 1947 which limits individual holdings to 150 hectares or a total taxable value of RM 200,000 (whichever is greater). However, the Social-Democratic majority in the diet of Land Schleswig-Holstein, passed a law expropriating all estates of more than one hundred hectares.

The French Zone

In the first three years of occupation, economic conditions in the French Zone have been even less satisfactory than in the bizonal area. Because of insufficient food imports and substantial exports and requisitions for the use of French occupation personnel, food rations have been even lower than those in the British and American zones. The food shortage was only partly relieved by the fact that the zone did not admit any significant number of Allied or German displaced persons. Industrial recovery was hampered not only by the lack of food, but also by inadequate imports of raw materials for processing.

Unlike the bizonal area, however, the French Zone seems to have yielded a net profit to the occupying power, with exports—primarily of meat, lumber, chemicals, equipment, and manufactured goods—exceeding in value the imports of coal, raw materials, and grain. Removals of machinery are also reported to have been more severe than in the American and British zones.

Developments in the Soviet Zone

Soviet policy in Eastern Germany seems to have been guided by two principal objectives: (1) to exact maximum reparations; (2) to use Eastern Germany as a base from which to extend Soviet influence throughout Germany; or, failing this, to convert Eastern

Germany into a satellite state within the Soviet sphere of influence.

Unlike the Western powers, the Russians probably never considered the primary purpose of the occupation to be one of military, industrial, and ideological disarmament. They always appeared to look upon the occupation from the point of view of the contribution it could make to the economic and military potential of the Soviet Union.

At first they believed this purpose to be served best by the removal to Russia of large quantities of industrial equipment. It soon became apparent, however, that the Russians generally lacked the skilled labor and technical know-how required to dismantle, reassemble, and operate this equipment efficiently; consequently, this method of exacting reparations proved to be even more wasteful than would normally be expected. Soviet policy then switched to reparations out of current production. Roughly one-third of the industrial capacity remaining in the zone was transferred to Soviet ownership, but left in place to be operated for Soviet account using German labor, fuel, and raw materials.

At the same time, the Russians effected in their zone drastic political, economic, and social changes designed to safeguard Soviet influence. Although some of these reforms were in accordance with the traditional program of the German non-Communist Left, such spontaneous support as might have been won by these measures was rapidly dissipated as a result of the arbitrary and partisan manner in which they were executed. The ruthless methods of economic exploitation employed by the Russians naturally did not help to make the Soviet system popular among the German people. However, any effective opposition was forestalled by the terroristic measures which the Russians instituted.

DISMANTLING

Large-scale dismantling of plants, installations, and individual machines began immediately after V-E Day, first in Berlin, Brandenburg, and Silesia; later Thuringia and the state and province of Saxony were the main targets. Altogether, more than one thousand plants seem to have been affected. At the end of May, 1946, the Commander in Chief of the Soviet Occupation Zone, Marshal

Sokolovsky, announced that the removal of plants in the zone had been substantially completed by May 1. About that time an American correspondent estimated that industrial capacity had been reduced to about 50 per cent of 1938.[42] In accordance with the Allied reparations plan, removals seem to have been concentrated in the engineering, electro-technical, and chemical industries; however, "peaceful" industries—such as sugar refineries and other food processing plants, wood-working, textile, leather, printing, and paper plants—which were supposed to be exempted from reparations are also reported to have been dismantled. In addition, telephone exchanges, telephone cables, and the second track on all but three railroad lines have been removed. In connection with the dismantling of certain plants (including Junkers, Zeiss), it was reported that several thousand skilled workers were forcibly removed to Russia.[43]

INDUSTRIAL PRODUCTION

At the same time the Russians made a determined effort to reactivate the remaining industry in their zone. Soon after V-E Day, a German central economic administration was installed in Berlin, and was charged with the preparation of quarterly production and distribution plans for the zone. Its authority over the various state governments was subsequently strengthened by a series of measures which went parallel to those taken in the combined American and British zones, except that in the Soviet Zone, the central agencies came to rely increasingly on Communist-dominated organizations (such as the so-called Socialist Unity party, the trade unions, the peasant organizations, and economic control committees) for the implementation of their policies on the state and local levels.

These organizations were also used in attempts to increase production by means of special incentives in kind distributed through the trade unions and peasant associations. At the same time, piece-wages were introduced in all key industries and steps were taken to enforce work discipline.

The initial recovery of the zone was also aided by drastic financial measures. Except for an exemption of RM 300 to RM 400 on small accounts, all bank and postal savings accounts acquired prior to May 8, 1945 were frozen. All banks and security exchanges were closed; the contents of safe deposit vaults seized; the public debt and obligations of banks, Sovietized and nationalized enterprises, and expropriated landed estates were repudiated; and all transactions in old securities prohibited. Insurance policies (except life insurance policies up to RM 10,000 and social insurance benefits) and the retirement fund of government employees were cancelled. While these measures were widely criticized as inequitable since they imposed great hardship on many small savers and in some instances interfered with the resumption of private business, they increased the compulsion to work and to sell by making it necessary to pay for rations and to meet tax and other cash obligations out of current earnings.

However, after a fairly rapid recovery during the first eighteen months, to about 40 per cent of the level of industrial production in 1938, further progress began to be hampered increasingly by some of the same factors which impeded recovery in the Western zones, together with some difficulties which were peculiar to the Soviet Zone. The Soviet Zone was traditionally dependent on supplies of hard coal from Upper Silesia and of steel from the Ruhr, but since the German surrender, shipments of these basic commodities were reduced to a trickle. The shortage of coking coal seems to have prevented any substantial utilization of even the relatively insignificant iron and steel capacity which is located in the zone. The lack of steel, in turn, was probably the most serious limiting factor in the recovery of many other industries. As a result of the steel shortage, the exhaustion of stocks of other raw materials, the stagnation of interregional trade, high absenteeism and low productivity of labor, and bottlenecks created by excessive removals of equipment in critical industries, the industry of the zone soon lost its initial advantage over that of the other zones.

CURRENCY REFORM

When the currency reform went into effect in Western Germany, the Soviet authorities matched it in their zone with a currency conversion of their own. The latter, unlike the former, was not limited to a purely monetary operation; its discriminatory features made it an instrument for the redistribution of wealth. Although the actual amount of new currency issued has not been revealed, it may be inferred from SMA Order No. 111 and subsequent ordinances of the German Economic Commission that the over-all reduction of money in circulation was much less than in the West. Entire categories of money holdings were exchanged at the rate of one for one, including personal currency holdings up to RM 70, currency holdings of Soviet personnel up to the limits of their monthly or bi-weekly earnings, savings deposits up to RM 100, and all credit balances of public authorities, nationalized enterprises, Soviet corporations, and the Soviet Military Administration. Holders of individual savings accounts up to RM 1000 and holders of insurance policies were entitled to a preferential conversion rate of 5:1 and 3:1, respectively. Current accounts of industrial and other business concerns were converted at the 1:1 rate within the limits of their weekly turnover or wage bill. Private debts were not devalued. All other money holdings or postwar credit balances were converted at the rate of 10:1. However, accounts which upon investigation were held to have been wrongfully acquired became subject to confiscation. The balances accumulated prior to May 9, 1945 remained frozen, but it was announced that they would be converted into a loan to be repaid over a period of twenty-five years beginning in 1952.

In contrast with the West, the currency reform in the East was not supported by large imports and the prospect of an even larger flow of food and raw materials; nor was it stringent enough to permit a partial relaxation of price and allocation controls, even if it is assumed that such a course would have been compatible with Russian methods and objectives in the Soviet Zone. As a result, the reform failed to restore initiative and confidence. Black market prices remained almost as high, and food and other consumer goods remained as scarce as before the reform. Industrial production stagnated as deliveries of coal, steel, and other goods from Western Germany were cut off following the Soviet blockade of Berlin, while the Soviet Union and its satellites were either unable or unwilling to substitute imports from the East.

In an effort to counter the ERP, the German Economic Com-

mission announced a two-year plan for the Soviet Zone; but even
for the end of 1950, it was unable to hold out greater hopes than
the attainment of an industrial production target equal to 81 per
cent of the 1936 level (or 69 per cent of that in 1938), and a 2000
calorie average ration,[44] goals which were within reach or had
been surpassed in the Bizonal Area in the fall of 1948.

REPARATIONS FROM CURRENT PRODUCTION

In spite of the low level of production, however, an amount of
between $600,000,000 to $1,000,000,000 per year (at 1947 world
prices), representing between one-half and one-third of the net
industrial output of the Soviet Zone, appears to have been taken
as reparations or requisitioned for the use of the occupation forces.

In June, 1946, Marshal Sokolovsky was reported to have stated
at a meeting of leading German administrative officials in Berlin-
Karlshorst that of a total industrial production equal to RM 2,000,-
000,000 in the first quarter of 1946, only RM 300,000,000, or 15
per cent, were requisitioned for reparation and occupation account.[45] However, the figure of RM 2,000,000,000 seems to represent gross production. In 1936, the net value of industrial production in the Soviet Zone, after elimination of double counting
of raw materials, semi-finished and finished products, was equal to
only about RM 2,000,000,000 per quarter. In the first quarter of
1946, it probably did not exceed RM 600,000,000. The value of
reparations from current industrial output, therefore, seems to have
been about 50 per cent of the total.[46] In the field of consumers'
goods, the Russian share was alleged to be between 60 and 80
per cent.[47]

At the purchasing power parity rate of RM 1 = $.50, the total
value of reparations deliveries from the current production of the
Soviet Zone may therefore be estimated at $150,000,000 in the first
quarter of 1946. With subsequent increases in production and
tighter Soviet control over industry, this rate has probably increased to $250,000,000 per quarter. The Two-year Plan promised
a reduction of Soviet takings to 25 per cent of the net value of industrial production which, at the target level of 81 per cent of that
in 1936, would still amount to more than $250,000,000 per quarter.[48]

FOOD SUPPLY

Unlike the Western zones of Germany, the Soviet Zone is normally self-sufficient in food. Before the war, it produced the equivalent of more than 3,000 calories per person per day. In 1945, severe fighting in the area east of the Elbe River interfered with the spring planting and caused considerable damage to standing crops, and livestock herds and farm equipment were depleted through looting and requisitions. Crop yields were further reduced in many instances because the lack of horses and equipment prevented cultivation. These conditions, added to the wartime depletion of the soil, reduced food production in the Soviet Zone (in terms of calories) to less than two-thirds of the prewar level in spite of the diversion of crops from livestock feeding to direct human consumption. In the absence of imports, the entire needs of the occupying forces as well as those of the indigenous population, swollen by millions of refugees from the east, had to be supplied from this reduced production and the remaining stocks. As a result, the weighted average nonfarm consumption, including non-rationed and black market supplies, declined to about 1,400 calories per person per day, but local consumption rates varied from 1,800 to 2,000 calories in some areas of the province of Saxony to less than 1,000 in areas along the new Polish border. Food consumption of "normal consumers" averaged 1,200 calories but varied from 1,600 to 1,800 calories in the best areas to less than 800 in the worst. In the western parts of the zone, conditions were thus roughly comparable to those in the Western zones. In the area between the Elbe and Oder rivers, which had suffered most from devastation and which was most overcrowded by refugees, conditions of famine prevailed. In the city of Frankfurt an der Oder, which was one of the gateways for refugees and released prisoners of war entering Germany from the east, more than 12,000 persons out of an average population of about 60,000 were reported to have died in the first six months following the surrender from starvation and epidemics fostered by malnutrition.[49] In Berlin, the death rate was reported to have reached a level of seventy-five per thousand per annum during the months of May, June, and July, 1945, more than five times the normal rate.

Beginning in November, 1945, efforts were made to equalize

food consumption throughout the Soviet Zone. A uniform ration scheme was introduced which discriminated in favor of large cities to make up for the lesser availability of unrationed and black market supplies. Farm deliveries were encouraged by permitting producers who had surrendered their quotas to sell any surplus over these quotas in the free market. As a result of these measures and better harvests, the food situation improved somewhat, but except for short periods in the spring of 1946 and 1947, the average rations and total consumption rates seem to have remained below those prevailing in the American and British zones. This was due in no small part to substantial requisitions for the use of the occupying forces and for export.

REORGANIZATION OF THE ECONOMY

In contrast with the Western powers, the Russians proceeded almost immediately to reorganize the economy of Eastern Germany from top to bottom. At first it appeared that the primary purpose of these measures was to establish complete Soviet control over the economy with a view to assuring the fulfilment of Soviet reparations orders. It soon became apparent, however, that these measures fitted into a pattern imposed on all countries dominated by the Soviet Union, and aimed at the complete integration of Eastern Germany into the Soviet orbit.

The first of these steps was the seizure of virtually all important industrial and commercial enterprises by Marshal Zhukov's Order No. 124, of October 30, 1945, which provided for the sequestration not only of properties of governmental and Nazi organizations and leading Nazis and war criminals, but also of all "ownerless" property and property of "any other persons designated by the Soviet Military Commander."

In the spring of 1946, all sequestered properties were divided into three lists: List A, comprising a large number of small and medium-sized enterprises, and a few large plants; List B, comprising mostly small plants and artisan shops; List C, comprising practically all remaining large enterprises in the key industries of the zone, as well as some smaller concerns.

The plants in Lists A and B were turned over to the state and local authorities who in turn disposed of List B properties by returning them to former owners who had been found innocent or mere "followers" of the Nazi party, or by giving or selling them to victims of Nazism, resettlers, and war victims. Properties in List A, comprising about 3,000 plants employing some 350,000 workers, were transferred to public ownership by decree, except in the state of Saxony, where nationalization was approved by a plebiscite. In the spring of 1948, it was reported that the socialized sector accounted for about 40 per cent of the remaining industrial capacity of the Soviet Zone.

The enterprises in list C, however, were expressly excluded from nationalization and remained under the direct control of the Soviet Military Administration. The latter proceeded to organize some 220 of the largest of these plants into Soviet trusts, one for each industry, under Russian management, employing altogether some 300,000 to 400,000 persons, and combined under a single Soviet holding company. These Soviet corporations are reported to include all important plants in the synthetic oil, chemical, iron and steel, nonferrous metal, potash, cement, and engineering industries; several large power plants and brown coal mines; and the part of the Zeiss optical works which was left in Germany. Some important cigarette, leather, textile, and musical instrument factories are also alleged to have been taken over. These enterprises, which account for about 30 per cent of the industrial output in the zone, seem to have been seized as reparations.[50] Their output is reported to go almost exclusively to Russia; since the proceeds are not credited to German export account, they apparently are considered as reparations.

Since the Soviet corporations are given the highest priority on fuel and raw materials and can offer to their workers high wages, premiums in kind, and other privileges, they not only enjoy a tremendous competitive advantage over the German sector of the economy, but at the same time, by creating desirable and secure employment which brings with it food and goods for barter, produce vested interests in their survival.

As a result of the expropriation measures, practically all the remaining important industrial properties are now either under direct Soviet control or under public management. Land ownership was subjected to an almost equally far-reaching reform. Under the land reform decrees, estates of all persons and corporations owning more than one hundred hectares (with some exceptions such as land owned by the churches) were expropriated without compensation, including buildings, equipment, and other assets, as well as mortgages and rights of third persons. As of July, 1946, when the land reform was virtually completed, more than 6,000 properties covering altogether almost 2,300,000 hectares had been affected by the decrees. In addition, 2,000 Nazi properties under one hundred hectares, totaling about 80,000 hectares and almost 400,000 hectares of state-owned land had been confiscated. Of the total of about 2,750,000 hectares, however, only slightly more than half was arable land.

About two-thirds of the land was divided among some 300,000 families, mostly agricultural laborers, resettlers, small owners, and tenants. (Charges of political favoritism in the selection of these settlers were made by all non-Communist groups). In general, five hectares was the maximum size for a homestead created or augmented in size by the land reform. Recipients must pay to the state a sum equal to the current value of one year's crop in ten to twenty annual instalments. Land obtained through the land reform cannot be divided, transferred, or mortgaged.

The remaining third of the expropriated land was transferred to public ownership and set aside for state forests, agricultural experiment stations, model farms, and agricultural schools.

It is interesting to note that even under this relatively drastic law, only about 100,000 out of a total of approximately 1,000,000 German farm families expelled from Eastern Europe could be resettled as small farmers.[51]

Tractors and other heavy agricultural machinery, industrial facilities located on the confiscated estates, as well as a large part of the barns, buildings, livestock, and of the light machinery and implements, were not turned over to small holders but were transferred to so-called Farmers' Mutual Aid Committees. Like the Russian Machine and Tractor Stations, these committees, through their control over farm machinery and repair and processing facilities, have become powerful instruments of the state; as machines replace men and animals, the peasants' dependence on them increases.

In spite of rewards and political pressure, however, thousands of new settlers, lacking the capital, livestock, equipment, housing, farm buildings, and in some instances the experience, necessary to sustain even a minimum standard of living on holdings of such small size, abandoned their newly acquired farms. The ultimate success of the land reform will depend in large measure on the speed with which adequate buildings, equipment, roads, and other utilities can be made available.

ECONOMIC PROSPECTS

As a consequence of the war and defeat, Germany sustained what may be the sharpest percentage reduction in national wealth suffered by any nation in modern times. The loss of the area east of the Oder and Neisse, accompanied by the expulsion of its ten million German inhabitants stripped of virtually their entire property, deprived Germany of about one-tenth of its assets. This region was Germany's most important food surplus area, accounting for about one-fifth of the monetary value and one-fourth of the caloric value of its agricultural production; it also included more than one-tenth of Germany's coal reserves and about 7 per cent of its industrial capacity.

In the west, the separation of the Saar district, though it did not burden Germany with an additional number of expellees, deprived it of a significant part of its natural and industrial resources. In 1937, the Saar accounted for only 1 per cent of Germany's population, but included one-tenth of Germany's coal deposits, and 12 per cent of its steel production. At the favorable terms of trade for its principal export products (coal, steel, chemicals, glass) currently prevailing in the world markets, the area is capable of producing an annual surplus of about $100,000,000 over its own needs.[52]

In the remainder of the Reich, it is estimated that as a result of wartime destruction and undermaintenance, which more than offset wartime investments, the long-term industrial and transport capacity declined by about 15 to 20 per cent from the prewar level. Losses in housing and household furnishings probably amount to more than one-third of the prewar value. Losses in agriculture through depletion of the soil, reduction in livestock numbers, deterioration of equipment, and destruction and seizures may amount to about 10 per cent of the agricultural property.

If allowance is further made for past and scheduled reparations removals, the loss of the merchant marine, and the loss of foreign assets, including patent rights and secret processes, the total reduction in per capita national wealth from the prewar level may be estimated at about one-third.

The economic significance of Germany's manpower losses is no less real, but more difficult to assess, than its losses in material wealth. Although the total number of mouths to be fed within Germany's present borders is greater than in the Old Reich before the war, the number of able-bodied men has declined by about four million killed and perhaps half as many again who are largely or totally disabled. As of March, 1947 between two and four million more were being held as prisoners of war.[53] As a result, the number of able-bodied men in the age group from twenty to forty declined by more than one-half, from 16 per cent of the total population before the war to less than 8 per cent; and the women outnumbered the men by more than seven million, or 27 per cent.[54] War losses and possibly the withholding of productive manpower in Eastern Europe account for the small proportion of able-bodied men among the millions of expellees that were received in the Western zones; the expellees are therefore considered as an economic liability, at least in the short run.

If it is assumed that all of the two million German prisoners of war reported to the Allied Control Council will be returned, the total war loss will amount to about seven million men killed, missing, or seriously disabled. This represents 20 per cent of the prewar labor force in terms of numbers, but a much higher percentage in terms of earning capacity. This loss may, however, be compensated in part by the increase in the number of employed women and juveniles who normally would not have sought gainful occupations.

The situation will be further aggravated if, as appears likely, "rump Germany" remains split by the "iron curtain."

Eastern Germany, which includes about 30 per cent of the population of present-day Germany, stands to lose more heavily by partition than the Western zones. Cut off from its customary sources of supply of steel and various types of equipment, denuded of much of its own industrial capacity, it will be dependent for its recovery on supplies of hard coal, steel, and raw materials from the East. Although Eastern Germany's role as a supplier of urgently needed industrial goods to the less developed countries of the Soviet Bloc will become increasingly important as its industries are revived, it will probably have to accept less favorable terms from the trade monopolies of its Eastern neighbors than would be available to it in the freer markets of the West.

On the other hand, the Soviet Zone, being self-sufficient in food and having a generally more balanced economy, will be able to support itself with a relatively smaller volume of foreign trade than the more densely populated and more specialized Western zones; its readjustment problems are therefore less serious.

For Western Germany, exports will be a matter of life and death.

Before the war, Western Germany had to import fully one-half of the food requirements of its nonfarm population, or about seven million tons of food per year. Since that time, its population increased by about 20 per cent. Even at the extremely low consumption levels prevailing during the first three years of the occupation, which were only barely sufficient to "prevent disease and unrest," the United States and British governments spent $643,000,000 in 1946 and $727,000,000 in 1947 for essential imports into their zones. About three-fourths of these expenditures went for imports of food from the United States. During the same period, exports from the bizonal area did not exceed $143,000,000 in 1946 and $222,000,000 in 1947 (mostly coal), leaving a deficit of about $500,000,000 each year.

But Western Germany cannot be kept on the dole indefinitely.

To maintain an adequate diet and to sustain its manufacturing industries on the limited scale provided by the revised Level of Industry Plan, Western Germany must import food, textile fibers, petroleum, and other raw materials to the value of about $3,000,-000,000 per year, in terms of 1948 prices. To pay for these imports, Western Germany must rely on its principal resource, the technical skill of its workers and managers. More than ever it will have to become one of the workshops of Europe, and indeed of the world; a processor of raw materials. Separated from its agricultural and semi-industrialized hinterland, it is completely dependent on world trade beyond the power of economic retaliation. For Western Germany, or even for a reunited Germany within the Potsdam boundaries, a return to the autarchic policies of the last few decades is out of the question.

If the idea of a de-industrialized German nation living on the products of agriculture and small-scale industry could ever be seriously entertained in weighing the fate of sixty-six million people living in an area of 180,000 square miles within the prewar boundaries of the German Reich, its absurdity becomes even more obvious when applied to the problem of feeding fifty million Germans in an area only half this size. In size, in population, and in general economic characteristics, Western Germany resembles the United Kingdom, and its problems are much the same as those which England would face if confronted with the destruction of one-fifth of its industries and transport and one-fourth of its buildings, the loss of its entire merchant marine, the loss of its remaining foreign assets, separation from the rest of the British Commonwealth, and the influx of several million Britons from overseas.

To be sure, Western Germany can make further progress in developing its agricultural production; but such progress will most likely take the form of an expansion of the production of high-value garden crops and livestock products, yielding a large return per acre of land and per man employed, which would be based in part on imported fertilizers and feedstuffs, rather than on an increase in the production of staple crops which use much land and little labor and in which Germany is unable to compete with the vast expanses of the New World. Whether these products will be consumed domestically or exported will depend in part on the prosperity of Germany's urban economy in relation to that of neighboring countries; but in any event, exports of such luxury goods will be rather limited by the intense competition in this field.

In industry, some further expansion is possible in the light industries (including textile and leather products); but in this field, as before the war, German exports will probably continue to face considerable sales resistance, particularly in view of the probable closing of the Eastern European markets and the development of consumer goods industries in many of the less developed areas of the world.

In order to earn the foreign exchange necessary for its imports, Western Germany will therefore have to rely in the main, as in the past, on exports of industries in which it has a comparative advantage in the world market; that is, machinery, transportation equipment, heavy electrical equipment, optical and precision instruments, and chemicals—all products which yield high returns in foreign exchange in relation to the input of coal and other raw materials.

In the three years which have elapsed since the German surrender, the nations of the West have come to realize that the economic plight of the German people presents a formidable threat not only to the survival of democracy in Germany itself, but to the stability, security, and well-being of Europe as a whole. The Western occupying powers have gradually turned away from the predominantly negative policies embodied in the Potsdam Agreement and JCS 1067 toward a policy of active support of German economic rehabilitation. This change in policy was motivated by three principal considerations:

1. The realization that Western Germany would have to be subsidized indefinitely by the occupying powers unless its production reached a level well above the targets originally contemplated.

2. A growing awareness that a reasonably rapid economic recovery in Germany is necessary to give peaceful and democratic forces there a chance to assert themselves. Present conditions, if

allowed to continue, could not fail to breed violent political extremism.

3. The increasing conviction, not only in the United States and Great Britain but also among Germany's Western neighbors, that the economic revival of Germany is essential to the economic revival of Europe. In the countries of Western Europe, this change in outlook was speeded by their changing reconstruction needs. As long as these countries were competing with Germany for short world supplies of food, coal, and raw materials needed to reactivate their industries, they naturally felt that their own urgent requirements should take precedence over those of Germany. Gradually, however, as post-surrender shortages of critical raw materials were overcome and the countries of Western Europe reached the stage of full employment of their industrial and manpower resources, their most pressing import needs shifted to industrial equipment and other manufactured products. Before the war, Germany had supplied more than one-third of their net import requirements for these commodities.

The first major step toward the rehabilitation of the German economy was taken when the governments of Great Britain and the United States on December 2, 1946 agreed on a one billion dollar pump-priming advance to their combined zones to be extended over a period of three years, two-thirds of which was intended to be used to cover the entire cost of food imports in 1947, thus releasing any proceeds of German exports for the purchase of raw materials and equipment needed for the rehabilitation of the bizonal economy. In addition to this long-term advance, the Reconstruction Finance Corporation was authorized to make short-term self-liquidating loans for the purchase of cotton, to be repaid with the proceeds of exports of cotton textiles.

For various reasons, the results of the first year of operation of this scheme fell short of the goal. An unexpected crop failure in Western Europe reduced the quantities and increased the cost of Germany's food imports. The food shortage and an unusually severe winter interfered with production. Of the reduced volume of production (particularly of coal), a relatively larger share had to be retained to meet essential domestic requirements, leaving less available for export. Moreover, exporters were hampered by complicated licensing and pricing procedures and restrictions on contacts between German and foreign businessmen. The practice of strictly limiting payments to German exporters to the official ceiling prices in Reichsmarks held little inducement to manufacturers who found it considerably more profitable to offer their products in the domestic barter market. To overcome this difficulty, an export incentive plan was put into effect in the late summer of 1947 by which manufacturers and workers in export industries were given the right together to dispose of 10 per cent of the foreign exchange proceeds of exports. When production for export finally increased toward the end of 1947, the bizonal Joint Export-Import Agency found that because of the growing dollar shortage, some German export products, particularly textiles, could not be sold. The bizonal authorities, on the other hand, were reluctant to purchase for dollars such "luxuries" as fish, vegetables, and fruits which were offered by some of Germany's neighbors.

WESTERN GERMANY AND THE ERP

When the sixteen Western European nations assembled in Paris to consider Secretary Marshall's historic proposal for a European Recovery Plan, they recognized the important role which Western Germany would have to play in it: "Other Western European countries cannot be prosperous as long as the economy of the Western Zone is paralyzed, and a substantial increase of output there will be required if Europe is to become independent of outside support."[55]

The European Recovery Program provides for American aid to the participating countries, including Western Germany, amounting to about $5,500,000,000 in the first full year of the program.[56] Of this amount, about $1,100,000,000, or 20 per cent, is earmarked for Western Germany (including the French Zone). For the entire four and one-fourth-year period of the program, the United States Government estimated the total cost of the program at $17,000,-000,000, of which between three and one-half and four billion would go to Western Germany. Western Germany's share in the program is thus roughly proportional to its share in the population and economic resources of Western Europe; but in the view of the Harriman Committee, it is too small if actual reconstruction needs are considered.[57] This view is shared by the Herter Committee.[58]

Because of the extremely low level of economic activity now prevailing in Western Germany, however, that area is expected to benefit more from the ERP, relatively, than the rest of Western Europe. To put it in a different way: Western Germany is expected to yield higher returns, in terms of output per dollar invested, than any other participating country.

The magnitude of the proposed investment in German recovery may best be gauged by comparing it with the inadequate efforts of the past few years. Between July 1, 1945 and June 30, 1947, grants and loans by the United States amounted to more than $11,000,-000,000. Only $550,000,000, or 5 per cent of this, went to Germany. If allowance is made for British expenditures on behalf of Germany, this amount increases to $800,000,000, which was barely enough to keep the people alive. By contrast, grants and loans extended to Great Britain during the same period amounted to $3,300,-000,000, and those extended to France to $1,500,000,000.

It is estimated that with ERP aid, Western Germany will more than double its imports, from $800,000,000 in 1947 to $1,900,000,-000 during the first year of the program. To break the bottlenecks in its recovery, imports during the first year of the program include not only food and raw materials, but also steel, machinery, and transport equipment which Germany normally produces for export. The usual exports of equipment and repair parts will at first be deferred so as to hasten the rehabilitation of German industry, and total exports in 1948-49 will probably not exceed $800,000,000. While this policy will increase the net outlay for Western Germany during the first two years of the program, the added cost will be more than defrayed in the long run by speeding the achievement of a self-supporting economy and by increasing the volume of exports which Western Germany can contribute to the later stages of the program.

The ERP will contribute to German recovery not only through its direct material impact, but also through its psychological effect. While its success will depend on the achievement of internal economic stability, it will itself facilitate the necessary fiscal and financial measures by easing the existing shortages of food and other essential goods. By holding out hope for a gradual improvement in the standard of living, it will help to restore confidence and the will to work. Last but not least, it will provide the basis for the reintegration of Germany into the European family of nations.

The Economic Prerequisites for German Democracy

Can the ERP provide an adequate economic basis for the development of a stable, peaceful, and democratic society in Germany? The answer is a qualified yes. But ERP alone is not enough. It will achieve its objectives only if it is the first step in a process of economic integration of Germany into the European and world trade communities, and provided Germany solves its own internal problems of economic organization and social adjustment.

These external and internal adjustments will be difficult regardless of whether Germany remains divided or whether it is reunited within its Potsdam boundaries; from a purely economic point of view, the difference is merely one of degree. It is possible, however, that continuing partition will give rise to intolerable political tensions which might defeat any economic recovery program.

In evaluating the prospects of German democracy, it is difficult to overemphasize the importance of economic stability and a rising standard of living. In spite of the territorial losses imposed by the Treaty of Versailles, peaceful and democratic tendencies predominated in Germany in the late 1920's when the effects of war and inflation had been overcome and the standard of living was recovering to the prewar level. Beginning in 1930, depression and mass unemployment weakened the democratic labor organizations and the moderate middle-class elements which supported the Republic, revived the old nationalistic issues and brought Hitler to power.

The ERP will go a long way toward helping to overcome the extreme poverty and insecurity which today are the main obstacles to a democratic development among the fifty million Germans in the West. But it will not bring full recovery to the prewar standard of living. Even in the last year of the program, when industrial production in Western Germany is expected to recover approximately to the 1936 level, the standard of living will fall far short of that level. The caloric value of the diet will be nearly normal, but the per capita supply of high-quality foods, clothing, housing, manufactured goods, and imported luxuries will be from 25 to 50 per cent below the prewar average.[59]

Even under favorable conditions, Germany will not fully recover from the war and its aftermath for many years to come. In the period from 1925 to 1929, when political and economic conditions in Germany were stable and foreign aid was forthcoming in substantial volume, annual net investments over and above replacements of worn-out capital equipment averaged RM 6,000,000,000. But even at this relatively high rate of capital accumulation, the reconstruction of the German economy may be expected to take between twenty and thirty years.

It is not surprising, therefore, that most Germans look forward with considerable anxiety to the time when ERP ends. This also helps to explain their acute distress over the continuing removal of industrial plants and equipment as reparations. According to present plans, some 920 industrial plants are to be removed from Western Germany (including the French Zone), two-thirds of which are not war plants. Less than half of these plants have been transferred so far. The dismantling of additional plants, it is held, will involve a loss to Germany several times as great as any possible benefit to the recipients. To the argument that this capacity cannot be used in Germany anyway because of shortages of fuel, raw materials, and transport, the Germans reply that these shortages exist only because Germany does not receive a fair share of the available world supplies. They also point to the waste of skilled labor and other resources employed in the dismantling that are thus withdrawn from more productive tasks. There can be little doubt, moreover, that the discouraging spectacle of the tearing-down and removal of their means of livelihood has a disastrous effect on the morale and will to work of managers, technicians, and workers alike.

But even if it is granted that the material effects of the scheduled plant removals may be small during the next few years, the lack of these plants will severely limit further economic progress once Western Germany reaches the modest goals set by the ERP. It will then not only retard the recovery of the German standard of living, but it will also reduce Germany's ability to sustain itself and eventually to repay its debts. The revised Level of Industry Plan calls for a steel production in Western Germany of less than eleven million tons. In 1929, the only year of real prosperity which the Weimar Republic had, and five years before the Nazi rearmament program started, Western Germany (including the Saar) produced for home consumption and export more than sixteen million tons of steel.

However, a clause of the United States Foreign Assistance Act opened the possibility of a further revision of the dismantling program. During the debates preceding the adoption of the Act, several members of Congress questioned the compatibility of the program of plant removals with the objectives of the European aid plan. The Congress therefore instructed the ECA Administrator to "request the Secretary of State to obtain the agreement of those countries concerned that such capital equipment as is scheduled for removal as reparations from the three Western zones of Germany be retained in Germany if such retention will most effectively serve the purpose of the European recovery program." [60] The governments of France and of the United Kingdom agreed that there was a "need to examine certain portions of the reparations list" in the light of the ERP, and an Industrial Advisory Committee was set up by the Economic Cooperation Administration to make such a study. [61]

Since Germany's industrial economy is based on coal and steel, its future is bound up with that of the Ruhr. An International Authority, vested with the power to allocate the output of the coal and steel industries of the Ruhr as between German consumption and export, as contemplated by the six-nation conference in London, will hold Germany's fate in its hands. [62]

It is likely, however, that in actual practice, this power will not be

abused. During the period of occupation, the powers which share
the responsibility for the economic administration of that part of
Germany which includes the Ruhr (at present, the United States
and the United Kingdom) will retain a predominant voice in the
Ruhr Authority. It is in the interest of these powers, and particularly of the United States which carries the burden of financing
Germany's recovery, to see that Germany is not denied a fair share
of the output of the Ruhr and that it receives a fair price for those
quantities of coal and steel which are exported.

When the occupying powers relinquish their prerogatives, the
present shortage of coal and steel in Europe will probably have
been overcome, and the main task of the International Authority
will be to ensure (1) that the resources of the area are not again
used for the purpose of aggression; (2) that the volume and direction of the exports of Ruhr coal and steel are determined by the
untrammelled play of economic forces. Monopolistic restriction and
discrimination in the sale of Ruhr products—whether motivated by
German or Allied interests—would be contrary to U.S. policy
and inconsistent with the purposes of the European Recovery
Program.

International control of the Ruhr will be permanent only under
two conditions:

(1) If the International Authority acts as a true "public utilities
commission," bearing in mind the interests of producers and consumers of all participating nations; and

(2) if it is the forerunner of a European economic union which
includes Germany as an equal partner.

In the long run, Germany will not be viable in any case, economically and politically, except as a member of an integrated European community within a system of free world trade. Germany,
even more than the rest of the highly industrialized and overcrowded countries of Western Europe, is dependent on international trade for its survival; and more than any other country, it
stands to gain by joining a European association of nations. A
European economic union would afford a peaceful and productive
outlet for the energy and skill of its people which have so often
been misguided in the past.

A complete integration of Germany into the European economic community and a freer system of world trade will, of course, require adjustments on the part of Germany as well as in other participating countries. But in the end, Germany as well as the rest of Western Europe cannot but profit from the abandonment of the autarchic policies of the last few decades.

The recovery of German industry and agriculture and the integration of the German economy into European and world trade in turn will tend to strengthen those forces within Germany—the trade unions, parts of the small and medium peasantry of the West and South and parts of the urban middle class whose interests were bound up with German foreign trade—which have been traditionally inclined toward democracy and internationalism.

The admission of Germany as an equal member of a European union offers the best hope for a satisfactory solution not only of Germany's economic problems, but also of its political problems. "The essence of the problem . . . is to re-create a Germany with full powers of a centralized government and with an unimpaired industrial capacity . . . a Germany powerful and enjoying full equality among the nations, so Western in its outlook that it can be trusted and so attractive to Germans that it can win the Eastern Germans for the West."[63]

The problems of internal organization facing Germany are no less formidable than the adjustments required by its changed external circumstances. The policymakers' task will be threefold: (1) To provide for a more equitable distribution of income and wealth; (2) to speed reconstruction; and (3) to preserve economic freedom and financial stability. To some extent, these three objectives may appear to be mutually contradictory; their reconciliation will try the strength of Germany's democratic institutions.

The war and its aftermath has left millions of Germans destitute. Those able to work may start again from scratch; but there are millions of helpless people who must depend largely or entirely on social insurance benefits or relief. Public assistance scales, including payments to disabled veterans and war widows and orphans, have been kept at extremely low levels and will have to be increased. Many of those now dependent on public welfare payments had accumulated legitimate savings but saw them depreciated by the currency reform, while holders of real wealth left undamaged by the war remained untouched. Clearly, corrective measures are called for which will equalize so far as possible the burden of war losses within Germany by means of taxation or mortgaging of real property. The proceeds of such a capital levy would be made available in the first instance to those unable to work, and secondly to small savers generally. Allied and German authorities are agreed on the urgency of such legislation. German experience after the last war and the subsequent period of inflation has shown the formidable threat to democracy presented by a middle class suddenly pauperized through the depreciation of its savings. Resettlement and partial compensation of the German refugees and expellees from Eastern Europe will also be required if this group is not to become a hotbed of nihilism and irredentism. Public opinion surveys indicate that in the eyes of the German people, the equitable distribution of the war burden will be a crucial test of democracy.

The second criterion by which the success of democratic government will be gauged is the progress of reconstruction. The people will look to the government for the maintenance of full employment. It will expect the government to prevent the misdirection of resources and to assure a proper balance between current consumption and investment.

The Bizonal authorities have estimated that in order to achieve the production targets of the recovery program, total net investments (including increases in inventories) amounting to twelve billion dollars will be required during the next four years. This represents 11 per cent of the anticipated gross national product, compared to a peak of 12 per cent reached in 1928. The provision of adequate low-cost housing for workers at industrial centers and for expellees and bombed-out people is highest on the list, with capital requirements amounting to more than two billion dollars, followed by public utilities and transport, with about one billion each. Coal production, which lagged behind the general trend of recovery in recent months, threatens to become a bottleneck unless worn-out equipment is replaced, new shafts are sunk, and new seams are opened up; $600,000,000 are to be invested for this purpose.[64]

It will be extremely difficult to finance these investments without resorting to an inflationary expansion of credits. Even in periods of prosperity, such as the late 1920's or the late 1930's, voluntary savings did not exceed about 10 per cent of the gross national product. There is reason to believe that for some time to come, in spite of high interest rates, voluntary savings will fall far short of this amount. The German people have seen their savings wiped out twice within the span of a generation, and it will take many years of financial stability before confidence is restored. Incomes will be lower than before the war, and taxes will be higher. The tendency to spend will be greater because of the urgent need to replace durable consumer goods which have not been available for years. These factors may be counteracted to a minor extent by granting to savers tax privileges and priority claims on new housing and durable consumer goods in short supply. Business savings may be stimulated by extending a differential tax advantage in favor of undistributed profits which are plowed back into industry.

Another non-inflationary source of investment funds may be found in the Deutsche mark proceeds of imports financed by the United States. At the present time, about two billion Deutsche marks are thus withdrawn from circulation annually. This source of internal financing will, of course, disappear with the cessation of foreign aid. Some non-inflationary credit expansion will also be possible as the productivity of the German economy increases. Finally, there may be some voluntary influx of private foreign capital, particularly if Germany offers guaranties for the repatriation of a reasonable amount each year to cover amortization and net returns. It may be expected, however, that these relatively painless methods will not yield sufficient funds to finance the proposed investment program. Forced savings, through taxation or compulsory loans, will therefore have to be relied upon to fill the gap.

The popular demand for greater social equity and the need for funds to finance long-term investments will place a considerable burden on the public budgets. In the fiscal year 1947-48, the public

budgets of the Bizonal Area showed a surplus of one billion Reichsmarks of revenues over expenditures. Of the RM 16,500,000,000
collected in taxes and fees, less than 10 per cent was employed for
investment purposes, while 15 to 20 per cent was required for wages
and salaries, about 20 per cent for social welfare payments, about
10 per cent was transferred to regional and local governments (primarily for welfare payments), about 10 per cent was spent for
subsidies, and about 30 per cent was required to cover occupation
costs including expenditures for Allied displaced persons.

Since that time, tax rates have been reduced, and total tax revenues
will probably decline by about 20 per cent in 1948-49. To be sure,
certain expenditures, including subsidies for coal and steel, occupation costs, and outlays for the care of displaced persons will be
reduced. Some economics will also be effected in government
wages and salaries. Public employment in the Bizonal Area increased from 400,000 in 1936 to almost 700,000 in 1947. It
should be possible to reduce this number, even if allowance is made
for the fact that public authorities have assumed increased responsibilities compared with the prewar period, and that obligations
formerly centralized in the Reich office in Berlin have been transferred to the Bizone. Certain other expenditures, however, are more
likely to increase than to decline. Interest will have to be paid on
the new public debt of the *Länder*. The Western zones have also
had to assume formal responsibility for part of the deficit of the
Western sectors of Berlin. There are considerable pressures to raise
social welfare expenditures, social insurance benefits, and pensions.
Finally there is the urgent need for long-deferred public investments. It will be impossible to meet these obligations without recourse to deficit financing unless new sources of taxation are opened
up. In addition to increased taxes on luxury consumption, and taxes
on windfall profits arising from the currency reform (including
those resulting from the liquidation of commodity hoards and the
devaluation of debts), an increase of income tax rates is probably
unavoidable. In view of the weakness of Western Germany's administrative machinery, it will not be easy to enforce increased tax
collections at a time when taxpayers will have to meet heavy obliga-

tions in connection with the capital levy for the equalization of war burdens.

Obviously, a policy of high taxes, balanced budgets, and general austerity will not find ready popular acceptance. But the alternatives are even more repugnant. One alternative is open inflation which, while encouraging investment, would do so at the price of an enormous waste of resources and an undesirable concentration of wealth on one hand, and impoverishment and labor conflicts on the other. In the long run, an uncontrolled inflation would prove to be politically and socially intolerable and economically disastrous.

The other alternative is a return to wartime regimentation, with its comprehensive system of direct allocation and price controls coupled with an attempt to freeze the excess purchasing power in the form of long-term savings. The experience of recent years has shown that this approach tends to lead to an inefficient allocation of resources and is difficult to enforce over an extended period of time; moreover, it requires for its administration a huge bureaucracy which may abuse its powers. Fiscal controls, no matter how painful they may appear, involve less regimentation once they are adopted; but to be successful in an impoverished country, they require institutional measures tantamount to a far-reaching social reform.

Thus Germany is confronted with a choice between inflation, *Zwangswirtschaft,* and a measure of socialism, a dilemma which will present a formidable challenge to German democracy. The future of German society will largely depend on how this challenge is met.

Official statements would seem to justify the expectation that, west of the iron curtain at least, the German people will be allowed to work out in a democratic manner, without foreign interference, the particular compromise between individual freedom and social control of economic processes which best answers their needs. Germany's future governmental structure, while providing for a degree of political decentralization which will allow sufficient scope for the play of regional checks and balances, will not deny to the central government economic powers similar to those possessed by other modern federal governments, including the power to collect federal taxes and the right to set up its own executive organization in the *Länder*. The German people will also be allowed to decide, without foreign interference, the particular methods of public control to be imposed on large-scale industries of a monopolistic character, including their transfer to public or semi-public ownership if they so desire.

At first, conditions in Germany will not be favorable for a free economy. Generally speaking, the higher the standard of living and the greater the equality of opportunity, the better will be the chances for economic freedom of choice and freedom of opportunity.

Chap. 5 The Reconstruction of Government & Administration

HANS MEYERHOFF

GERMANY UNDER ALLIED OCCUPATION is a country without a national government. This distinguishes it from all other ex-enemy nations and sets the broad framework of problems which confront the four occupying powers in the reconstruction of government and administration.

Three principal factors of different origin contributed to the absence of a national government in occupied Germany. (1) The military formula of unconditional surrender never extended the hope to German groups, that, by overthrowing the Nazi regime, the Allied powers would be prepared to negotiate a peace with an anti-Nazi, sovereign German government. Furthermore, the only major attempt on the German side to overthrow the Nazi regime—even in the absence of Allied commitments—the putsch of July 20, 1944, ended in failure. (2) The gradual military penetration of Germany confronted the Allied powers with the need for making local administrative appointments long before the final collapse of the central Nazi government in Berlin. (3) After the Nazi collapse, the Allied powers, while rejecting a dismemberment of Germany, agreed that the political and economic conditions in the defeated country were such that "for the time being, no central German government shall be established."[1]

The only agency charged with responsibilities for Germany as a whole was the Allied Control Council (ACC), set up in Berlin. But since there is no corresponding central German agency through which the Allies could jointly enforce their policies throughout the Reich, the ACC had become an agency primarily recommending and coordinating Allied policies rather than the highest Allied executive body in the Reich.[2] Real executive power has devolved upon the four Allied commanders in chief in their respective zones of occupation. The reconstruction of a new, democratic state machinery did not start with the establishment of a central national government, subject to joint four-power control, but evolved gradually from below within the framework of the directives of each power in its zone of occupation.

Thus Germany came to be divided into four virtually independent zonal units. The problem of surveying the revival of a post-Nazi, democratic state and government machinery has two different aspects: (a) how each power has conceived this task in its zone of occupation, and (b) how the developments in the various zones can be reconciled so as to restore eventually some kind of economic, administrative, and political unity to the Reich—to which the Allied powers also committed themselves at Potsdam.[3]

These two sides of the problem, in turn, are influenced by two further factors. In the first place, the administrative reorganization in the various zones is rooted in certain historical conditions. The apparatus used by the occupying powers rests upon the traditional structure of German administration. The bureaucracy, at the disposal of the occupying powers, bears the imprint of special factors, characteristic of the historical development of the German civil service. The blueprints—both Allied and German—for a future Reich are again sketched against a background of issues and forces peculiar to German history.

In the second place, developments have not been uniform in the four zones of occupation. While there are certain general principles guiding Allied policies—again agreed upon at Potsdam—the way in which the four powers have come to interpret and apply these principles in the field of government and administration differs considerably according to the political meaning which the four powers have given to such general principles as decentralization, denazification, and democratization. The differences of interpretation stem, in this field as in others, from the different social and political systems of the four powers as well as from the different objectives they pursue in post-Nazi Germany.

Thus it is against a background of historical conditions peculiar to Germany, on the one hand, and Allied intentions after the Nazi defeat, on the other, that the reconstruction of forms of government has taken place in the four zones of occupation.

HISTORICAL BACKGROUND

A few historical factors most pertinent to the contemporary problem may be briefly sketched as follows: [4]

1. What is known as the German Reich came into being only in the course of the nineteenth century as a result of a federation among a large number of independent sovereign states of the most varying sizes and political power. At the time of the Vienna Congress in 1815, some thirty-five independent principalities and four free cities, which had survived an even larger and more chaotic assemblage under the Holy Roman Empire, formed the first loose kind of a German Confederation (*Deutscher Bund*). In 1871, when the first real national unification took place in the form of the German Empire, there were still twenty-five states which were members of the Reich. In addition, the territorial structure of the Reich was further complicated because of the geographical size of its most powerful member, the state of Prussia.[5] Because of its size, Prussia was divided into twelve provinces (*Provinzen*), administrative units not to be found in any of the other states.

This territorial structure remained essentially intact throughout the Weimar Republic and the Nazi regime. In 1918, the number of states—now deprived of their dynastic superstructure—was reduced to seventeen; but many of them remained petty, artificial regional units which had no other justification for surviving than the powerful vested interests connected with the traditional state machinery. Moreover, it proved impossible to overhaul this cumbersome administrative structure by eliminating the bulky size and political weight of Prussia. Numerous attempts aiming at some kind of a radical Reich reform, which would have done away with a number of the petty state units and would have dismembered Prussia, were made at the time of the Weimar Constitution and afterwards; but all these efforts failed.[6] Since the Nazi regime did not alter the formal structure of the states and provinces, they survived essentially unchanged into the post-Nazi period.[7]

2. When the political unification of Germany took place in 1871, this fulfillment of intensely nationalist, popular aspirations did not coincide with the establishment of a liberal, democratic, parliamentary regime. Unlike those of other European countries, the liberal components of the nationalist movement during the nineteenth century did not enter into the final product of the first unified Reich. Germany never had a successful liberal, bourgeois revolution in its history. Attempts to ride the bourgeois revolutionary waves sweeping Europe in 1830 and again in 1848 failed in Germany as in other central and eastern European countries. This development in Germany was due not only to the resistance of the vested dynastic and bureaucratic interests of the individual states, most of which had governments without popular representation,[8] but also to the persistent rivalry, throughout this period, between the two most powerful German states—Austria and Prussia. Thus the satisfaction of nationalist aspirations was possible only under the political and military victory of Prussia the government of which was thoroughly antiliberal and authoritarian and which, owing to its size and its military as well as economic resources, gained a pre-eminent influence under the imperial constitution.[9]

This development, aside from its general political consequences, has also left a marked imprint on the status, functions, and personnel of the civil service in Germany. German, and particularly Prussian, civil servants have gained the reputation of high standards of bureaucratic efficiency. And it is true that, in the course of the last century, the German civil service became a profession with a highly developed machinery for admission, qualifications, hierarchical levels, efficient techniques, and professional integrity. The German civil servant came to represent the prototype of the expert in governmental affairs, the man with the know-how to execute any political decisions, essentially nonpolitical: an expert technician who could and would serve any master without responsibility for the political consequences of such service.[10]

The case of the German civil service, however, points up the fallacy in the concept of a so-called nonpolitical, professional bureaucracy. Such a notion is probably fictitious in any case; it is doubly so when a bureaucracy is not subject to any checks other than the mere formal requirements of education and professional training. In actual practice and sentiment, the higher civil service in Germany was a thoroughly conservative, reactionary, and autocratic body and a political force of the first magnitude. First, it exercised a monopoly over all administrative affairs hardly ever subject to supervision by a popularly elected parliament. Second, it was composed for the most part of members, usually the second or third sons, of the military class and wealthy land and property owners. Insofar as members of the rising middle classes gained entrance to the higher civil service, they did so only after they had been successfully assimilated—either by virtue of membership in a class-conscious students' organization or by training as reserve officers—to the feudal pattern of German bureaucracy. Third, it quickly developed an *esprit de corps* which was hardly less authoritarian, nationalist, and snobbish than that of the military caste and which considered every popular aspiration towards sharing in its functions as an immediate threat to the authority of the state and its own vested interests. Thus there came into being the type of a professional, nonpolitical public servant in Germany whose technical proficiency was admittedly great, but whose ignorance of and lack of sympathy with liberal, democratic principles was only equalled by that of the German militarist and university professor.

Obviously, there were changes during the Weimar Republic. Throughout Germany the civil service became an instrument of representative, elective governments and was infused with a number of democratic elements. Nevertheless, the Republic failed to undermine the power of the traditional institutions and elite because all changes were predicated upon a highly legalistic procedure. The Republic recognized, on the whole, as inviolate the traditional bureaucratic rules and rights concerning qualifications for and status in the civil service. Thus people with a permanent status could not be dislodged except by disciplinary action. And if certain people were removed for political, i.e., nondisciplinary, reasons, they were entitled to an equivalent position in a different branch of the civil service. It is obvious that these procedures did not lead to any basic institutional reforms or to any large-scale replacements of the traditional body of civil servants by democratically-minded newcomers. And the intricate network of paragraphs, procedures, and channels of authority, which remained firmly in the hands of the old administrative experts, served in many cases (particularly in the fields of the judiciary and education) as a convenient and effective device for diverting or even sabotaging the implications of democratic policies.

The Nazis quickly disposed of all democratic elements installed during the Republic and then proceeded to turn the civil service on all levels into a thoroughly Nazified and party-supervised body. This did not prove to be too difficult an operation since the number of democratically-minded civil servants was not very large anyway, and since the traditional bureaucratic corps—many of whom had successfully served under the Empire and the Republic—found service under the new masters quite in harmony with their code of professional ethics as well as with their traditional social and political predilections.[11]

3. As in all modern societies of a certain industrial development and social differentiation, there has been in Germany a persistent trend towards the accretion of greater power in central, national administrative agencies as against the governmental functions reserved to the federal states.

This concentration of power in central controls was first noticeable in the economic field. In the course of the last century, most of the smaller German states formed a "customs union" with Prussia abolishing tariff barriers and establishing a kind of economic unity even before the Franco-Prussian War culminated in the political unification of the Reich. The Empire itself still represented a highly federated constitutional structure. Thus despite the political unity of the Reich, symbolized in the person of the emperor,

the various federal states remained the principal regional governmental and administrative agencies. The constitution itself left to
the individual states a large number of important functions.[12] The
Reich arrogated to itself only a minimum number of crucial legislative fields.[13] In addition, the power of the popularly elected National Assembly (*Reichstag*) did not compare with the political
influence exercised by the Second Chamber (*Bundesrat*), representing state interests.

World War I, however, caused a further upsurge in nationalist
sentiments as well as a further concentration of economic and
political power. The war cemented the nationalist bonds of the constituent members of the Reich against traditional regional and
dynastic loyalties. The people reacted as a unified body against
what they considered hostile threats to their *national* existence.
Moreover, the rapid expansion of German industry in the years
before the war and the war measures designed to marshal this industrial potential for military purposes led, as in other countries,
to new central economic agencies.[14] Finally, the last years of the
war witnessed, under Ludendorff's guiding hand, the first attempt
of an actual totalitarian merger of political and military power.

Under the Republic, these trends towards an increasing scope and
weight of central controls found expression, first, in constitutional
changes which gave the Reich a number of functions it had not
previously exercised (e.g., in finance, economics, labor, justice);
and, second, in the reduction of the political power of the Second
Chamber (now called *Reichsrat*). It is to be noted that this concentration of political and economic power ran parallel with the
introduction of the first parliamentary democracy in the Reich as
well as in the various federal states. Prussia, in particular, once the
prototype of authoritarian government, became in many respects the
most advanced and liberal state of Republican Germany. It is therefore erroneous simply to equate a particular governmental form,
such as a federal or centralized state, with democratic or authoritarian principles. The German Empire was highly federated, but
authoritarian; the German Republic was more highly centralized,
but a parliamentary democracy; the Nazi regime, finally, was a

Occupation Policy

totally centralized and authoritarian state. The form of a state is quite negligible in comparison with its political content. The locus of power does not lie in the formal, constitutional structure itself, but rather in the type of institutions created under this framework and the type of ruling groups using these institutions.

Throughout this period, the unity of the Reich was never seriously threatened. While there are in Germany, as in most other countries, rather marked differences in the ethnic composition, linguistic habits, and religious affiliation in the various parts of the country, these differences alone have not been such as to give rise to politically significant separatist movements since 1871. Nor have the familiar administrative squabbles, again characteristic of all federal states, over the respective sphere of competence between the governments of the Reich and the states ever constituted a threat to the political unity of the Reich.

What conflicts there were, during the Weimar Republic, between the central government and the various states were always motivated by a struggle for political power *throughout* the Reich. Thus, when in the period of the collapse in 1918-1919, revolutionary governments came into power in Bavaria, Brunswick, and other places, the Reich government used nationalist, militarist forces to overthrow these governments. Again in 1923, the central government sent the *Reichswehr* out against the governments of Thuringia and Saxony which consisted of popularly elected majorities of radical Socialists and Communists. These interventions were directly motivated by the threat which these revolutionary state regimes held for the interests of the ruling groups in the Reich government. In the same year, the Reich government faced the separatist threat of a highly conservative, reactionary government in Bavaria. But even here where particularist trends had always been strongest,[15] the real issue was not a constitutional conflict of asserting state rights against the central government or vice versa, but the fear that the political course of the central government might be such as to conflict with the interests of the ruling groups in Bavaria. And it was characteristic that this Bavarian movement, which included many factions and culminated in the abortive Hitler Putsch of November 9, 1923, adopted as its final slogan the "March on Berlin." In all these cases, therefore, legal constitutional issues were used only as a decoy either for maintaining or for extending a certain kind of political and social regime *throughout* the Reich.[16]

The Nazi state carried the ideas of bureaucratic centralization, political authoritarianism, and racial nationalism to an extreme. While the Nazis never got around to abolishing the traditional state structure of Germany, as they had plans to do, the individual states lost all democratic, self-administrative powers and were converted into mere executive agencies of the totalitarian government of the Reich.

To sum up: The historical factors pertinent to the Allied task of reorganizing government and administration after the Nazi defeat were briefly: (1) a territorial division of Germany which had remained comparatively intact since the days of the Empire; (2) a tradition of government and civil service which, except for the interlude of the Weimar Republic, had been the prerogative of conservative, authoritarian class interests and which had finally come completely under Nazi influences; (3) a trend towards increasing concentration of economic and political power which again reached its height under the Nazi regime.

What was significantly new in the picture was (a) the absence of a central German government and (b) the division of Germany into four zones of occupation.

THE NEW TERRITORIAL UNITS

Since Allied military forces penetrated deeply into Germany before the final collapse and surrender of the Nazi regime, the actual process of building a new, non-Nazi government and administration began on the lowest regional levels of municipalities, counties, and districts.[17] These local units were only gradually reintegrated into the larger states and provinces. Thus the occupying powers operated, from the very beginning, through the existing German administrative machinery and gradually restored the traditional pattern on all levels. Nonetheless, the old structure has been changed in two major respects: (1) Prussia has disappeared as a state; and (2) revisions have taken place in the various zones, partly improving on, partly still further complicating the traditional pattern. Of these changes the dissolution of Prussia is obviously the more important.

Prussia has disappeared (a) because the zonal divisions split up the old state so that any central control was automatically out of place, (b) because of territorial losses in the East.[18] Since Allied policy-makers are agreed on preventing the re-emergence of a large, potentially powerful Prussian state unit in the future Reich, it is almost certain the Prussia, as it has existed in the past, will never rise again.

Revisions in the old administrative structure aiming at a more functional territorial organization have taken place in the British and American zones. The traditional picture has practically remained intact in the Russian zone, chiefly because the old territorial units (with a few minor changes) were quite well suited to serve again as administrative centers.[19] In the British and American zones, however, plans have been under way to bring about a number of internal structural changes.

The British first set up a new state called North Rhineland Westphalia (including the Ruhr) and then proceeded to simplify the traditional patchwork of small states in the remainder of their zone by creating two more state units of substantial size, Lower Saxony and Schleswig-Holstein, and by giving the Free City of Hamburg the status of a fourth state.

The major administrative reorganization in the American zone has created the new regional unit of Hesse, which combines the former state of Hesse and the former province of Hesse-Nassau (except for a few counties on the left bank of the Rhine under French administration).[20]

At the same time the zonal divisions have also created a number of new regional administrative units and technical difficulties which did not previously exist in Germany. This is due largely to changes caused by the belated addition of the French zone of occupation.[21] These changes have particularly affected the Rhineland and the states of Wuerttemberg and Baden. In each case, the old German units were cut roughly in half owing to the zonal division between the British and French occupation, on the one side, and the American and French occupation, on the other. Thus the northern part of the former Rhine Province forms a new administrative unit together with the former province of Westphalia under British occupation. The French authorities, on the other hand, have merged the southern part of the Rhine Province (including a few counties of the former province Hesse-Nassau) with the old Palatinate into a new administrative unit called Rhine-Palatinate. Again, American authorities have combined the rump pieces of northern Wuerttemberg and northern Baden into a single new administrative unit, while the southern parts of these two states, under French occupation, continue to function as separate administrative entities.

Thus certain favorable developments affecting the territorial reorganization of Germany are, for the time being at least, matched by certain new difficulties created by the zonal divisions. The situation is further complicated by the uncertainty surrounding the status of the Saar and the final disposition of the Eastern territories. The economic incorporation of the Saar, demanded by France, has been agreed to by the governments of the United States and Great Britain. It has also been endorsed by the Saar population. In the elections (October 5, 1947) for a Saar Assembly which will be charged with framing a constitution, the parties favoring or accepting the prospect of economic union with France gained an overwhelming majority. The Communists as the only party campaigning against economic union were a small minority of less than 10 per cent of the total vote. The future status of the Saar, however, is still in abeyance since the Soviet Union has so far withheld approval of the French request for economic union and since it is not yet clear whether the Saar will retain any genuine measure of political and administrative autonomy within the framework of economic union with France. The majority of German political groups, outside the Saar, is opposed to what it considers the virtual loss of this area which Germany regained by virtue of a plebiscite in 1935.

As far as the Eastern territories are concerned, only part of East Prussia, including Königsberg (renamed Kaliningrad), has been definitely cut off from Germany as a result of the Berlin Conference. With regard to the other Eastern areas, at present under Polish administration, Great Britain and the United States have stated both at the Moscow and London conferences of foreign ministers that they do not wish to consider the present Oder-Neisse boundary as final. German public opinion and political parties, except for the Socialist Unity party in the East and the Communists in the West, have supported Anglo-American requests for a revision of Germany's eastern boundaries as fixed at the Berlin Conference. The Soviet Union and Poland have sharply opposed any suggestion aiming at such a revision.

These problems, however, are political rather than administrative. Whatever their final solution may be, the decision will be made on political rather than administrative grounds. Nor is any such solution likely to affect too much the future internal territorial structure of the Reich itself. Therefore, if Germany is ever reconstituted as a unified Reich, it might still be possible to merge the zonal territorial units which have developed during the occupation in a way which will simplify the traditional artificial federal structure inherited from the past and create a smaller number of more functional administrative regional units within Germany. Meanwhile, various proposals have been made to revise the territorial structure in the Western zones—particularly with a view to re-establishing the traditional boundaries of Wuerttemberg and Baden; but the three powers have so far taken no action in this direction.

The territorial units, however, represent only the framework by which the system of a federal government is held together. Their formal arrangement does not provide a clue to the functions and substance of such a government. Thus it is not surprising that, while there is a certain homogeneity of the federal pattern itself in the four zones, there are rather marked differences in the substantive changes which the four powers have carried out in the respective governments of each zone.

The guiding principles for the reconstruction of a new democratic government were also laid down at the Berlin Conference. These principles are: (1) denazification, (2) democratization, and (3) decentralization.²² All three principles are sufficiently broad and vague as to allow for any number of interpretations.

DENAZIFICATION

The purge (or, as this process is known in Germany, "denazification") was the most urgent task facing the occupying powers. It was obviously impossible to reconstruct a democratic governmental machinery without personnel which would be considered reliable to carry out Allied policies. The important questions, however, on which the occupying powers differed, were (a) how the unreliable, Nazi-infected personnel was to be weeded out or controlled, and (b) what kind of people were to be trusted to reform German administrative affairs in conformity with Allied objectives. On these questions, Allied policy has differed widely in the Eastern and Western zones of occupation.

In the Eastern zone, the purge of the old pre-Nazi and Nazi civil service pursued clearly defined political objectives. While the occupation authorities laid down general directives, all detailed measures of denazification were left to the anti-fascist bloc of the four political parties. In fact, owing to the paucity of both qualified and reliable administrative personnel at the time of the collapse, the reconstruction of the civil service has run parallel with the revival of the parties themselves. This method served a double purpose. On the one hand, it helped to encourage the growth of new political life; on the other hand, it helped to insure a fairly thorough penetration of the traditional corps of civil servants with politically reliable men. "Reliability," therefore, was defined primarily in political terms rather than in terms of professional qualifications. And while it was obviously impossible—owing to the tradition and the total *Gleichschaltung* of the civil service under the Nazis—to dispense entirely with the services of trained professional experts with a dubious political background, these men were not put into positions of authority. Such positions were entrusted only to people who were politically reliable—which meant in the Eastern zone primarily people from the two left-wing parties, later merged under pressure in the Socialist Unity party. This seems to have been true particularly on the lower levels of administration where the other parties were frequently excluded altogether. But even on the level of states and provinces, where the parity principle prevails among the new parties, representatives of the working classes (politically most reliable from the Soviet point of view) have always had a predominant share in the decision on replacements and the execution of policies.

In addition, traditional bureaucratic prerogatives were more widely distributed than before. Works' Councils and trade unions were drawn into the administration of the expropriated and nationalized industries; and representatives from youth, women, and peasant groups, usually under Communist domination, serve in advisory and executive capacity particularly in a number of communal affairs.

These measures have had various effects. They have undoubtedly reduced the monopoly position of the traditional corps of civil servants. They have further increased the degree of the new kind of politicization infused into the administrative branches of government. Together with the political appointments to administrative posts, however, they have also built up a large body of a new bureaucratic elite from the ranks of the left-wing social classes. Thus there has been no decrease in the number of government personnel. On the contrary, as in all other zones, the bureaucratic body has swelled to bigger proportions and importance. But there has been a radical change in the composition of the bureaucracy, and the large body of new civil servants with vested interests and dependencies of their own forms the backbone of the new type of society which is emerging in this part of Germany.

The administrative purge in the other zones proceeded according to different principles. While there were regional differences these variations were differences in degree rather than in kind. The over-all pattern of British, American, and French policy has been fairly similar. The new parties were at first specifically excluded from participating in the purge; and all initial manifestations of militant, anti-Nazi action by radical left-wing elements were quickly suppressed as threats to military order and security. In the beginning the purge was conducted exclusively by the various occupying powers. It consisted essentially in setting up certain categories defining more or less "active" Nazis (by length of membership, for example, or rank and kind of service in the party) who were subject to automatic dismissal (and possibly arrest) and in replacing these people by others who were professionally qualified but did not fall under these categories. The enforcement of this policy resulted, because of the high percentage of Nazis in the civil service, in quite a considerable number of dismissals.[23] And since denazification, in the general sense, extends to the whole field of public life (i.e., besides the administrative purge, to a purge of industry, business, the professions, education, press, etc.), its social and political implications, in theory, might have been far-reaching.

In practice, however, this approach to the problem soon ran into difficulties because the policy was primarily negative and did not provide enough positive guidance. It was easy enough to know who was to be dismissed; it was much more difficult to know who was to be appointed. In fact, the method guiding reappointments clashed in most cases with the principles underlying the dismissals. Since the army authorities were concerned, first of all, with the need of getting the technical administrative machinery running again smoothly and as quickly as possible in order to ease the burdens of occupation and to prevent popular unrest and disease, political motives were generally subordinated to considerations of administrative efficiency in making new appointments. Thus the policy subscribed, on the positive side, essentially to the criterion to which the German civil service had formally adhered in the past; namely, that the holders of public office must be, first of all, professional experts who can keep the administrative machinery running smoothly and efficiently, and, therefore, that political considerations, other than the formal criterion of open identification with the Nazi regime, need not enter into the decisions concerning dismissals and reappointments. The result was twofold. (1) Since efficient performance was the chief criterion on the positive side, this policy obviously tended to strengthen the grip of the traditional bureaucracy; for it justified, as far as German public officials were concerned, the selection of people from the old civil service or from the ranks of discharged veterans who had the formal qualifications for efficient performance. And the people who had these qualifications, of course, came in general from the same social class with a similar political background as those who were dismissed. (2) The policy has been under attack from both political sides in Germany—from the Left because it was considered too formalistic, lenient and devoid of political sense; from the Right because, if carried out according to the letter of the law as embodied in the official pronouncements on denazification, it would have been too radical and revolutionary.

Under these circumstances it is not surprising that, when the American authorities realized that the details of over-all denazification were too great a task for an occupying power, they turned the matter over to the Germans themselves.[24] The results of this new policy have been far from satisfactory. The German authorities proceeded according to the pattern which was laid down previously. Special chambers were set up in the various communities to judge individual cases again according to certain categories of more or less active Nazis and Nazi sympathizers. It soon became apparent, however, that this procedure would run into a number of serious difficulties.[25] First, it was difficult to find prosecutors and judges for the Purge Chambers, because many of them were subjected to threats and intimidation, social ostracism, and even direct personal reprisals. Next, when procedures were actually inaugurated, the sentences under the prescribed categories, have, in many cases, been so light and lenient as practically to exonerate the accused. The whole procedure has had numerous internal political repercussions.

It has also confronted the occupation authorities with the need for constantly reviewing the whole policy on this subject. In November, 1946, General Lucius D. Clay, then Deputy United States Military Governor for Germany, issued a stinging rebuke to the German authorities for the laxity and flaws with which they had executed the denazification program. Said General Clay: "I can only state that we are at present highly disappointed in the results [of de-Nazification] and that we have yet to find the political will and determination to punish those who deserve punishment. It becomes more and more obvious that the de-Nazification procedure is rather being used to restore as many people as possible to their former position than to find the guilty and punish them. I fail to see how you want to prove your ability for self-government and your will to democracy if you escape or evade the first unpleasant and difficult task that has fallen to you."[26]

What had happened, of course, was that two years after the Nazi defeat the majority of the people whose cases were coming up before the chambers were judged by their peers, i.e., by men who generally came from the same social background and held similar political views as the accused, except that they lacked the flaw of *direct* identification with Nazi activities. It was, therefore, only natural that the judges would be most inclined to find any number of "extenuating circumstances," because they shared with the accused the belief that the potentially far-reaching implications of the program must be carefully curbed lest they result in radical social and political changes. The lack of anti-Nazi militancy of these groups, now primarily in charge of denazification, reveals most clearly the homogeneity of class and political interests which exists between the old and new bureaucratic elite.[27] Meanwhile, as the impetus to cleanse the body politic of Nazi influences fades in the course of time and the Allied powers are preoccupied with other problems concerning the political and economic future of Germany, the denazification program which at the outset of occupation overshadowed almost every other internal issue is being wound up rather quietly without causing much public interest or any basic changes in the traditional composition and structure of the civil service.

DEMOCRATIZATION

Democratization, used here in a highly restricted sense, refers to the creation of representative, elective bodies of government.[28] It represents, as it were, the positive aspect of the Nazi purge. Originally all government jobs under the occupation were appointive positions, and the consequences following from the methods used to make the new appointments[29] have had a direct bearing on the problem of how to provide the representative underpinnings for this new governmental structure. For it is obvious that the new people put into power by Allied appointment would so use their newly-won power as to create the conditions which are most favorable to their winning an electoral approval.

This principle seems to have been adopted outright in the Russian Zone. The whole approach here has been guided by the obvious aim of creating such a social and political atmosphere as will guarantee that what the Soviet Union considers a "democratic government" will gain electoral approval. Thus the first communal elections in the Soviet Zone, in September, 1946, came at the end of a long period characterized by basic social and political reforms; the political parties had been active in an anti-fascist bloc for a year and a half. The political purge had struck hard against the old bureaucratic and economic elite. The new parties and governments had taken the initiative in dividing the estates of the East-Elbian Junkers, in nationalizing mines and banks, and in expropriating industrial enterprises owned by Nazis or war criminals. The churches had been barred from political activity. The traditional system of education had been remodelled. Trade unions had gained a prominent place in economic-political affairs. Youth, women's, and peasants' organization had been politicized under radical, left-wing leadership. Cultural leagues had served as political instruments for the same purpose. Finally, the two left-wing parties had been "unified" under Russian pressure. All these changes were carried out without a popular mandate in the sense that they were undertaken on the initiative of the Russian authorities and the political parties before holding a popular election which would measure the strength of these parties. In fact, they were considered indispensable prerequisites for the elections because they were intended to pave the way for an electoral victory of the class of people and the political parties which, according to the Soviet conception, represent the most reliable component of a democratic government. As the election returns in the Eastern zone have shown, this aim, despite careful preparation, was achieved only by a narrow and precarious margin.[30]

In contrast, the American Zone progressed farthest in fulfilling the formal conditions for a democratic revival. After initial hesitation, democratic political parties were permitted to operate. Moreover, various efforts were made from the beginning to provide the appointed governmental agencies with some kind of a representative basis. This was generally done through municipal or provincial advisory bodies selected on a corporative principal, i.e., composed of representatives of various economic, professional, and religious groups together with representatives of the political parties. Since these selections were derived from the traditional institutional and class structure of German society, they obviously weighted the distribution of political power in favor of the old social elite. Finally, elections throughout the zone were held at the earliest possible time —first for the counties, then for the municipalities, and finally for the three states. The newly elected state parliaments were then charged with the task of drawing up democratic constitutions for each state.

The British, like the French, at first postponed elections in order to maintain a much more direct control over all administrative affairs on all levels than that practiced in the American Zone.[31] The British have sharply distinguished between administrative agencies inherited from the old Reich administration and those traditionally part of the regular provincial administration. The locus of administrative power lies with the special agencies charged with the former central Reich functions. The provincial governments have frequently found themselves discharging purely routine matters. Moreover, it is only the latter which have gradually been brought under some kind of democratic control as a result of the elections which were held throughout the zone in 1947.

Secondly, the British, in contrast to the occupying powers in all other zones, have also introduced changes in the German electoral system. The electoral method they have devised in their zone combines the traditional German system of proportional representation with the traditional British system of majority election. The general principle is that, in any given electoral contest, a candidate is elected on the basis of a majority vote and that only a certain percentage of unused votes (*Reststimmen*), which would ordinarily be lost in a majority election, are distributed among the various political parties for the election of additional candidates. In a multi-party system such as had always prevailed in Germany, this electoral procedure gives great advantages to the majority parties and considerable disadvantages to minor party groups.

New problems of democratic controls have arisen in the three Western zones in connection with their economic and political unification. These developments are discussed in the following sections.

DECENTRALIZATION

At first sight the task of decentralizing the German administration would seem to be much easier than that of purging it of Nazi elements or imbuing it with a democratic spirit. In the absence of a central government, the individual states, now the largest and most important administrative units, have naturally fallen heir to the governmental functions previously exercised by the Reich. Similarly, the former Prussian provinces have now taken over the affairs previously reserved to the state government of Prussia. Decentralization, therefore, appears to have been accomplished by the simple expedient of not having a central authority.

This statement, however, must be qualified in two respects. In the first place, it is questionable to what extent decentralization has been more than the simple expedient just referred to. According to the decisions at the Berlin Conference, it was specifically linked with the "development of local responsibility." [32] The idea behind this decision was that the Germans, without much experience and tradition in democratic practices, were to learn the lessons of democracy from scratch. Democratic processes were to be initiated and stimulated, first of all, in the affairs of the community in which the individual might be able to participate most directly and through which he might learn something of the meaning of democratic rights and responsibilities. Hence, the emphasis on strengthening the self-administrative functions of local government.

It is doubtful whether this aim has been accomplished anywhere. For the most part, the elimination of a central Reich authority has so far resulted simply in a high degree of regional centralization rather than in a genuine measure of decentralized self-administration on lower levels. Instead of placing the emphasis as before on one centralized, national government, there are now a number of independent regional governments whose degree of centralization, however, is patterned after the model of the old central authority of the Reich.

In the second place, the Berlin Conference recognized the need for certain centralized agencies the absence of which, in a complex society like Germany, would lead to grave economic risks and serious administrative confusion. It, therefore, stipulated that "certain essential central German administrative departments . . . shall be established, particularly in the field of finance, transport, communication, foreign trade and industry."[33] This article has come to play a crucial part in the determination of Allied policies. It has been on the agenda of every meeting of the Council of Foreign Ministers since the Berlin Conference. It has provided the basis for persistent efforts on the part of American and British authorities to overcome zonal barriers and bring about the economic unification of Germany. These efforts, in turn, have plunged the four powers into an acrimonious debate on the political future of Germany. As of the end of 1948, the central economic agencies envisaged at the Berlin Conference had not yet come into being, and there was less hope than ever that this type of economic centralization (preliminary to a political unification of Germany as a whole) would ever be achieved by the four powers.

In the absence of such agreement, central economic controls have been set up on various zonal levels. This tendency towards zonal coordination began first in the Russian Zone. In October, 1945, a Central Administration was formed in the Russian Zone consisting of thirteen economic departments. This Central Administration was not a government. The state governments retained regular legislative and executive powers, which reduced the functions of the Central Administration chiefly to those of planning and supervision except in the field of finance where its powers were binding. In February, 1948, a new Central Economic Commission was set up in the Soviet Zone. This Commission is composed of twenty-six members.[34] The members serve on an appointive basis. The decisions of the Economic Commission are binding upon all subordinate administrative branches in the zone. This is a marked increase in executive powers over those held by the former Central Administration—a development which indicates that the Soviet authorities were faced with the need for improved economic controls similar to that which prompted the Western powers to create their Bizonal Economic Organization. Soviet statements, however, have rejected this interpretation and have continued to dissociate themselves from the developments in the West as well as from any attempts to establish central economic agencies for Germany as a whole.

While the American and British authorities have repeatedly urged the establishment of central economic agencies for Germany as a whole, neither at first went as far as the Russian authorities did in perfecting a central machinery on the zonal level. The first coordinating device in the American Zone was the Council of States (*Laenderrat*) consisting of regular monthly meetings of the three prime ministers, their staffs, and a permanent secretariat. The British began zonal coordination in still a different way. To absorb the administrative powers, formerly exercised by the Reich, they set up a number of economic and financial Coordinating Offices throughout their zone. In addition, they also created a Zonal Advisory Council (*Zonenbeirat*), a body of twenty-eight members drawn from the civil service, the parties, and other social groups and exercising little genuine influence.

In December, 1946, joint economic controls were set up for both zones through the Bizonal Economic Administration. Twice reorganized within the next year, this organization eventually emerged as an agency consisting of the following branches:

1. The Economic Council: a parliamentary body with legisla-

tive powers. It comprises 104 deputies chosen by the various state diets roughly in proportion to the strength of different political parties in the state elections.

2. The Council of States: a second chamber representing state interests and exercising a suspensory veto over the legislation of the Economic Council except in matters of expenditure and taxes. It is composed of two delegates from each state selected by the state government.

3. The Executive Council: the executive branch consisting of the five chiefs of the administrative agencies[35] and a chairman elected by the Economic Council.

4. A Supreme Administrative Court for the two zones and a central bank.

Without a clearly defined political or legal status, this bizonal organization encountered numerous difficulties in exercising effective central powers vis-à-vis the individual state governments on the one hand and vis-à-vis the occupation authorities on the other. Thus German officials and political groups soon became increasingly vocal in calling for a solution which would provide a firmer and clearer constitutional basis for the administration of the two zones. Meanwhile, with the implementation of the Marshall Plan for Western Europe, there was also an increasing need for a more effective exploitation of the economic resources in Western Germany as well as for a closer integration of this region with Western Europe. These needs, together with the failure of the Bizonal Economic Administration to provide an adequate administrative machinery for meeting them, led to the decisions of the London Conference of the six Western powers (United States, Great Britain, France, and the three Benelux countries) in March, 1948 concerning a new political consolidation of the three Western zones.

The London Conference agreed (1) to merge the American, British, and French zones under "a federal form of government" with "adequate central authority," (2) to place the Ruhr under international control, with Germany to be given a voice in its administration, (3) to include Western Germany in the Marshall

Plan. The Conference further recommended the prompt coordination of economic policies among the three zones; but, at the time of this writing, the Bizonal Economic Organization had not yet assumed trizonal jurisdiction; only the foreign trade organizations of the three zones have been placed under joint central control. Meanwhile, however, various steps have been taken to implement the decision to set up a new constitutional regime for Western Germany. The three military governors issued general directives to the prime ministers of the states in their respective zones on the principles of "a democratic constitution" for a "governmental structure of a federal type" as well as on the powers reserved to the occupation authorities.[36] After some hesitation the German officials accepted these proposals; and since September, 1948, a "Parliamentary Council," composed of sixty-five members representing all the states in the three zones, has been meeting in Bonn to work out a constitution which would form the basis for a political unification of the Western states without prejudging the question of the ultimate unification of Germany as a whole.[37] Simultaneously with the promulgation of this constitution, expected in December, 1948, the three powers will issue an "occupation statute" defining the special fields and interests over which they will continue to exercise exclusive jurisdiction.

THE PROBLEM OF FEDERALISM

There emerges, underneath the bewildering variety of administrative forms and policies in the different zones, the final problem of the future status of Germany as a whole, the crucial problem of how to put the four pieces together again or, at least, of how to overcome the widening split between the three Western zones, on the one hand, and the Eastern zone on the other. This is a problem which far transcends the level of administrative affairs. For, from an administrative point of view, there would be no difficulty in setting up the various central departments on which the Big Three agreed at the Berlin Conference.

What has so far stood in the way of realizing this aim is the simple fact that the unity of the Reich is again, as in the past, a political problem involving a struggle of power among the Allies as well as among social and political groups inside Germany. The constitutional issue involved in this problem (i.e., the question of what form of state is the best guarantee for a democratic Germany), is much less important than the political questions: (a) what do the various powers mean by "democracy"? and (b) what role are they willing to assign to a future Germany in international affairs? Over these questions the Germans will obviously exercise little or no self-determination at all. Therefore, insofar as German groups have joined the issue of working out a new constitutional framework for the Reich, they have done so largely by following the lead and supporting the intentions of those Allied powers with whom they have identified their own social and political interests.

The German point of view on this problem is well expressed in a statement by Jakob Kaiser, formerly Chairman of the Christian Democratic Union in the Soviet Zone: "The future constitutional form of the German state is determined, to a great extent, by the will of the occupying powers. . . . In view of these circumstances, we must all agree that Germany's future internal structure will assume a federative form. Let us endorse the laws of federative organization: the Reich functionally *(sinnvoll)* organized into states *(Laender)* . . . However, let us unite in the will that we must not let it come again to the development of states within the state. May God prevent that Germany ever be thrown back again into an association of sovereign states *(Staatenbund)*."[38]

This statement makes several points which are probably shared by a majority of the German people themselves. (1) The future status of the Reich will be determined ultimately by the will of the four powers. (2) Insofar as the German people and German political groups can make their influence felt at all, they probably sympathize at present with some kind of a federal state. The experience under the Nazi regime, associated with the most rigorous central controls, has led a majority of Germans to believe that there is a causal nexus between excessive governmental centralization and political totalitarianism. (3) Federalism, however, must not mean separatism or sovereign powers to any individual state. It should be a federalization along functional regional, economic, and cultural lines; but the unity and ultimate sovereignty of the Reich must not be impaired. These general views also formed the basis for the debates on the forthcoming constitution for Western Germany. Accepting the general directive for a federal type of government, the "Parliamentary Council" at Bonn has already agreed (a) that this type of federalism must not interfere with certain rights and powers exclusively reserved for a central government and (b) that, whatever the final form of the new regime in Western Germany may be, the constitution must leave the door open for the formation of a central government for all of Germany in the future. None of the officials or political groups in the Western zones, therefore, is prepared to accept the creation of a separate state in Western Germany, which would formally acknowledge the final division of the Reich.

From the German point of view, the preservation of national unity is of fundamental importance. It is more than a technical problem of re-establishing some kind of administrative uniformity among the many states developing under different occupation policies. It is even more than the realization that the various parts of the Reich are economically interdependent and that without central controls, any large-scale planning for economic reconstruction after the war is impossible. It is perhaps primarily the realization that national unity constitutes the last genuine political asset after defeat. From this point of view, the question goes far beyond renouncing the Nazi heritage. The loss of national unity would mean a renunciation of all political aspirations in recent German history.

All the major political parties, therefore, are national parties. Although still operating on a zonal level, all of them consider this phase of their activities only preparatory to a political life encompassing the entire nation.[39] Furthermore, all major political parties agree that there should be no dismemberment of what is left of the Reich and that there should never be a return to the pre-1871 status of a confederation of independent, sovereign states (*Staatenbund*) of Germany. Therefore, the political and economic unity of the Reich as established in 1871 still remains the unquestioned constitutional premise from a German point of view.

While there is general agreement on this point among German groups, the parties are divided on the degree of federalism or centralism which they envisage for a future Germany.[40] In general, the parties of the Right (Liberal Democrats and Christian Democrats) favor a considerable degree of federalization, while the parties of the Left (Social Democrats, Communists and Socialist Unity party), who have traditionally maintained that a centralized organizational apparatus and centralized administrative and economic controls are indispensable for a political victory of the working classes, favor a higher degree of centralization. This division, as we shall see in the final section below, has assumed new forms and meanings under the impact of Allied occupation policies; but insofar as the Germans have a voice at all, present differences among them reveal that, as in the past, the issue of centralism vs. federalism is being contested along political and class lines rather than on the basis of purely constitutional considerations.

THE NEW GERMAN CONSTITUTIONS

A similar conclusion emerges from a cursory glance at the background and nature of some of the constitutions adopted in various parts of Germany. In 1948 all the German states except those in the British Zone had worked out constitutional documents providing a legal basis for their democratic revival. In addition, representatives in the West as well as in the East were busy drafting preambles, articles, and basic rights for the constitution of a future united Germany. Considering briefly a few of the basic types submitted or enacted, we shall see that, in the absence of a national government, the new constitutions reflect primarily the political interests of the social groups in charge of drafting them.

The constitution for the state of Hesse, where the Socialists have a plurality which is almost a majority, provides for a parliamentary form of government in the Weimar tradition. All legislative powers reside in one assembly, and the prime minister and his government are directly responsible to the assembly. There is no state president, no second chamber; there are no emergency powers. The constitution retains the separation of state and church in the field of education; it explicitly affirms Hesse to be part of a German Reich with the proviso that any article in the Hesse constitution in conflict with the future constitution of the Reich would be invalid. The constitution was framed after the pattern of the Weimar Republic both with regard to the powers of the state government itself and with regard to its future position vis-à-vis a central government.[41]

In contrast, state rights and prerogatives were automatically strengthened in the Bavarian constitution where middle class and conservative ruling groups are most concerned with consolidating their power against a future Reich government which may be of a different social and political complexion. The original draft was so extreme in this direction that it was subsequently revised. It proposed a state president for Bavaria; it adopted the Swiss model of government according to which a government, once elected by the diet, is no longer directly responsible to the diet and cannot be deposed for four years; it strengthened the executive by providing it with emergency powers against which there was little parliamentary or judicial protection; it set up a second chamber; it recognized the special position of the church by restoring the principle of denominational schools; and it granted to the state the rights of citizenship and the conduct of foreign affairs. Some of these provisions were revised in the final form submitted to the electorate. The article proposing a state president was defeated because the majority of the Socialist deputies voted against their own leadership. The second chamber was adopted only as an advisory body without legislative powers. The emergency powers of the government were subjected to judicial review by a constitutional court. And the final draft included a reference to certain priority rights of a future Reich Government as well as the superior powers of zonal and bi-zonal agencies and Military Government. But even the final, approved draft revealed—in its emphasis on a strong executive, in its social and economic clauses, as well as in the preferential status accorded the church—the social and political interests characteristic of the conservative majority in Bavaria.

The constitution for Wuerttemberg-Baden represents a kind of "liberal" compromise between the Hesse and the Bavarian version corresponding to the middle class political forces holding a parliamentary majority.

The constitutions for the states in the French Zone again try to provide specific safeguards for state rights and interests, generally in conformity with French plans for the future federal reorganization of Germany as a whole. Otherwise, they conform to the normal pattern of a parliamentary democracy, but again reflect the predominantly conservative forces in power by the preferential status accorded to church interests. The states in the British Zone have not enacted any constitutions, but have also drawn up various drafts and participated in the work of the "Parliamentary Council" at Bonn charged with the drafting of a constitution for Western Germany.

This constitution, the final form of which is not yet available at the time of this writing, will consist of a series of compromises within the general framework of a federal, parliamentary democracy. This follows from the fairly even balance of political forces in the three zones. Roughly speaking, the Socialists have a majority in the British Zone and in Hesse: middle class and right-wing groups dominate the political scene in Bavaria and in the French Zone. Thus it is not surprising that progress in the "Parliamentary Council" at Bonn (the Germans refused to call it a "Constituent Assembly") has been slow and that there will probably be a number of uneasy compromises on such basic issues as the position of the Federal President, the status and powers of the second chamber, the kind of election system (probably a complicated mixture of proportional representation and the plurality system), the function of plebiscites, and the precise scope of central powers (particularly in the field of finance and taxation). But there is general agreement on the following points: that the constitution be theoretically applicable to all of Germany, that the states delegate powers to the central government in the fields of interior administration, finance, economics, postal services, railroads, labor, agriculture (food), and justice, that there be two chambers (an assembly popularly elected and a second chamber representing the states), that the government be responsible to parliament, that there be safeguards against the undue use of emergency powers, that there be a Federal Administrative Court, and that there be a charter of basic rights. Thus the final document is not likely to be a particularly startling or original product, nor will it be more than a formal guarantee that democratic practices will ultimately prevail in Western Germany. The way in which the constitution will be translated into practical politics will again depend, as it did in the past, on the kind of political groups which will eventually come into power under the constitution. Nevertheless, this development constitutes a substantial advance towards self-government in Western Germany, even though the new regime will be subject to an "occupation statute" defining the fields over which the occupation powers exercise exclusive jurisdiction. These include foreign affairs, foreign and internal trade, the Ruhr, reparations, level of industry, decartelization, disarmament, and demilitarization as well as all matters affecting the security of the occupation forces.

Constitutions have also been worked out and adopted in the five states in the Russian Zone. Here the initiative and final decision lay with the Socialist Unity party; and the legal documents again reveal the special political interests which they are intended to serve. The constitutions of the various states are uniform and fit into the draft for an all-German constitution as it has been worked out by the so-called "People's Council" in the Soviet Zone (corresponding to the "Parliamentary Council" in the West) under the influence of the Socialist Unity party.

This draft is based on two major principles: (1) a unitary Reich in which the individual states are nothing else but administrative subdivisions and (2) a unitary locus of political power in the popular assembly to which all other branches of government are subordinated.

The Constitution of the "People's Council" theoretically proposes a two-chamber system; in fact, however, the popular assembly reigns supreme. The "chamber of the states" does not have any significant legislative powers. The states are primarily administrative organs of the central government. In fact, the concentration of powers in the central government extends also to the level of district and municipal administration. Likewise, the functions of a Federal President (originally dispensed with altogether) are largely ceremonial. The government is formed by the majority party, but with the participation of all other parties—thus continuing the official "block policy" of the Eastern zone. The government is fully and exclusively responsible to parliament. Laws duly promulgated by parliament are free from judicial review. Other "mass organizations" besides the political parties (e.g., trade unions) are permitted to put up lists of candidates for the election to the assembly. The section on civil rights is taken over substantially from the Weimar Constitution; but the absence of judicial review of parliamentary or executive action together with a number of other qualifying phrases reduces the official guarantee of civil liberties enjoyed by the individual vis-à-vis the state. The position of church and state is also defined in the manner of the Weimar Constitution; but there is a special caveat against the abuse of religion for "political purposes." Finally, the constitution gives legal status to the social and economic reforms planned or already executed in the Soviet Zone. In brief, the document tries to combine a highly centralist administrative structure with a type of government concentrated in a single, all-powerful parliament, characteristic of all Communist-sponsored constitutional documents since the war.

Meanwhile, it would be wrong to give too much weight to the constitutional documents as they are being discussed or as they have been enacted at the time of this writing. They seem curiously premature and devoid of political reality. Despite the spate of words and the volume of print devoted to the subject, it is rather difficult to take these efforts very seriously.[42] The noble tenor of the documents[43] seems to be strangely out of tune with the actual conditions of the country and the people for which they were written. Despite all good intentions to get the various parts of Germany started again on the road of constitutional government, it is quite evident that the actual powers of the various constitutional regimes, in whatever zone, are still severely limited by the superior rights and reservations of the occupying power. Moreover, as long as the future of the Reich remains unsettled and has, in fact, become the major source of conflict between the East and the West, the influence of the constitutional documents on the shape of democracy in Germany will be quite insignificant in comparison with the forces acting upon the different zones of the Reich as a result of Allied policies in general and of the East-West conflict in particular.

ALLIED POLICIES ON THE FUTURE OF GERMANY

This raises a problem which obviously transcends the scope of this chapter. It is impossible, in this context, to fit the whole problem of the future status of Germany adequately into the general framework of inter-Allied relations. Instead, we shall simply try to state briefly some of the attitudes taken by the four powers on the problem of setting up a national German government. Three fairly distinct views have emerged on this point in the course of inter-Allied negotiations since the Nazi defeat: a French, a British-American, and a Russian point of view.

The French point of view is, in many ways, the clearest and simplest. Not being signatories to the Protocol of the Berlin Conference, the French have not felt bound by the decisions of that conference. Hence, they have, from the very beginning, taken the line (a) that the establishment of a central, national German government be postponed as long as possible and (b) that, if a national government be established in the long run, the powers of this government vis-à-vis the powers of the various federal states of Germany be as weak as possible. This approach is motivated, on the one hand, by concern over the military security of France, on the other hand, by a recognition of the political power factors in post-Nazi Europe.

Having been the victims of German aggression thrice within seventy-five years, the majority of French people are agreed that the principal aim of peacemaking after this war must be to make Germany, once and for all, incapable of future aggression. To achieve this aim, they have argued, the political and economic potential of the Reich must be weakened as much as possible. From the political point of view, this means the weakening of a national German government and the encouragement of particularist, federalist trends in Germany—even if this should lead to outright separatist movements. The French distrust any powerful central German government regardless of its political complexion. From the economic point of view, this means that the heart of the German industrial potential in the Ruhr must be brought at least under international control, preferably be cut off entirely from a future Germany. Unless these two conditions are fulfilled, the French have declared themselves unwilling to consider seriously the establishment of any German national agencies such as envisaged at the Berlin Conference. It is evident that this line of reasoning is not only derived from considerations of military security, but also from the realization that a strong Germany has always been the most powerful factor in Europe. Therefore, only if Germany is sufficiently and permanently weakened can France hope to be the leading, purely continental, European power.

The British and American points of view have on the whole coincided in working towards the earliest possible fulfillment of the commitments made at the Berlin Conference. This has been, on the one hand, a purely economic problem recognizing the need for certain national agencies because of the economic interdependence of the various zones. On the other hand, it has been assumed, from the very beginning, that the national economic agencies would constitute the framework around which might gradually be built a future political government of the Reich.[44] But while urging the early establishment of central economic controls preparatory to the eventual political unification of the Reich, British and American constitutional plans have also favored a greater distribution of governmental powers among the federal states than was the case under the Weimar Republic. On the one hand, these plans would not assign to the constituent members of a unified Germany as much power and independence as is envisaged by the French constitutional proposals; on the other hand, they differ from the highly centralist conception which underlies Soviet statements on the distribution of powers in a future Germany. It has been difficult to reconcile these Anglo-American views with the French attitude towards Germany. While the French, in the London Conference of the six Western nations, agreed to the merger of the three zones and to the establishment of a new political regime in Western Germany, they did so most reluctantly, and have ever since been frequently critical of the implementation of the London decisions—particularly with reference to the future status of the Ruhr.[45]

It has been impossible to reach a similar agreement with the Soviet Union. Ever since the last meeting of the Chiefs of State at the Berlin Conference, the controversy over what the future status of the Reich should be has gradually narrowed down to a division between the conception held by the Soviet Union, on the one side, and the three Western powers on the other. The consolidation of Western Germany has been the target of sharp criticism on the part of the Soviet Union. This criticism, in turn, has undoubtedly helped to advance rather than retard the establishment of a new political regime in the Western zones.

The Soviet position does not derive from any opposition to a national German government per se. On the contrary, the Soviet conception of the state as well as the Marxist view that the working classes can only hope to attain power in the state through highly centralized political and administrative controls both favor a strong national government. As far as Germany is concerned, therefore, the Soviet Union has actually tried to set itself up as the protagonist of German political unity. Its criticism of the policies of the Western powers is based on the assumption that the economic unification of the Western zones is designed to lead to the political division of Germany. This has been the predominant theme during the Moscow Conference (March-April, 1947) as well as during the London Conference of Foreign Ministers (November-December, 1947). During the London sessions, in particular, the Soviet Foreign Minister concentrated on issuing frequent appeals in favor of German unity as part of his counter-offensive against the unification of the Western zones. For the same purpose, Soviet authorities have also enlisted the help of German political groups in sponsoring so-called "People's Congresses" all over Germany which are supposed to serve as propagandistic rallying points for the cause of political unity. While the initiative for these People's Congresses has primarily lain with the Socialist Unity party or the Communists, the problem of political unity is of such over-riding importance and appeal to German minds that it has also had an effect on other political groups. Thus some bourgeois and right-wing political groups, particularly in the Eastern zone, have associated themselves with the idea of a People's Congress, and the non-Communist parties in the Western zones which have dissociated themselves from this Communist-sponsored enterprise are, to a certain extent, caught in a dilemma between their strong theoretical affirmations in behalf of German unity, on the one hand, and their actual participation in the political regime of Western Germany on the other.

Thus the underlying controversy between the Soviet Union and the Western powers has not been concerned with the question of a national government per se, but rather concerned with the timing of the establishment of such a government and with its political composition. The Soviet Union has made the formation of the central economic offices envisaged at the Berlin Conference dependent upon the prior fulfillment of certain other measures likewise agreed upon at the Berlin Conference. These measures are: demilitarization, democratization, and reparations. And while differences over the progress of demilitarization and democratization can be effectively used on either side in the war of words,[46] it is quite clear by now that the really important struggle is waged over the issue of reparations. Both during the Moscow and the London conferences of foreign ministers negotiations broke down on this point. A discussion of this issue is found elsewhere in this book;[47] here it is sufficient to note that this problem, too, is ultimately meaningful only in terms of the struggle between the East and the West for supremacy in Germany as a whole. Central political and economic controls in the hands of a Reich government would simply shift this struggle, now being waged between the Eastern and Western zones, to the national level. Judging from the present political sentiments prevailing in Germany, this would probably jeopardize, at least for several years, the Soviet sphere of influence in Eastern Germany rather than help to extend such influence into the Western zones. Since neither side can afford a weakening of the position it now holds, a continuation of the present deadlock is practically inevitable. Moreover, while both sides as well as the political regimes emerging in the Eastern and Western zones will continue to be committed to a unified Germany, the deadlock will, in fact, lead to a prolonged interregnum of a divided Germany.

This is quite apparent from the effects of the Berlin crisis. Retaliating against the decisions of the London Conference of the six Western nations (and, more specifically) against a currency reform introduced in the Western zones after the London Conference), the Russians have imposed a blockade on all road and rail traffic into and out of Berlin. The result has been the division of Berlin into two parts, the Eastern sector and the three Western sectors, the collapse of four-power rule in Berlin, the establishment of rival governments in Berlin,[48] and the virtual suspension of the Allied Control Council, the supreme inter-Allied agency originally set up for the administration of Germany as a whole. Whatever may be the final solution of the Berlin crisis, these developments are not likely to be reversed for a long time to come.

Chap. 6 Political Party Developments

VERA FRANKE ELIASBERG

THE POLITICAL PARTIES OF GERMANY even today have an unreal quality. Since they are operating in conquered and occupied territory, genuine political power lies beyond their reach. The many elections which have taken place in the various zones have also been somewhat insubstantial since the candidates could commit themselves to policies only in a remote sense and the voters cast their ballots as general expressions of opinion, rather than in the expectation of being able to influence decisions. Furthermore, German party and electoral activity has taken place under the watchful and not unbiassed eyes of the occupation authorities. It would, therefore, be misleading to view the present party system of Germany as a definitive indicator of German political trends. So much depends on the ultimate solution of the German question that any judgments as to Germany's political potential made before that time, must be in the nature of provisional guesses.

Nevertheless, under the occupation there has been a gradual devolution of some authority to German governing agencies, with the result that party contests have begun to acquire a greater robustness. As this process continues, the political stakes are taking on greater significance and meaning and the parties are finding genuine and popular roots in economic and social interests.

As a consequence of these general conditions any study of contemporary politics in Germany must make a sharp distinction between overt, observable developments and underlying potentialities of unknown strength. Just as it was unsound to accept the doctrine during the Nazi era that Germany was entirely united in support of the regime, so is it similarly unreasonable today to take the programmatic adherence to democracy of the German parties as indications of a unanimous and wholehearted conversion. Political movements and traditions do not die such sudden deaths. Germany's right-wing antidemocratic tendencies today are not organized as parties. They are to be observed rather in the form of small underground groups (at the moment of little significance), of factions and regional units of established parties the tendencies of which are now protectively colored, and of widespread attitudes of resentment, distrust, and indifference among the general population. Together these movements and tendencies constitute potential anti-democratic movements the importance of which will wax or wane in relation to the conditions of existence in Germany and the progress of international relations.

This study of German political parties deals first with the historical characteristics of the zones of occupation, then describes the strength and characteristics of the parties in the Western and Russian zones, and in conclusion draws certain tentative implications from these trends for the future of German political development.[1]

POLITICAL CHARACTERISTICS OF THE FOUR ZONES

The various zones of occupation at present exhibit very dissimilar political structures. While these differences result largely from the varying policies of the occupying powers, they to some degree reflect regional political differences which antedated the occupation. Germany is relatively young as a united nation. Different regions have different political traditions, and under the Weimar Republic there were substantial regional variations both in the relative strength of the parties and in their character.[2]

The *Russian Zone* includes those parts of Germany which historically have the weakest democratic tradition. It is economically the most heterogeneous and politically the most unbalanced zone. The agrarian regions east of the Elbe, especially the state of Mecklenburg and the Prussian province of Pomerania, had an almost feudal structure only a generation ago. On the other hand, the region around Halle and Dessau is the center of the newest and most modern German industries which mushroomed between the two world wars. The state of Saxony and parts of Thuringia are the home of the oldest German industries with the lowest wages, the worst working conditions, and a great amount of homework.

During the Weimar Republic the Russian Zone always showed a tendency to support the extreme parties. Thus Pomerania gave a majority to the nationalistic parties from 1924 on, while the Halle-Merseburg region in central Germany was always a Communist stronghold. In Berlin itself, the Communists were almost as strong as the Social Democrats. Moreover, the Social Democratic party was much further to the left in Saxony, Thuringia, and Berlin than in most other regions. The middle parties were always weak, partly because the Russian Zone contains only insignificant Catholic districts. Aside from the district of Magdeburg and the city of Berlin, the democratic parties of the Weimar Coalition secured a majority in the elections of 1919, but never subsequently.

The *British Zone* is on the whole the most intensively developed part of Germany, industrially as well as agriculturally. It is also the most densely populated part of Germany. Almost half of all cities with more than 100,000 inhabitants, the stronghold of the labor movement, are located in this zone. A strong liberal tradition, dating back to the Napoleonic wars, exists in the Rhineland. Likewise, the great commercial cities of Hamburg, Luebeck, and Bremen had a republican form of government for centuries. There are Catholic majorities in the Rhineland and part of the Ruhr area, where about half of the Catholic voters supported the Center party. In the Ruhr area and in Hamburg the Communists were very strong. The agricultural and Protestant districts of Holstein and Hanover early showed a trend toward the nationalistic parties; later they became strongholds of National Socialism. In spite of this and the influence of the big industrialists, the British Zone as a whole returned majorities for the democratic parties in most elections during the Republic. Of all regions in Germany, the Cologne-Aachen area showed the smallest percentage of Nazi votes in the elections of November, 1932. The homogeneity of the Weimar Coalition was also greater in the British Zone than elsewhere, as the Social Democrats were more moderate than in central Germany, and the Center party, based largely on the Catholic trade unions of the Rhineland and the Ruhr, more progressive.

In the *American Zone* the extreme parties of the Right and Left remained weak until 1930 because there were few economic extremes, such as those resulting in the British Zone from large industries and in the Russian Zone from large estates and because the population was mainly Catholic.

A certain liberal tradition exists in all three states of the American Zone. In Bavaria, however, this is overshadowed by the stronger tradition of conservative Catholic particularism. Southern Bavaria is the most strongly Catholic section of Germany; the dominant Bavarian party under the Republic was the extremely conservative Bavarian People's party. This party was backward in cultural, educational, and economic questions and it had little love for democracy as such. The Bavarian labor movement never recovered from the suppression of the Munich Soviet of 1919; the Social Democratic party was rather weak and very moderate, while the Communists were negligible in strength. The Protestant section of Northern Bavaria, Franconia, tended to be anti-particularist but very nationalistic and generally conservative. During the early years of the Republic, Bavaria was in many respects the most reactionary German state and furnished the National Socialist movement its most fertile soil. Later, however, Bavarian conservatives veered away from Nazism, which they found too centralist, militarist, and potentially revolutionary.

Both Wuerttemberg and Baden have liberal traditions, dating back to the Rhenish Confederation. Baden has a Catholic majority, Wuerttemberg a strong Catholic minority. The Center party in Baden was in general progressive, and the state government there was always composed of the parties of the Weimar Coalition. The labor movement was never very strong, and the Communists were negligible. In Wuerttemberg there was a strong Protestant middle class, from which the German Nationalist party derived some support. The region was also more industrialized than Baden and had a stronger labor movement. There was some Communist strength in the metal industry of Stuttgart.

The state of Greater Hesse, which has a Protestant majority, is not as homogeneous as the other two states of the American Zone, having been formed by the merger of the state of Hesse (with the exception of the region on the left bank of the Rhine) and the Prussian province of Hesse-Nassau. In the industrial sections, especially around Frankfurt, the labor movement was rather strong. Some districts in the vicinity of Kassel went Nazi very early.

The *French Zone* was carved out of the British and American zones and to some extent shares their characteristics. It is predominantly Catholic throughout. The southern parts of the Rhineland, Baden, and Wuerttemberg resemble in general the northern parts of those areas which are in the British and American zones. A slight difference exists in the Palatinate and the southern Rhineland, where prolonged French control after the last war resulted in a somewhat more nationalistic outlook on the one hand and a small separatist movement on the other. But even under the most favorable conditions, resulting from German inflation and the breakdown of passive resistance in the Ruhr, the Rhenish separatist movement never succeeded in winning the support of any substantial part of the population. The Saar which was detached from Germany for fifteen years is today again considered a French protectorate rather than a part of occupied Germany.

The dissimilarities of the various regions, while arising in part from different traditions and different economic structures, might have been lessened had the four occupying powers followed common policies. But the division into four airtight zones has tended to accentuate them instead, particularly because each area has been assigned to an occupying power which has more or less tended to reinforce its historical tendencies.

EMERGENCE OF THE PARTIES

The collapse of the Hitler regime left a near-vacuum in German politics. The Nazi party melted away; its members disappeared from public view and its organizations ceased to exist. On the other hand, the older parties had not yet had an opportunity to rebuild their shattered organizations; only rudimentary groups emerged from the underground.

In the reorganization of German political life, as in other fields, the occupation authorities in the various zones followed widely different policies. But different as they were, the policies of the four occupying powers had one result in common—they all hindered the spontaneous development of political organizations.[3]

In the first months after the collapse of the Hitler regime, there were as yet no separate military governments for the three Western zones. All three were subject to the terms of the SHAEF directive on the military government of Germany, issued in April, 1945. This directive stated: "No political activities of any kind shall be countenanced unless authorized by you." Under its authority, underground groups which had come out into the open after the Nazi collapse were dissolved and their activities prohibited. In several cities, applications for permission to form parties were rejected. No meetings were permitted, nor were any newspapers allowed except those published by the Military Government. Thus for several months after the Allied occupation of Western Germany political life remained practically nonexistent.

In the Russian Zone, on the other hand, the directive of Military Government demanded the immediate establishment of political parties along carefully prescribed lines. On June 10, 1945, political parties were officially sanctioned by a decree of Marshal Zhukov. By the end of June, four parties had been established and were permitted to form zone-wide organizations, hold mass meetings, and publish newspapers which, of course, were subject to strict Russian censorship. Two of these parties, the Social Democrats and the Communists, were both in name and in their own opinion the legitimate successors of the same parties of the pre-Hitler period. The other two, the Christian Democratic Union and the Liberal

Democratic party, had no exact equivalents under the Republic.

The leadership of the Communist party had been brought back from exile in Moscow by the Red Army. From the first day, the Communist party had a functioning Central Committee, the majority of whose members were the same as in 1933. On June 11, the day after the legalization of parties, it was able to publish its program, and it had a head-start in rebuilding its organization.

The nucleus of the revived Social Democratic party was formed in the last days of the Battle of Berlin. By June 15, the Central Committee *(Zentral-Ausschuss)* had been established and a program published. Members of the Central Committee had been prominent in the old Social Democratic party, although none of them had been a member of the pre-1933 Executive Committee. All of them had remained in Germany under the Nazi regime and several had been in prison.

The Christian Democratic Union was in a sense the successor of the old Center party, but unlike the latter, it sought support not only from Catholics, but also from Protestant elements and in general all those non-Nazis who felt themselves to the right of the Social Democrats. Its chairman was Andreas Hermes who had been prominent in the Center party. Among the signers of the party's program, published on June 26, were several leading Christian trade unionists, some scientists, some former members of the Democratic party, and miscellaneous anti-Nazi conservatives.

As for the Liberal Democratic party, there is a persistent rumor that it was formed by order of Marshal Zhukov who declared that there must be four parties. The sponsors of the party, except for two who had formerly represented the Democratic party in cabinets of the Weimar Republic, were politically unknown. By July 5, 1945, the organization of the party's leadership was achieved, at least on paper, and it had published its program.

All four programs, published as appeals to the German people, seem at first glance very vague and strangely similar.[4] This was not surprising since at that time, a month before the Potsdam Declaration, nobody in Germany had any real basis for predicting even the main features of the country's future. Its frontiers, its economic basis, the zonal borders and their effects, the boundaries of Allied control and German self-administration—all were unknown. Problems and prospects were nebulous, and so were the programs of the four newly formed parties. These, in any case, were as yet only central committees with no mass basis.

All four programs start with a gloomy picture of Germany in ruins, all are full of denunciations of Nazism and militarism, and all declare that Germany's only chance for survival lies in its transformation into a truly democratic state. Despite important differences on such questions as religion, private enterprise, and the vehemence with which they assert German guilt the similarities are more striking than the divergencies. Each party emphasizes the necessity of close cooperation of all anti-fascists. The program of the Communist party concludes with the statement:

The Central Committee of the Communist Party is of the opinion that the foregoing program of action can serve as the basis for the creation of a bloc of anti-fascist democratic parties (the Communist Party, the Social Democratic Party, the Center Party, and others). We are of the opinion that such a bloc can form a firm foundation for the struggle for the complete liquidation of the remnants of the Hitler regime and for the establishment of a democratic regime.[5]

The other parties understood that this invitation would not have been published by the Communist party except at suggestion of the Russian Military Government. They therefore responded, and on July 14, 1945, the four parties established an Anti-Fascist Bloc.

There were those who doubted whether democracy would be furthered by the precipitate rebuilding of political parties "from above" at a time when the sole concern of most people was finding something to eat and a place to sleep. Yet by comparison with the Western zones political life in the Russian Zone at least presented the appearance of progress.

A four-party system had been established which was to become the pattern for the reorganization of political life in the other zones. All four parties considered themselves not merely as zonal, but as nation-wide organizations with headquarters in Berlin which would function for all of Germany as soon as political activities were permitted in the Western zones. Yet by the time political parties had developed in Western Germany, there had been profound changes in the pattern of the Russian Zone, which had served as their model. The cleavage between Eastern and Western Germany thus found expression in the party structure of the two spheres of influence.

The Potsdam Declaration of August 2, 1945 superseded the SHAEF Directive on political activity. It urged, "All democratic political parties, with rights of assembly and of public discussion, shall be allowed and encouraged throughout Germany."

The ban on political activities had been violated in greater or lesser degree by those Germans, a not very numerous group, who were politically-minded. They quietly went about laying the groundwork for their organizations. Their success depended in large part on the attitude of the local military authorities. Military Government's reliance in the Western zones on religious leaders gave those groups who later founded the Christian Democratic Union a better start, especially in the rural areas. Moreover, the undamaged organization of the churches facilitated the progress of the C.D.U. In the larger cities this was to some extent counterbalanced by the stronger organizational tradition of the labor movement. This was reinforced by the fact that some shop steward elections and a few local trade unions had meanwhile been permitted. These trade unions were required to be nonpolitical, but they served as a meeting ground for Social Democrats, Communists, and Christian trade unionists. Personal contacts which had continued to exist among members of the pre-Hitler parties began to take systematic form, local leaders began to emerge, and the nuclei of the future political parties came into existence. The political alignment followed closely the four-party pattern of the Russian Zone.

On August 13, 1945, the American Military Government announced that in accordance with the Potsdam decisions, the formation of political parties and labor unions would be permitted. A directive of August 27 stated: "Military Government officers may accept and approve applications to form political parties at the county (Kreis) level." It was the desire of the American occupation authorities to assure the democratic character of the parties by letting them grow from below. But this confinement to local units was a serious handicap since it prevented party offices in the larger cities from acting as headquarters for the surrounding areas. Freedom of movement was severely limited both by Military Government regulations and by the lack of transportation. Without buildings, offices, typewriters—even paper and pencils—the new parties faced tremendous technical difficulties. They had neither facilities nor authorization to publish newspapers, pamphlets, or other propaganda material.

When one considers these difficulties, the development of the new parties was surprisingly rapid. On September 2, 1945, the American-controlled radio of Frankfurt a/Main announced that the military commander of the city would accept applications to form political parties. By September, 17 Social Democratic and Communist organizations had been established and held their first public meetings. By November, 212 local party organizations of the four major parties had been recognized in the American Zone and these parties were permitted to function on a state-wide basis. Although a number of purely local groups emerged, most of the newly formed organizations regarded themselves as parts of one or another of the four parties.

The development of political parties in the British and French zones was, on the whole, similar to that in the American Zone but started somewhat later. The formation of parties was not sanctioned in the British Zone until September 14, 1945, but once authorized the parties developed faster than in the American Zone. The zonal congress of the Social Democratic party in Hanover on October 5 was the first political congress in post-Hitler Germany. This congress, at which fraternal delegates were present from the other Western zones and Berlin, was of great importance for the development of the Social Democratic party. At the same time the Communist party held its first district conference, for the Ruhr and Westphalia, in Dortmund. And on December 19, at Godesberg, the Christian Democratic Union held its first zonal conference, with fraternal delegates from other zones.

The French Zone was the last to permit the organization of political parties. One reason for this was that a section of the French administration tried to organize a separatist movement. This achieved some success in the Saar, but little elsewhere. The formation of parties was therefore authorized in the Saar on November 11, 1945, whereas it was not until December that it was permitted in the rest of the French Zone. Even after formal authorization had been given it took some time before the parties were actually recognized. Thus the American-controlled DANA agency reported on February 22, 1946: "Following the recent resumption of Communist Party activities in the French zone, permission has also been given the Social Democratic Party to pursue political activities." The French administration, particularly in the Palatinate, appeared to favor conservative or reactionary elements, many of whom had been Nazis or closely connected with them. (Thus, in a number of cases, officials dismissed by the American authorities as Nazis were shortly thereafter appointed by the French to positions in their zone.) This was probably due to the fact that these elements, hoping to save themselves and their property, now showed separatist tendencies. On the other hand the labor parties, particularly the Social Democrats who were strongly opposed to separatism, found themselves obstructed by the French administration and the Germans whom it had placed in office, and developed under greater difficulties than in the other zones.

Strength and Characteristics of the New Parties

By the beginning of 1946 the main lines of political development in the Western zones were more or less set, and the principal characteristics of the various parties, insofar as these could come to the surface under the occupation, were evident. In the Eastern zone, the effects of Russian pressure were just beginning to be felt and had not yet blurred the political picture as they were subsequently to do.

The original Central Committees in Berlin and local groups elsewhere had expanded into zonal organizations, both in the East and the West. The parties began to compete with each other for influence and positions in the local and provincial German administrations. The trade unions developed into mass organizations, in which the labor parties vied with each other for control.

Moreover, the parties began to exert pressure on Military Government on questions of policy. Thus the labor parties held that the denazification policy was not far-reaching enough in the case of more important figures—particularly those who, while fully cooperating with the Nazis, had been sufficiently well-connected to be able to avoid actually joining the Nazi party. The Christian Democratic Union and Liberal Democratic party on the other hand held that the denazification was too rigid and mechanical in regard to the small fry and that it disrupted essential services. Likewise, the parties endeavored to secure influence over the newspapers and other means of forming public opinion. Other questions with which the parties concerned themselves were those of food distribution, reconstruction, and especially personnel. Thus, despite the initial efforts of both the British and American Military Government to secure "nonpolitical" officials, a majority of the German administrators were either members of or closely connected with one or another political party. The Germans who held office were regarded by the population as representatives of their parties, and this fact became increasingly important as the local governments received new powers and functions.

There were two great obstacles to the development of the parties in all zones. In the first place, the average German was so preoccupied with the difficulties of daily life that he had little time or energy for anything more. But there was in addition a widespread suspicion of everything political. Large numbers of Germans were sick of parties and programs. They distrusted all slogans, and dismissed everything as propaganda. There was a widespread feeling that everything they were offered was something which had already been tried and failed. This feeling was not altogether without justification, since the parties were rather similar to those of pre-Hitler days and presented few new ideas or leaders. Moreover, the German people were still almost as isolated from the outside world as they had been under Hitler. Little information on world events was available to them or sufficient information about conditions in the other zones of Germany, and they had no satisfactory basis on which to arrive at opinions.

Meanwhile, disappointment and dissatisfaction with the occupying powers grew. Since the people had the feeling that all questions were decided from above, and that they themselves had nothing to say, they tended to lay the blame for all their difficulties at the door of Military Government. And the parties, for their part, were regarded by many people as mere instruments of Military Government, lacking any power to make independent decisions. There was, of course, a great deal of truth in this. Germany's fate was in the hands of the victorious powers, not the German parties. Even in minor local matters, all decisions could be nullified by any Military Government official. The parties thus had no real power and no responsibility, and without self-government there was no real basis for democratic political life.

THE CHRISTIAN DEMOCRATIC UNION

In the American Zone, the first to hold elections, the strongest party is the Christian Democratic Union (in Bavaria called the Christian Social Union).[6] To some extent it resembles the Christian parties which have developed since the war in other European countries, notably the Popular Republican Movement in France and the Christian Democratic party in Italy. But while these parties, like the pre-Hitler German Center party, are essentially Catholic, the Christian Democratic Union seeks to unite Catholics and Protestants in one party. In so doing, it has broken sharply with German tradition.

The basic doctrine of the C.D.U. is that much of the evil in the contemporary world arises from the disregard of Christian morality; hence its reformation requires the application of Christian principles in all spheres of life, including politics. Thus, the *Appeal of the Christian Democratic Union* asserts: "From the chaos of guilt and shame into which the deification of a criminal adventurer has plunged us, a new order of democratic freedom can emerge only if we return to the civilizing moral and spiritual forces of Christianity, and make these sources of strength ever more accessible to our people."[7]

One of the leading Protestants in the party, Pastor Otto Fricke of Frankfurt, has declared: "We want all Christian people to have a common approach to public questions. We can reconstruct German life only on the basis of Christian doctrine, the Ten Commandments, and the Sermon on the Mount."

Germany is not the only country which is today experiencing a religious revival, but in Germany there have been additional factors which reinforced this tendency. The destruction of moral and traditional values in the Nazi era and disillusionment and demoralization in defeat have turned large numbers of people to Christianity as a source of moral principles. The aggressively anti-Christian ideology of the Nazis and the role of the churches as the only institutions not completely dominated by the totalitarian state made them a rallying point for many people. Moreover, Christianity was regarded by many as the antithesis not only of Nazism but of Communism, the threat of which was dramatized by the presence of the Red Army on German soil.

Christian principles, however, are subject to varying interpretations. Hence the C.D.U. has drawn into its ranks people of widely divergent points of view. Thus, while the first official program of the C.D.U. does not use the phrase "Christian Socialism," it calls for a planned economy and nationalization of monopolistic key industries. At the same time, however, it advocates the preservation of private property.

The first conference of the Christian Democratic Union, at Godesberg in the British Zone, drew up a program calling for moral regeneration, based on a search for the causes of Germany's downfall; for peace and international justice; for federalization of Germany; for proportional representation; for denazification; and for a guarantee of work, food, clothing, and shelter for all by the application of Christian economic principles.

While the Christian doctrine of forgiveness as expressed in the party's attitude towards denazification and the fact that it was the one important party not committed to a complete reorganization of the economic system made it attractive to reactionary elements, the C.D.U. does not want to become the rallying point of these groups. It seeks, rather, to create a party which will transcend class lines and traditional differences. But in its effort to win the workers, it suffers from one serious disadvantage, as compared to the old Center party. The latter drew much of its support from the workers organized in the Christian trade unions, which in turn strongly influenced its policies. But today all workers are organized in one "nonpolitical" trade union movement, in which the various parties compete for influence. And in this competition the C.D.U. is at a disadvantage as compared to the more experienced Social Democrats and Communists.

Even the left wing of the C.D.U. finds itself in sharp opposition to the Social Democrats on the relation between church and state, particularly in respect to education. This is one point on which the entire C.D.U. is united. In general, the lack of internal homogeneity of the C.D.U. has given rise to far greater differences between its affiliates in the various areas than have developed in the case of the other major parties.

In the Catholic parts of Western Germany the Christian Democratic party is the successor, although on a broader base, of the Center party, one of the pillars of the Weimar Republic. In Bavaria, however, the pre-Hitler representative of political Catholicism was the Bavarian People's party—strongly authoritarian and antidemocratic. It is therefore neither surprising nor accidental that in Bavaria we find the Christian *Social* Union replacing the Christian *Democratic* Union. And in Bavaria, too, extreme right-wing elements have succeeded in penetrating the party more deeply than in most other parts of the country. Thus, in the formative stage of the party its Wuerzburg and Viechtach branches were dissolved by the Military Government because of large-scale Nazi infiltration into them.

Just as the Bavarian People's party stood well to the right of the Center party, so the Bavarian Christian Social Union is more conservative than the Christian Democratic Union in most other areas. The first leader of the Bavarian C.S.U. was the reactionary Friedrich Schaeffer, who originally had been appointed Minister President by Colonel Charles Keegan. When Military Government later disqualified Schaeffer from holding public office, the party leadership went to Joseph Mueller. Mueller, who had also been prominent in the Bavarian People's party, had taken part in the July 20 movement and utilized his position at the Vatican to make contacts for this oppositional group. He recognizes the necessity of government control of the economy during the initial period of reconstruction; but he does not favor any far-reaching land reform measures or a permanent planned economy and emphasizes the importance of encouraging private enterprise.

A very different view was expressed by the periodical *Frankfurter Hefte* which represents the progressive wing of the C.D.U. in Greater Hesse. In an editorial entitled "The Hour of Social Reform" (June, 1946) this publication calls for the socialization of all large-scale and key industries.[8] Under this heading it includes natural resources, heavy industry, large banks, and large-scale enterprises in all branches of the economy. It emphasizes that by socialization it does not mean state ownership leading to state capitalism, but rather cooperative ownership by the workers themselves. It further asserts that a planned economy is essential in order to avoid the depressions and large-scale unemployment which result from a "free" economy. And it declares: "An aspect of our socialism is that in our country some concept of planned economy must be closely integrated with the old western doctrine of the free but responsible personality in order to give the new economic order its typical form." Subsequently the C.D.U. in Greater Hesse voted in the Constituent Assembly for the socialization of the basic industries.

In the elections for the Constituent State Assemblies in the American Zone the C.D.U.-C.S.U. emerged as the strongest party in two of the three states. In Bavaria, where the population is more than 90 per cent Catholic, the C.S.U. received 52.4 per cent of the total vote.[9] In the newly created state of Wuerttemberg-Baden, where the Protestants predominate, the C.D.U. failed to achieve a majority, although it was the strongest single party. Its share of the vote was 38.4 per cent. In Greater Hesse, which is predominantly

Protestant and has a relatively larger industrial working-class than either of the other states in the American Zone, the C.D.U. ran second to the Social Democrats. The latter polled 42.6 per cent of the vote, whereas the C.D.U. obtained 30.8 per cent. In the entire American Zone it did much better in the rural areas than in the cities.

The C.D.U.'s share of the vote was considerably greater than that of the pre-Nazi Center party. In the Reichstag elections between 1928 and 1932, the Center party averaged in all of what is now the American Zone slightly over 26 per cent. The corresponding percentage in 1946 was 40.9. This increase was in large part due to the disappearance of the old right wing parties, whose former adherents now supported the C.D.U. in the absence of party organizations conforming more closely to their views.

In the British Zone the Christian Democratic Union was from the very beginning under the conservative leadership of Konrad Adenauer, former Lord Mayor of Cologne. He is the spokesman of those forces who consider the C.D.U. a bulwark against too far-reaching social reforms. In the most important state of the British Zone, North Rhine Westphalia, the C.D.U. became the shelter for the industrialists of the Rhine and Ruhr who, being mostly Protestants, as a rule did not belong to the old Center party but rather to the nationalist right-wing parties. On the other hand, the C.D.U. tried to continue the tradition of the Center party which in the Rhineland was based to a large extent on the support of the Christian trade unions.

It is difficult to see how such divergent views can, in the long run, be reconciled. Hence it is not surprising that in some industrial centers where the influence of the Catholic workers is strong, a split has already taken place. A part of the C.D.U. left-wing in Rhineland-Westphalia, disturbed by the policies of Adenauer and the infiltration into the party of conservative industrialists, sought to create a party which would exclude these groups and seek support primarily from the Catholic workers. In the spring of 1946 the Center party was revived in Westphalia under the leadership of Karl Spiecker who had returned from exile in Canada.[10] Under the

Weimar Republic, Spiecker had been prominent in the left wing of the Center party and had held high positions in the party and the governments of Prussia and the Reich. The program of the new Center party pledged to uphold the principles of its forerunner: it wanted to be the party of the "center," not a right-wing party like the C.D.U., and it wanted to remain a predominantly Catholic party. The new Center party had some success in the industrial centers of the Rhineland, but like all splinter parties in present-day Germany it is, at least up to now, only of local importance. In the state of North Rhine Westphalia it polled 6.2 per cent in the elections of October, 1946 and 9.8 per cent in April, 1947.

The elections of October 13, 1946, for the district and city councils of the British Zone were the first test as to whether the Christian Democrats would succeed in overcoming the traditional cleavage between the Catholics and Protestants. They passed this test with flying colors. In the whole zone the C.D.U. received 36.9 per cent of the total vote (only one half per cent less than the Social Democrats.) In the states of North Rhine Westphalia and Oldenburg the Christian Democrats, with 45.4 and 40.5 per cent of the total vote, came out as the strongest party. In the Protestant states of Schleswig-Holstein and Brunswick the C.D.U. was by far stronger than the Liberal Democrats or any other non-labor party. Before 1933 the Center party was practically nonexistent in Schleswig-Holstein, receiving less than 1.5 per cent of the vote. Now the C.D.U. received 38 per cent. In Hamburg, where the Center party formerly accounted for barely 2 per cent, the 1946 elections gave the C.D.U. 27 per cent of the vote, although two other non-labor parties appealed to the same middle-class groups. The picture was similar in the Protestant cities of Bremen, Kiel, and Luebeck. On the basis of this evidence there can be little doubt that the C.D.U. has become the great rallying point for the middle classes who are united across religious lines by the fear of Russia and social revolution.

Simultaneously with the first elections in the British Zone, district council elections took place in the French Zone. They resulted in an overwhelming success for the Christian Democratic Union which polled 55.6 per cent of the vote. Only about two million people voted in the French Zone, but the striking victory of the C.D.U. must be regarded as another important step in the rise of the Christian Democrats to the position of the dominant party in Western Germany.

The C.D.U. suffered a slight setback in the State Assembly elections in the British Zone in April, 1947. Its share of the total vote decreased from 36.9 to 32.2 per cent. But the Christian Democrats remained the strongest party in the state of North Rhine Westphalia, the heart of Western Germany.

In the municipal elections in the American Zone (December, 1947 in Wuerttemberg-Baden; April and May, 1948 in Hesse and Bavaria) the C.D.U. lost rather heavily. In Bavaria the C.S.U.'s vote decreased from 52.4 to 37.8 per cent. The bulk of these votes went to the new Bavarian party and to the Refugee party (see below, "Smaller Political Groups"). In Hesse and Wuerttemberg-Baden the C.D.U. lost several per cent to the Liberal Democratic party and independents. But it would be misleading to draw definite conclusions from a comparison of local elections with those for state parliaments.

In Eastern Germany the Christian Democratic Union is considerably to the left of the C.D.U.-C.S.U. in the West and strongly opposed to the policies of Adenauer and the now dominant right-wing faction of the Bavarian C.S.U. But the development of the party in the Russian Zone has been strongly influenced by the policies of the Soviet Military Government and will be described later.

The Liberal Democratic Party

The Liberal Democratic party tries to rally those middle-class and bourgeois groups who, because of their traditional anti-Catholicism, are not willing to support the Christian Democrats. It advocates liberalism in the economic sphere as well as in cultural and educational policy. It is the only major party in postwar Germany which openly comes out for free enterprise with no state intervention. In its first Appeal it declared that: "The establishment of a unitary German economy on the basis of private ownership and economic freedom is the prerequisite for initiative and successful economic activity."[11] Such a program has an unrealistic ring in present-day Germany, where most people find their chance of survival determined by emergency planning, delivery quotas, rationing and price control.[12]

The leaders of the L.D.P. are either political unknowns or persons formerly associated with the old Democratic party, who in the last years of the Weimar Republic were already only individuals with small followings.

In the elections for the Constituent State Assemblies in the American Zone the Liberal Democratic party received its highest vote, 19.5 per cent of the total, in the state of Wuerttemberg-Baden. This was considerably better than its showing in Bavaria, with 5.6 per cent, or in Greater Hesse, with 15 per cent. In the elections of October, 1946, the L.D.P. received 6.7 per cent of the total vote in the British Zone, and 7.1 per cent in the French Zone. Its support seems to come mainly from the urban Protestant middle class. But even in the purely Protestant states of the British Zone it is too weak to be a serious competitor for the Christian Democrats. In the 1947/1948 municipal elections in the American Zone the Liberal Democratic party improved its position slightly. Its gains were greatest in the cities of Hesse.

Like the C.D.U., the L.D.P is known under different names in the various parts of Germany. Thus it calls itself the Democratic People's party in Wuerttemberg-Baden and the Free Democratic party in the British Zone.

The Liberal Democratic party in the Russian Zone is far to the left of the Western Liberal Democrats,—at least in its official proclamations. Although without any real influence, it came out as the second strongest party in the elections in Eastern Germany. But this fact was the result of the policy of the Soviet Military Government and will be discussed in detail below.

THE SOCIAL DEMOCRATIC PARTY

Today the Social Democratic party is, as it was under the Weimar Republic and the Empire, in the first place the party of organized labor. But it has also attracted followers from other social groups. At the beginning of 1946 it seemed likely to become the strongest party in Germany. It received a serious setback, however, as a result of the unification of the Social Democratic and Communist parties in the Russian Zone. This development will be treated separately.

The Social Democratic party owes its popular support largely to the fact that it, more than any other German party, was consistently pro-democratic and anti-Nazi. This appears to have outweighed its political blunders, weaknesses, and frequent lack of militancy under the Weimar Republic in the minds of not only the great bulk of its former adherents but large numbers of other Germans as well. Both its old and new followers look to the S.P.D. as the exponent of democratic socialism. In Germany the socialist movement was always in the forefront of the fight for democratic and humanitarian ideals. And for millions of Germans the word "socialism" has an almost religious appeal—a fact on which the Nazis attempted to capitalize by calling their movement National Socialist.

In the new program of the Social Democratic party, adopted at the party congress in Hanover on May 11, 1946, the party's adherence to the three principles of socialism, democracy, and humanism is restated even more clearly and emphatically than in 1918-19. The program attributes the catastrophe of Germany and Europe to "the destruction of the political power of the working classes, which diverted democracy from its course." And it states that "the defection of the German bourgeoisie, and of that section of the labor movement which failed to recognize the political importance of democracy for the working-class, constitutes the historical guilt of the German people." The program declares that democracy "is the best form of political struggle for all creative forces . . . necessary for Socialists not merely for reasons of power politics but on moral grounds." But it emphasizes the inadequacy of political democracy by itself, asserting: "Because of the special historical development and the peculiarities of the spiritual development of Germany, socialism is necessary to German democracy. German democracy must be socialist, or the counterrevolutionary forces will destroy it once again." At the same time, it stresses the importance of traditional liberal ideals, stating that, "There can be no socialism without freedom of information and freedom of criticism. Nor can there be any socialism without humanity and respect for human personality." [13]

This passage defines, as it is intended to, the barrier which divides Social Democrats from Communists. The former, adhering to the Western concept of democracy, find no way of reconciling themselves to the totalitarian approach of the Communists.

The economic content of the program is not essentially different from the traditional Social-Democratic position. But circumstances give it an immediacy and a widespread appeal which it never before possessed. The foundations of the old system of private property have been seriously undermined by the involvement of many industrialists and financiers with the Hitler regime and by the destruction of the war. And in a country where only the most rigid equalitarianism can assure even subsistence for all, there is considerable support for the statement in the Social Democratic program that "present-day Germany is no longer in a position to support a private capitalistic profit economy. The existing property relationships are an obstacle to reconstruction." Whereas in 1919 many Social Democratic leaders were of the opinion that "you can't socialize misery," there is today no disagreement in the party as to the necessity of instituting a planned economy and socializing all raw materials, public utilities, key industries, and those which tend to become monopolies. And remembering the role of the landed proprietors in undermining the Weimar Republic, the party calls for a thorough-going land reform, but on a basis of cooperative farming of large units, rather than the division of the land into uneconomic dwarf farms.

In international affairs, the Social Democratic party recognizes the obligation of Germany to pay reparations, so far as these are compatible with economic realities. It is fundamentally internationalist, declaring its belief in the "United States of Europe, a democratic and socialist federation of European states. . . . Not parts of Germany, but all of Europe, should be internationalized." But while recognizing that the day of unlimited national sovereignty is past, it asserts national freedom as a democratic right.

The continuity of the Social Democratic tradition is both an advantage and a disadvantage for the party. On the one hand, it has led to a high degree of reliance on surviving pre-Hitler functionaries. This creates difficulties in developing leadership among the younger age groups, a problem which the Socialists have in common with all the other German parties. On the other hand, the loyalty and experience of its former members stood the S.P.D. in good stead in rebuilding its organization. Thus it was the first German party to hold a congress (in May, 1946) with elected delegates.

Kurt Schumacher, chairman of the S.P.D., is one of the few national leaders to emerge since the downfall of the Hitler regime. Before 1933, he was Reichstag deputy and newspaper editor in Stuttgart. He was arrested in 1933 and spent more than ten years in various prisons and concentration camps. His stature was increased by his leadership in the fight of the S.P.D. to preserve its independence in the face of the Russian sponsored campaign for its merger with the Communist party. One factor which contributes to his popularity is his independent position in relation to the occupying powers, whose policies he does not hesitate to attack.

In the party struggle in Germany it first appeared that the Christian Democratic Union would be the most successful in channelizing growing national resentment in its own support. Increasingly the Social Democrats, mostly through the speeches of Schumacher, have come out in opposition to the Eastern territorial settlement and efforts to separate the Ruhr and the Saar from future German control. Schumacher's defense of German integrity has been broadened to include demands for an increased industrial level and limits on reparations and dismantling of industries. He has had to combat separatist and particularist trends within some local organizations of the party. Thus the Social Democratic organization of Flensburg was expelled because of its advocacy of annexation of parts of Schleswig-Holstein to Denmark. The district organization of the Saar was sharply reprimanded for supporting the French policy of incorporating the Saar into the French economic system.

While in the elections for the Constituent State Assemblies in the American Zone the S.P.D. lagged considerably behind the C.D.U., it was much stronger than it had been in any Reichstag election in the Weimar Republic. At its high point, in the elections of 1928, it received 24 per cent of the vote in Bavaria, 23 per cent in Wuerttemberg and Baden, and 31 per cent in Greater Hesse. In all of what is now the American Zone it averaged slightly under 25 per cent. The corresponding percentages in 1946 were 28.2 per cent in Bavaria, 31.8 per cent in Wuerttemberg-Baden, and 42.6 per cent in Greater Hesse. The over-all average is 32.6 per cent.

The Socialists showed their traditional weakness in the rural areas where they polled only 29.5 per cent of the vote throughout the zone. In the city council elections, on the other hand, the Social Democratic vote averaged 39 per cent.

In the predominantly Catholic French Zone the Social Democrats received in the elections of October 13, 1946, 28.6 per cent of the total vote, barely half the total of the Christian Democrats.

The first elections in the British Zone, held at the same date, were a close contest between the Social Democrats and Christian Democrats. The S.P.D. received in the whole zone 37.4 per cent of the vote, closely followed by the C.D.U. which polled 36.9 per cent. The strength of the Social Democrats varied considerably in the different states of the British Zone. They received only 35 per cent of the vote in the predominantly Catholic state of North Rhine Westphalia. Forty-one per cent in Lower Saxony and Schleswig-Holstein. The S.P.D. was by far the strongest party in Hamburg and Bremen where it polled 44 and 48 per cent respectively. Its position changed only slightly in the elections for the State Assemblies in April 1947. For the whole of the British Zone it registered a slight gain, but in Rhineland Westphalia it lost approximately 3 per cent of the total vote to the Communists. In the local elections in the American Zone in December, 1947 and in the spring of 1948, the position of the S.P.D. remained on the whole unchanged. In the rural areas it lost some votes to independent candidates.

THE COMMUNIST PARTY

The Communist party had certain important initial advantages. It had derived great prestige, both from the Nazi concentration on Communism as *the* enemy and from the successes of the Red Army. It was the only party in Germany with the unlimited backing of one of the occupying powers. And it had a ready-made leadership and program to present to the German people at a time when all other parties were still in a formative stage. But these advantages were soon dissipated. The behaviour of the victorious Red Army and the Russian policy of large-scale industrial removals was a serious handicap in the Communist organizational campaign. The close relationship between the Communist party and Russia, while still an advantage from the point of view of organization and power, became a political handicap. Like other European Communist parties, that of Germany has ceased to talk of revolution, dictatorship of the proletariat, or internationalism. It declares that democracy is the only possible basis for a new Germany, demands antifascist unity, and uses strongly nationalistic language—except where Russian policy is concerned. But as always, its policies are determined by a strongly centralized bureaucracy, in no way responsible to the membership, and may be changed at a moment's notice.

With the backing of the occupying power, the Communists in the Russian Zone entrenched themselves in all the principal administrative positions. As a result, there has been a tendency for the K.P.D. to rely less on the industrial workers and more on bureaucrats of all types—public employees, officials of mass organizations, industrial managers and certain other groups of intellectuals. This tendency has been strengthened by the resentment of many workers, including former Communists, toward Russian removals of machinery. These removals seemed to the workers to threaten not merely their livelihood as individuals, but the social basis of the labor movement itself. In the minds of many workers this outweighed their approval of such Communist sponsored reforms as the expropriation of the large estates, the transfer of many industrial enterprises to public ownership, and workers' participation in the management of industry. The large-scale removal of livestock and farm machinery had similar effects on the rural population, who were in any case initially unsympathetic toward the Communists.

So rapidly did the Communists lose ground among the workers that they soon felt the need of consolidating themselves behind the façade of the Socialist Unity party (*Sozialistische Einheitspartei*, abbreviated S.E.D.), created by the forced merger of the Social Democratic and the Communist parties in the Russian zone. Their weakness in the labor movement may also help to explain the lenient policy of the Communists toward minor Nazis, whom it not only admitted to its ranks but actively recruited.

Whereas in the Eastern zone the K.P.D. has become *the* government party, in the West it retains its traditional role of opposition. Here it can best serve Russian interests by denouncing "Western imperialism" and German "reaction." Under this heading the Communists include not only big business elements which have sought shelter in the C.D.U., but Social Democrats as well. Communist criticism of the Western Allies is as open as the situation permits. With the deterioration of the relations between the Soviet Union and the Western powers, Communist attacks on British and American policy and on the Western-oriented German parties became much more forceful.

This showed itself in the elections for the Constituent Assemblies in the American Zone. Here the Communists received an over-all average of 8.2 per cent of the vote—6.4 per cent in Bavaria, 10.7 in Hesse and 10.2 in Wuerttemberg-Baden. These figures, approximately midway between the maximum and minimum votes received by the Communists under the Republic, represent a considerable diminution of Communist influence as compared to the Social Democrats. Surprisingly the Communists did not do much better in the cities than in the province as a whole. They polled only 6.6 per cent of the urban vote in Bavaria, 11.6 per cent in Greater Hesse, and 11.8 per cent in Wuerttemberg-Baden.

In the French Zone the Communists received 7.7 per cent of the total vote in the elections of October 13, 1946.

It was generally expected that the Communist party would show greater strength in the British Zone. The Ruhr area and the ports are traditional centers of Communist influence. The desperate food situation, the demolition of shipbuilding plants and the removal or destruction of industrial facilities of the Ruhr had created resentment against the British Military Government. Widespread discontent and disappointment were expected to find their expression in a rather substantial Communist vote. On the other hand there were indications that many workers in the British Zone associated the Communists with the industrial removals and dislocations resulting from the Russian demands for huge reparations and with the Russian and Polish annexations of large areas in Eastern Germany which led to the influx of hundreds of thousands of expelled people into overcrowded Western Germany. There was also resentment among Communist workers, particularly those who were active in the underground, against the party leadership. Some Communist underground workers believed that they were fighting for freedom and democracy, if not for everyone, at least for the working classes. They were consequently disillusioned by the authoritarian methods of the Russian Military Government and the Communist party in the Eastern zone, and especially with the attempt to compel the Social Democratic party to surrender its identity against the will of its members. In Bremen these general developments led two Communist members of the Senate to join the Social Democratic party as a protest.

The first elections in the British Zone showed that the Communists were not able to capitalize on the widespread discontent. The K.P.D. polled only 8.1 per cent of the total vote in the zone. Even in those industrial centers where before 1933 the Communists were twice as strong as the Social Democrats, they suffered a severe setback. To name a few important cities: In the Reichstag election of June 31, 1932, the Communists received 26.8 per cent of the vote in Düsseldorf, the Social Democrats 12.7 per cent. In 1946 the S.P.D. polled twice as many votes as the K.P.D. For Duisburg the respective figures are: Communists 26.8 per cent, Social Democrats 13.5 per cent in 1932; K.P.D. 87,325 votes, S.P.D. 213,885 votes in 1946. Essen gave the Communists 25.2 per cent, the Social

Democrats 12.7 per cent in 1932, whereas in 1946 the Social Democrats received 252,409 votes to 89,329 for the Communists. (It should be noted that under the new electoral system of the British Zone every voter was entitled to several votes.) In the whole area which today constitutes the British Zone, the Communist vote in 1932 was about three-fourths of the Social Democratic, whereas in 1946 it was approximately one-fifth.

The Communist party improved its numerical position slightly in the elections for the State Assemblies in the British Zone in April, 1947. It received 10.5 per cent in the entire zone, and 14 per cent in the state of North Rhine Westphalia. During the food crisis in the spring of 1947 it seemed that the Communists were slowly regaining their influence in the industrial centers. But the shop steward elections in the Ruhr mining districts in October, 1947 brought them a new setback in their most important stronghold. They received 406 seats, as against 617 for the Social Democrats, 185 for the Christian Democrats, and 140 for nonparty candidates. In 1946 the K.P.D. had won 417 seats, the S.P.D. 448, the C.D.U. 146, and nonparty delegates 52. The main reason for this new decline of the Communists was their hostile attitude to the Marshall Plan which had become the symbol of hope for the people of Western Germany. This trend showed itself again when the local elections of 1947/1948 in all three states of the American Zone resulted in a loss for the K.P.D. In October, 1948 it suffered an even greater setback in the district council elections in the state of Rhineland Westphalia, where its share of the total vote decreased from 14 to 8 per cent.

The K.P.D., far more than any other party, is led by former political exiles. Most of the members of the Berlin Central Committee spent the years of the Nazi regime in Russia. Many other officials of the party were former prisoners of war who received training in that country. Others were brought back from various European and American countries. The nominal head of the K.P.D. is the seventy-year-old Wilhelm Pieck. He is unique among German Communists in that he served on the Central Committee continuously, through all changes in the party line, since 1918. More important is Walter Ulbricht who first achieved prominence when the Communists were conducting their all-out drive against the Social Democrats and the trade unions in the years immediately before the Nazis came to power. But since the policy of the Communist party is being determined by the Russian Military Government, the composition of the German leadership is of little consequence.

SMALLER POLITICAL GROUPS

Besides the four major parties there are a number of small splinter groups in the Western zones. Whatever importance these have is purely local. For the most part they developed as a consequence of the early Military Government policy of permitting only local organizations. Many formerly independent groups have affiliated with the Liberal Democratic party and the Christian Democratic Union. Most of those still remaining are either extremely far to the right, or else separatist or highly particularist.

In Bavaria the Economic Reconstruction Association (*Wirtschaftliche Wiederaufbau-Vereinigung*) attained 137,000 votes—about 5 per cent of the total—most of which came from urban middle-class voters. This party emphasizes the protection of private property and financial claims in its program. Its leader, Alfred Loritz, became Denazification Minister in the first Bavarian coalition government. But in July, 1947 he was arrested on charges of black-marketing. Even further to the right was the Bavarian Monarchist party (*Heimat- und Koenigspartei*) whose program of an independent Bavarian monarchy drew a few right-wing supporters. The meetings of this party sometimes ended in riots, and it was eventually suppressed by the American Military Government on the ground that the re-establishment of the monarchy was contrary to Military Government policy. In summer 1947 the extreme particularists formed the Bavarian party (*Bayern-Partei*), a "states rights" party whose program can be summarized by the slogan "Bavaria for the Bavarians." In the 1948 municipal elections this party received 8.7 per cent of the total vote.

In the British Zone, several independent right-wing parties arose in the Protestant sections. Among these are the German Conservative party (*Deutschkonservative Partei*) in Schleswig-Holstein and the Republican party (*Republikanische Partei*) in Hamburg. The Lower Saxon State party (*Niedersaechsische Landespartei*) is the heir of the old Hanoverian party and advocates the separation of Hanover from Prussia and its establishment as a separate state in a federal Germany. A few extreme members of this party desire to see Hanover reunited to the British crown. In the first elections in the British Zone, the Lower Saxon State party received 20.8 per cent of the vote in the state of Hanover, a total larger than the C.D.U. which polled 19.7 per cent in this region. This party later changed its name to German party (Deutsche Partei).

In Schleswig-Holstein the South Schleswig Association (*Sued-Schleswig-Vereinigung*), which originally represented the interests of the Danish minority, was transformed into a political party and received some support from those Germans who resented the great influx of expellees into their province and who were attracted by the prosperity of Denmark.

The Rhenish People's party (*Rheinische Volkspartei*), centered in Cologne, wavers between an extreme particularism and separatism. Separatism, however, still seems as unpopular in the Rhineland as it was after the last war. Meetings of this party were frequently interrupted by shouts of "we want, not a free Rhineland, but a free Germany."

In the French Zone, Military Government has actively fostered the formation of separatist and particularist groups. In the Hessian Palatinate the Popular Social League advocates the creation of a separate state in that area as a part of a German federation. With the exception of the Saar the efforts of the French Military Government to encourage separatism in its zone appear to have been unsuccessful.

Popular sentiment, mindful of the difficulties caused by the profusion of parties under the Republic, is not favorable to the growth of splinter groups. But there exists one numerically strong group—the expellees from the East—who up to now have not been fully assimilated by the political parties. This group tends to form its own representation and to elect its own candidates, not necessarily in the state parliaments, but in the local administrations. Thus in Bavaria a separate refugee ticket received 12.3 per cent of the vote in the 1948 municipal elections. In other parts of Western Germany the expellees nominated their representatives as independent candidates. In Wuerttemberg-Baden independents received 18.2 per cent of the vote in the rural elections of December 1947; in Hesse the independents polled 28.5 per cent in rural areas. Since all major parties tried to win the expellee vote by including a fair number of refugees among their candidates, refugees elected on major party lists, together with those elected as "independents," actually formed a majority in several local administrations.

While antidemocratic and Nazi tendencies undoubtedly continue to exist in Germany, they are unable to manifest themselves in the form of parties because of Military Government policy. How significant these authoritarian and "crypto-Nazi" trends are it is impossible to say. Occasional roundups of former SS and SA officers engaged in underground activity, and acts of violence against the denazification tribunals have taken place in a number of regions, and suggest the existence of remnants of the Nazi movement. There is no evidence to indicate, however, that such a movement has a mass basis at the present time. Authoritarian groups have manifested themselves thus far only in small organizations of local significance. Nevertheless it must be assumed that such movements have a larger potential than would appear to be the case.

PARTIES IN THE NEW GOVERNMENTS

After elections had taken place in all three Western zones, the military authorities declared themselves ready to grant the political parties a greater measure of organizational independence and a greater share in government. The governments of the individual states had been installed at the beginning of the occupation by the military authorities without regard to the probable relative strength of the various parties. Thus at the end of the Schaeffer episode in Bavaria, the Social Democrat Wilhelm Hoegner was appointed Minister President although it was expected that the Christian Social

Union would be far stronger than the Social Democrats. On the other hand, in Hesse where the S.P.D. became the strongest party, the Liberal Democrat Karl Geiler was named Minister President. The situation was similar in the British Zone where in the traditionally Social Democratic Hamburg Dr. Petersen, at that time a member of the Free Democratic party and later of the Christian Democratic Union, was appointed Lord Mayor.

The gradual transformation to forms of government which were democratic at least in appearance was significantly influenced in the individual zones of Western Germany by the attitude of the occupying powers. Thus the diets chosen in June, 1946 in the American Zone were charged with the task of working out state constitutions which were submitted to popular referenda half a year later. Only then did there take place the election of regular diets on the basis of whose composition state governments were formed. The British, on the contrary, placed no value on formal constitutions. The state governments, originally installed by the military authorities of the British Zone, were repeatedly altered, and only after the diet elections of April, 1947 were the parties enabled to form governments from their own ranks. The French Military Government clung longest to the system of appointed and provisional governments and advisory state assemblies.

The consideration of constitutions for the states of the American Zone forced the parties for the first time to clarify their positions on a number of questions. The most important differences of opinion were those on socialization, relation of church and state and their roles in education, and—particularly in Bavaria—the degree of federalism and the rights which the individual states claimed for themselves. In the negotiations over the constitutions the bases for the future governmental coalitions were already being worked out. One of the basic patterns of the Weimar constitution repeated itself: the Social Democrats were able to press their demands in economic and social questions only in return for concessions in the field of education, cultural affairs, and the position of the church. The new constitutions were essentially a compromise between the concepts of the two strongest parties, the C.D.U. and the S.P.D.,

Political Party Developments 253

and clearly mirrored the relative strength of these two parties in the individual states. Thus the Hessian constitution is in every respect much the farthest left and at the same time the least federalistic. The Bavarian constitution is in many respects more conservative than that of Weimar and expresses the state particularism of Bavaria in so great a degree that General Clay thought it necessary to remind Bavaria that it is a part of Germany.

After the parliamentary regimes had been formed in the British and American zones, it developed that in the majority of states all parties were included in the government. The division of ministerial posts was in accordance with the relative strength of the individual parties. The reason for these all-party governments was most clearly formulated by the Social Democratic group in the diet of Wuerttemberg-Baden: "As long as there is no real democracy, that is, as long as the occupying powers are still the decisive factor in determining political and economic conditions, there can also be no true opposition"—also i.e., no genuine, responsible government parties. In Bavaria where the Christian Social Union had a clear majority there were such sharp internal differences that even agreement on questions of church and state did not suffice to permit a pure C.S.U. regime. The relatively progressive representatives of the Bavarian peasants' league in the C.S.U. diet group and the arch-conservative group of Hans Ehard and Alois Hundhammer were in opposition to their party chairman Joseph Mueller and formed a coalition government with the Social Democrats. After several months, however, this broke up and the various factions of the C.S.U. in Bavaria succeeded in getting together long enough to constitute a government from their own party.

In those states with Catholic majorities or strong Catholic minorities the Christian Democratic Union, like the Center party in the days of the Weimar Republic, claimed the Ministry of Education. Everywhere the Ministry of Economics went to the Social Democrats and in most states that of Agriculture to the C.D.U. The Social Democrats, for whose program the question of socialization was central, made the possession of the Economics Ministry a condition of their participation in government. But it has subsequently developed that the C.D.U.'s possession of the Ministries of Agriculture gave it positions of first importance.

The American inspired federalistic structure of Western Germany necessarily influenced the development of the parties in the direction of provincialism. Diet and cabinet members regard themselves primarily as representatives of their states, whose interests they seek to protect even when they are in conflict with the interests of Germany, or rather Western Germany as a whole. This tendency is strongest in the case of the C.D.U.-C.S.U. which has always been far more favorably inclined to a federalist structure than the traditionally centralistic Social Democrats. The conflict between the interests of the states and those of Western Germany as a whole, like the political and economic differences of the various parties, became much sharper when the United States and England created administrative organs for the two zones after their economic unification. For the first time since the collapse of Nazism, there was a chance to fight for positions of real power.

The Parties in the Eastern Occupation Zone

Although the Russian Military Government originally set up a four-party system in its zone it did not encourage competition among the parties. There was, moreover, immediately after the collapse of the Hitler regime, considerable spontaneous sentiment in favor of united action on the part of all democratic groups. This was especially true in the case of the labor parties. Hence little Russian pressure was required to secure the formation of the United Front of Anti-fascist Parties, formed in July, 1945. Within this united front, however, the parties at first preserved their own individual characteristics.

The Communist party, as previously indicated, derived its principal characteristics from its role as the preferred instrument of the Russian Military Government. Thus in Berlin the Communists received all the principal administrative positions and retained them even after the Russian Military Administration of the city was replaced by quadripartite control. The Social Democratic party in the Russian zone was somewhat different from its sister party in the West. This was partly due to the different traditions of the party organizations, but more to the presence of the Russian Military Government. In the Eastern zone, the Social Democrats tended to use more orthodox Marxian terminology and to stress the economic rather than the democratic and humanitarian aspects of socialism. Many of their leaders expressed suspicion of what they considered the capitalist and imperialist motives of the Western powers. On the other hand, they regarded Russia as a workers' state and the potential patron of a socialist revolution. However, it was not these ideological differences but the policy of the Russian Military Government which prevented the integration of the Eastern Social Democratic organization with that of the other three zones.

The Christian Democratic Union was both weaker and more radical than in the Western zones. This was partly due to the Russian preference for the labor parties, especially the Communists, and partly to the relatively small Catholic population of the zone. Nevertheless it remained a potential rallying point for those politically-minded people who did not wish to support the labor parties. As in the other zones, the Liberal Democratic party had, at the beginning, only a small number of supporters. Its surprisingly large vote in the Russian Zone is discussed below.

Immediately after the downfall of the Hitler regime there was widespread sentiment among the workers in favor of the formation of one united labor party. Many of them regarded the division in the labor movement as the principal cause of the success of fascism. In Berlin the Central Committee of the Social Democratic party several times proposed to the Communists that the two parties merge. But at that time the Communist leadership, expecting that with the backing of Russian prestige it would be able to secure dominance by itself, rejected these offers.

But the situation changed rapidly. The experience of the Red Army occupation and the Russian reparations policy destroyed Communist hopes for widespread popular support. Even though they received preference in the distribution of newsprint and radio time, and though the Russians supplied them with pamphlets by the hundreds of thousands, they rapidly lost ground. When it became clear that the K.P.D. was not going to dominate German political life in its own right, the Russian Military Government began to drop the policy that permitted free cooperation among the parties and to introduce, step by step, the pattern applied in the Eastern European countries where the key positions are in Communist hands and the various parties are dominated, not necessarily by Communists, but by conformists. Election results in Austria and Hungary in the fall of 1945 were taken as a warning of what free elections in Russian-occupied Germany might mean. The American Military Government's announcement of impending elections in its zone threatened to crystallize the political situation and weaken the position of the Communists still further. Since the results that it desired were apparently not to be achieved by laissez faire, the Russian Military Government resorted to active intervention.

The new Russian policy was demonstrated very clearly in December, 1945 when two leaders of the Christian Democratic Union, its chairman Andreas Hermes and Walter Schreiber, were removed as the culmination of a series of manoeuvres by the Russian authorities. These men had openly criticized certain features of the land reform, especially the very small size of the newly created farms and the expropriation without compensation. The Russian Military Government organized protest meetings of C.D.U. members in the provinces which passed resolutions against the Berlin leaders. The Communist press attacked the C.D.U. for supporting reaction and splitting the United Anti-fascist Front. Finally the Russian Military Government ordered the Berlin party organization to replace the two leaders in whom it no longer had confidence. The Christian Democratic newspaper was not allowed to print its own version of the conflict. Only the American licensed nonparty *Tagesspiegel* voiced some carefully worded criticisms of pressure by "other influences." Jakob Kaiser, a leading representative of the former Christian Trade Unions, and Ernst Lemmers, of the former democratic white collar union, took the place of the removed leaders.

The slogan of the "United Front of the Four Parties" was replaced in October, 1945 by agitation for "Anti-Fascist Unity of the Working Class." A campaign was launched for complete fusion of the Social Democratic and Communist parties.[14] Suddenly everywhere in the Russian Zone joint conferences of the two parties took place—often under the surveillance of Russian officers—and passed unanimous resolutions in favor of united action, common lists of candidates for elections, and of complete fusion. For weeks the Berlin Communist paper, the *Deutsche Volkszeitung*, conveyed the impression that the desire for unity of the parties was the motive behind every normal activity. Homes were repaired, and streets were cleared by the "united efforts of the anti-fascist workers' parties."

Both in Berlin and in the provincial districts the great majority of the Social Democratic rank and file objected to the Communist proposal of a merger on "the basis of equality," since this would give the Communists a much greater influence than was warranted by their popular support as indicated in the shop steward elections. They were afraid that the new party would be unable to shape its policy democratically. And finally they were hesitant to take a step that would drive a wedge between the Social Democratic organizations in the East and the West, where the Social Democratic leadership had clearly declared themselves against fusion on the grounds of the undemocratic structure of the Communist party, and, most important, its dependence on Moscow.

After several weeks of mounting pressure, the Social Democratic leadership in Berlin agreed to hold a joint conference with the Communists on December 20-21, 1945 to discuss the question of fusion. The conference was attended by the zone executives and the leaders of the organizations of both parties in the provinces, all appointed to their positions in the first weeks of the occupation and not freely elected by the rank and file. Military Government officers were present, which of course had some influence on those delegates who had to return into the Russian occupied districts.

The main resolution "For the Unity of the Working Class," advocating the merging of the parties into a single Unity party as a mutual short-term aim, was unanimously adopted. The Social Democratic members of the conference agreed only on the condition that the final decision for or against fusion be taken by a freely elected congress representing the Social Democratic organizations of all four zones. The resolution was immediately published in the press of both parties. But the Social Democratic paper was not permitted to print the reservations made by its representatives. As in the conflict within the Christian Democratic Union, only the American licensed *Tagesspiegel* criticized the conference for making decisions on party matters without consulting the membership. It was violently attacked as reactionary by the Berlin Communist paper and the Russian sponsored official paper of the city administration. A few days later, the Russian Military Government banned distribution of Western-sponsored newspapers in its zone. In the suburbs of Berlin posters appeared, signed by the chiefs of police, warning the population that anyone caught reading a banned newspaper would be punished.

On February 10, 1946, the Berlin leadership of the S.P.D. announced that a party conference for the Russian zone would be held on April 19 in order to decide on fusion with the Communists. Shortly afterwards the Communist leaders declared that the founding of the new Socialist Unity party (*Sozialistische Einheitspartei Deutschlands*) would take place on April 21, and that a draft of the program and the by-laws had already been worked out—all this weeks before the Social Democrats had been given a chance to decide whether or not the merger should take place.

The Berlin Social Democratic leadership's abandonment of the stipulation that only a nation-wide congress could decide on the merger meant yielding to the Communist demands. This turnabout was due to the tremendous pressure on the Social Democratic organizations in the Russian Zone.

In the first weeks of 1946, "joint unity conferences" were called by provincial Communist organizations. Since the membership lists of the S.P.D. organizations were in the hands of the Russian authorities and since the conferences took place under the supervision of Russian officers the Social Democrats had no alternative but to vote unanimously for the immediate merger. Before these conferences were called it had been shown what would be the fate of dissenters. Social Democratic officials who were known opponents of the merger suddenly disappeared, arrested by the Russian secret police. The concentration camps of Buchenwald and Sachsenhausen were reopened and many of their new inmates were dissident Social Democrats, some of whom had already become acquainted with them under the Hitler regime. Furthermore, jobs and ration cards often were dependent on one's attitude toward the merger.

Successful resistance to this combination of terrorism and bribery was impossible in the Russian Zone. But in Berlin the Western Allies shared control with the Russians, and although they gave little active support to the opponents of the merger, the latter did not feel themselves as completely at the mercy of the Communists as they did in the zone. A rank and file revolt broke out in the Social Democratic party, and at a conference of 2,000 functionaries on March 1 a motion for a plebiscite on the question of fusion was adopted by a two-thirds majority. This plebiscite was held on March 31 in the American, British, and French sectors, but the Russians refused to permit it in theirs. Of the 33,000 members in the sectors of the three Western Allies, 22,466 went to the polls and 19,529 of them voted against the merger. The Central Committee of the Social Democratic party ignored the plebiscite and proceeded to consummate the merger. The dissident members constituted themselves as an independent Social Democratic party, which eventually was recognized by the Allied Control Council and integrated in the Social Democratic organization of the Western zones.

The new Socialist Unity party, headed by the Communist leader Wilhelm Pieck and the former Social Democratic leader Otto Grotewohl, was set up on April 21, 1946, and immediately claimed more than one million members in the Russian Zone. From that date on the Social Democratic party was outlawed in the entire zone.

Simultaneously the Communist party carried on a vigorous campaign for the formation of a Unity party in the Western zones. But little support appeared in the ranks of the Social Democrats, nor did the S.E.D. succeed in convincing the military governments of the Western zones that it was democratic in origin and principles.[15]

The program of the S.E.D. placed primary stress on the economic aspects of socialism and the national interests of Germany, while somewhat less emphatically endorsing democracy. In its first Appeal the Socialist Unity party declared, "Our watchword is: no one-party system, but an end to the division of the labor movement. The future belongs to the Socialist Unity Party of Germany. Next to this million-strong party of socialism there can never at any time be any room in Germany for splinter groups."

In practice the S.E.D. has developed its organization on a near totalitarian pattern. Thus, whereas it was originally set up with an exactly even division of posts between former members of the Social Democratic and Communist parties, this apparent equality soon disappeared. Communists took over most of the key positions in the administration and mass organizations of every sort. The S.E.D. dominated the press in the Russian Zone and no dissenting opinions appeared in print. In the summer of 1946 it seemed that the Russian Zone was well on the way to one-party rule, or rather to the modern system of pseudo-democracy as practiced in Eastern and Southeastern Europe, where one party is in power and a few others are allowed to lead a shadow existence. The Socialist Unity party was well entrenched in the state as well as in economic and cultural life. The Christian Democratic Union and the Liberal Democratic party were permitted a degree of activity sufficient to maintain the appearance of a multi-party system.

The Russian sponsored S.E.D. propaganda brought to the German workers messages for which they were well prepared. It denounced the Western powers as apostles of capitalism, seeking to restore that system in Germany for their own benefit and with the aid of reactionary elements in Germany itself. Certain reforms were introduced in the Russian Zone and credited to the efforts of the S.E.D. However severe the restrictions which the Russians enforced in the course of collecting reparations, they consistently held out to the Germans the bait of friendly words and encouraged them to look forward to rebirth as a nation. They permitted the S.E.D. to make itself the vehicle for the expression of German national feeling. And finally, the loyalty of many workers in the

Eastern zone to their old political movement has in at least some degree been carried over to the S.E.D. For all these reasons a victory for the Socialist Unity party seemed assured when elections were announced.

But it was exactly in the traditional strongholds of the labor movement that the Socialist Unity party failed to achieve support greater than that of the combined totals of the Christian Democratic Union and Liberal Democratic party. The day after the first elections in the Russian Zone—those for the municipal and rural councils in September, 1946—the S.E.D. press celebrated "the great victory among our peasants." If one remembered the traditional cleavage between the German labor movement and the farmers, these eulogies to the "anti-fascist democratic spirit of our peasants" seemed surprising. But they were justified by election statistics. In all the rural areas the S.E.D. had won an absolute majority. In many big cities, however, the "bourgeois" parties polled the majority of the votes. This strange result is explained in part by the fact that people in the rural areas had in many cases no opportunity to vote for any other party than the S.E.D. because the C.D.U. and L.D.P. were not permitted to nominate candidates in places where they had no registered local party organizations with leaders confirmed by the Russian authorities.

The non-S.E.D. vote was split between the C.D.U. and the L.D.P. and the latter group, the more conservative of the two, came out the second strongest party. The C.D.U. received 19.8 per cent and the L.D.P. 21.2 per cent of the vote, much more than it polled in the Western zones. In fact, the heavy L.D.P. vote was the big surprise of the elections in the Russian Zone. This party was particularly strong in many of those cities which before 1933 had a large Social Democratic vote. The fact that many dissatisfied Social Democrats who were prevented from voting for their own party chose the L.D.P. and not the C.D.U. may partly be explained by the traditional distrust of the anticlerical German labor movement against any group calling itself "Christian." Undoubtedly many voted for the L.D.P., who might otherwise have voted for the Socialists, as a protest against Russian pressure.

In the final results for the first elections in the entire Russian Zone the S.E.D. achieved a majority of 57.1 per cent of the total vote in its own name and 59.9 per cent together with a number of affiliated organizations, such as the Women's League, Association for Mutual Farmers' Help, and Cultural League, which entered the elections in close alliance with the S.E.D.

The second elections, those for the state and provincial diets on October 20, 1946, showed on the whole the same trend, but the results were less favorable for the S.E.D. It received 47.7 per cent of the total vote; the Liberal Democratic party and the Christian Democratic Union polled 24.7 and 24.3 per cent. That is, their combined vote slightly exceeded that of the S.E.D. The remaining 3.3 per cent went to the above mentioned S.E.D. affiliated groups. Only together with them was the S.E.D. able to capture a bare 51 per cent majority.

Again it was the big cities which had the greatest number of non-socialist (or bourgeois) votes. The S.E.D. was strongest in the agricultural province of Mecklenburg-Vorpommern, the most conservative part of the Russian Zone. There it received, together with its affiliates, 53.4 per cent of the vote. The province of Saxony which comprises the middle German industrial area around Magdeburg, Dessau, and Halle—next to the Ruhr the most industrialized part of Germany—had the lowest vote for the S.E.D. and its allies, 48.2 per cent. All the more important cities of the Russian Zone, which under the Republic were famous as "red cities" because the two labor parties had more than 50 per cent of the vote, gave the S.E.D. smaller totals than the two labor parties had received in the pre-Nazi period. Leipzig and Magdeburg had "red majorities" even in the last free elections of 1932 when the Nazis polled one third of the total vote. Under Russian occupation they had lost this majority, a development which must have been a serious setback to Russian expectations.

In the industrial cities of the Western zones the combined vote of the two labor parties was greater in the 1946 elections than in most elections under the Republic. Only in the Russian Zone, where the united labor movement was officially hailed as a guarantee of a socialist majority, did labor lose votes in some of its traditional strongholds.

If further proof was needed that this paradoxical outcome was due to the fact that the Social Democrats had been outlawed in the Russian Zone, it was given by the elections for the city government of Berlin on October 20, 1946. There the Social Democrats had succeeded in maintaining their independence and they swept the city to an extent which surpassed all predictions, receiving 48.6 per cent of the total vote. The Christian Democrats came second with 22.2 per cent, while the Socialist Unity party received 19.8 per cent and the Liberal Democratic party 9.4 per cent. In the 1932 elections, the Social Democrats and the Communists polled in Berlin almost the same number of votes, 27.4 per cent each. In 1946 the Social Democrats received more than twice as many votes as the S.E.D. It came out as the strongest party in all twenty districts of Berlin, including the eight in the Russian sector.

The Berlin Social Democrats were nevertheless able to make only limited use of their electoral victory. Since the city of Berlin was subject to the control of a four-power Kommandatura in which decisions could only be made on a unanimous basis the Russian representatives were able to obstruct the taking over of the administration by the strongest party. In particular, they refused to permit the installation of the Social Democratic candidate for mayor, Ernst Reuter, because in the year 1922 he had left the Communist party in protest against its adventurist tactics in that period and was hence regarded as anti-soviet. Thus the people in Berlin and the Eastern zone were shown clearly how little power the political parties really possessed and how little they were able to influence even the details of decisions.

Half a year after its defeat in the Berlin city elections the Socialist Unity party secured an important victory in the elections for the Berlin trade union congress. To be sure, it elected less than half of the district delegates, but it got an overwhelming majority of the seats in the congress itself. Out of 436 seats, the S.E.D. won 361 as against 73 for the Social Democrats and two for the Christian Democrats. This electoral victory resulted partly from the strength of the S.E.D. machine in the trade unions and the extraordinarily complicated and confusing electoral system, but partly it was beyond doubt a consequence of the disappointment of many workers over the inability of the Social Democratic party to translate its victory in the city elections into practical results. One year later, when the struggle for Berlin entered a decisive stage, the non-Communist wing of the Berlin unions, organized as the Independent Trade Union Opposition (*Unabhaengige Gewerkschafts-Opposition*), was overwhelmingly victorious in the trade union elections in the Western-occupied sectors of the city. When the Communist administration of the unions sought to hold control nevertheless, an open split resulted.[16]

In the Russian Zone itself the election results were of little practical significance. For the sake of appearances the C.D.U. and the L.P.D. received some administrative posts in state governments completely controlled by the S.E.D. machine. But at the same time the possibilities of action and propaganda open to L.D.P. and C.D.U. were even more closely restricted. Above all, the paper allotments of their newspapers were constantly reduced. Moreover, the importation of non-Communist newspapers from Western Germany and Berlin was forbidden. Under these circumstances the L.D.P. and C.D.U. could possess no real vitality. But the repression of these parties did not increase the popularity of the S.E.D. It was regarded by a majority of the population more and more as a mere tool of the Russian occupation authorities. Compulsory participation in its demonstrations and congresses was only too reminiscent of the recently departed totalitarian regime. S.E.D. functionaries who had entered the united party of labor out of conviction were no less in danger of arbitrary penalization for their opinions than were members of the other two parties. The flight to the Western zones of such prominent functionaries as the former Thuringian Premier Rudolf Paul and the famous author Theodor Plivier did little to enhance the prestige of the S.E.D. But neither these events nor the widespread bitterness against the abduction of skilled workers and technicians to Russia could shake the control of the S.E.D. over the administration, the trade unions, and other mass organizations.

The Russian Military Government, however, ran into significant difficulties when during the London Conference it attempted to carry out a demonstration for German unity under the leadership of the S.E.D., and to achieve this purpose required the participation of the other parties permitted in the Eastern zone. As was to be expected from its previous behaviour, the Liberal Democratic party under the leadership of Wilhelm Kuelz made no difficulties about fullfilling the desires of the Russians. But Jakob Kaiser, chairman of the Christian Democratic Union, refused to participate in a congress which he felt would not genuinely represent the German people. Kaiser who had played a prominent role in the Christian trade unions under the Weimar Republic had participated in the 20th of July movement. As a result of the first conflict between the C.D.U. and the Russian authorities he was designated party chairman. Nevertheless, he had not only succeeded in preserving his independence, but had acquired in all four zones a reputation as the leader of the progressive forces in the C.D.U. (Like Schumacher, Kaiser was invited to the United States by the American Federation of Labor in the fall of 1947, but Russian dislike of the idea kept him from making this trip.) In Western Germany, Kaiser could probably have become the rallying point for opponents within the C.D.U. of the conservative leadership of Konrad Adenauer. He chose, rather, to remain in the Eastern zone in order to preserve by his personal influence a certain measure of independence for the C.D.U. in that region. But after his refusal to participate in the Unity Congress he was informed by the Russian military authorities that he and his deputy Ernst Lemmer no longer enjoyed the confidence of their party. The Russians held to this view despite the fact that the Central Committee for the entire Eastern zone reiterated its confidence in Kaiser and Lemmer. Kaiser still refused to leave Berlin and declared himself "chairman-in-exile" for the Russian Zone. In his place the Russian authorities appointed a committee headed by Georg Dertinger. The latter had formerly been a member of the right wing of the Center party and was reputed to be a close friend of Franz von Papen. The removal of Kaiser was a clear demonstration to the supporters of the C.D.U., and of course also of the L.D.P., in the Eastern zone that in the future there would be no tolerance for any form of political independence.

When it became clear that the S.E.D. was losing whatever popularity it had originally had, the Russians suddenly established two new parties. In June, 1948 the National Democratic party (*National-Demokratische Partei*) and the Democratic Peasants' party (*Demokratische Bauern-Partei*) were licensed in the Soviet Zone. A few months earlier, a new paper, the *Nationalzeitung*, had made its appearance in Berlin. It "spontaneously" published a number of letters from former Nazis and officers who expressed their wish for a political organization that would enable them to participate in the democratic reconstruction of Germany and in the fight for national unity. Their wish was promptly granted. Up to now very little has become known of the activities and the personnel of these new parties. Some former members of the Moscow Free Germany Committee (*National-Kommittee Freies Deutschland*) are among the sponsors of the National Democratic party. It seems that the Russians have built up skeleton parties for the "Democratic Bloc," to be pulled out of the closet when need arises.

PARTIES IN DIVIDED GERMANY

The sharpening conflict between the Soviet Union and the Western powers was, of course, reflected in Germany. Political developments in the Eastern and Western zones diverged sharply. This divergence made itself felt both in terms of governmental forms and in the programs of the parties themselves.

The Soviet Union and the Communists continuously stressed the goal of German unity, while rendering it in practice impossible, and in reality establishing a totalitarian regime in the East. The Western powers and the parties in their zones were confronted with the problem of creating a viable regime for Western Germany without at the same time taking the responsibility for making the split final. Their dilemma was rendered even more difficult by the fact that any attempt to integrate the three Western zones emphasized the division between them and the East.

At first both the occupying powers and the parties sought to evade this problem through half-measures and subterfuges. Thus the British and American authorities created an economic, but not political, joint administration for their zones. Unfortunately the boundary between economics and politics in the twentieth century is one that scarcely exists in theory and not at all in practice. Hence while the Bizonal Economic Administration was specifically declared not to be a government and to have no political functions, all its activities were inextricably involved with questions of political doctrine.

From the beginning, the Communists refused to recognize the legitimacy of the bizonal setup, charging that it was a step towards the partition of Germany. The other parties, feeling themselves justified in their course by the Allied assertion that the formation of the Bizonal Administration had no political implications, participated in it actively.

The Bizonal Administration consisted of a bicameral legislature and an executive committee. The lower and more important house of the legislature, the *Wirtschaftsrat* (Economic Council), was chosen by proportional representation from the legislatures of the various states according to population. In the upper house, the *Laenderrat* (Council of States), each state in the combined zones had two representatives. Members of the Executive Committee were elected by the *Wirtschaftsrat*, subject to the approval of the *Laenderrat* and of Military Government. They headed the various departments of the Bizonal Economic Administration and formed a quasi-government. There was, however, no single chief executive to coordinate the policies of the various departments.

The Social Democratic party and the Christian Democratic Union in particular, as the two largest parties, contested for influence over the Bizonal Administration. At first they formed a coalition, similar to those which exist in the various states. But this soon broke up, partly as a result of the unwillingness of the C.D.U. to concede the S.P.D. the positions which the latter felt it was entitled to and partly because of an unwillingness on both sides to compromise on questions of economic principle. This was in part due to a tendency on the part of the C.D.U. to move to the right as it gained in self-confidence. In this it was encouraged by the belief that its doctrines were more acceptable to the United States than those of the Social Democratic party. And by this time the United States was clearly dominant in the affairs of Bizonia, both because it was already paying the major portion of the deficit and because the Marshall Plan presaged an increasingly decisive American role in European affairs.

As a result, the C.D.U.—which together with the other non-labor parties had a majority in the *Wirtschaftsrat*—became the "government" party, while the S.P.D. went into the "opposition." The situation was rendered somewhat complicated by the existence of a Social Democratic majority in the *Laenderrat* and the continued coalition in most of the states, so that the "government" could do nothing without the consent of the "opposition." Somewhat paradoxically also, the "federalist" C.D.U. now controlled the central administration, while the "centralist" S.P.D. was more influential in the state governments.

Even before the London Conference of Foreign Ministers, the inadequacy of the Bizonal Economic Administration was clear to both the Germans and the Western powers. But it was still possible to regard it as something provisional and to hope that some form of all-German unity would emerge from that conference. If the Western powers and the democratic parties clung to this hope, the Soviet Union and the Communists encouraged and played on it.

For months before the conference there were inspired rumors in the Eastern zone that the Russians would propose democratic elections for a German central government and the evacuation of Germany by all four powers. In November the Socialist Unity party took the initiative in calling a meeting in Berlin to set up a People's Congress to speak on behalf of Germany before the London Conference of Foreign Ministers. The Social Democratic party refused to have anything to do with this congress; so did the Western C.D.U. and Jakob Kaiser, chairman of that party in Berlin and the Soviet Zone. The Communist character of the "united front" soon became obvious. During and after the London Conference the Russians and the People's Congress continued to wage an active propaganda campaign, designed to place the blame for a divided Germany on the Western powers. The People's Congress was turned into a permanent organization; representatives, almost entirely Communist, were included from the Western zones and it was indicated that this Congress was intended to be the nucleus for a German national government. Besides its general purpose of furthering Communist agitation, this move seems to have been motivated by a desire to make more difficult any effort to incorporate Germany in the Marshall Plan. The Communists also hoped that, since the seat of the People's Congress was in the traditional capital, Berlin, any attempt at unification in the West would appear to Germans as the creation of a dual or splinter government. To reinforce the effect of this propaganda, the Congress announced plans for the holding of a plebiscite on the question of whether the German people wanted their country united. (Such a plebiscite had been part of the S.E.D. program for some time.)

With the breakdown of the London Conference it became clear that no unification of all four zones would occur in the near future. At the same time, both the desperate economic situation of Germany and the necessity of organizing Western Europe in terms of the Marshall Plan made it impossible to continue indefinitely with makeshifts in the Western zones. Hence Britain and the United States agreed to expand the Bizonal Economic Administration and to enlarge its powers. The post of the bizonal chief executive was established, and the membership of the *Wirtschaftsrat* was doubled. Since the method of election was not changed, however, its political composition remained the same. Of 104 members the C.D.U.-C.S.U. and the S.P.D. each had forty, the Liberal Democratic party (or Free Democratic or German People's party) eight, the Communists six, the Center and the German parties (successor to the Lower Saxonian Party) each four, and the Bavarian Reconstruction party two. In the *Laenderrat* there were nine Social Democrats, five Christian Democrats, and one member each of the L.D.P. and the Bremen Popular Democrats.

Although the Bizonal Administration looked more like a government than ever, the Allies continued to emphasize that it was not.

At the same time they took on themselves complete responsibility for its establishment, although they had consulted German leaders and modified their original plans somewhat in accordance with German suggestions. These Allied declarations were necessary because of the unwillingness of the major German parties to accept any responsibility for anything which could be regarded as a step towards the division of Germany. Even as it was, the attitude of the parties toward the reorganized bizonal administration was distinctly reserved. Both the S.P.D. and C.D.U. emphasized that it had been established by the Allies rather than by the Germans. Partly because of this attitude and partly because in any case it could not have obtained the support of a majority in the *Wirtschaftsrat*, the S.P.D. refused to take any part in the Bizonal Executive Committee and nominated no candidates for it. It also criticized the bizonal setup on the ground that it was still too federalistic as well as because it failed to include Berlin. And it objected to the fact that members of the Executive Committee could not be removed by vote of lack of confidence in the *Wirtschaftsrat*, but only by Military Government. However, the Social Democrats announced that they would do nothing to obstruct the functioning of the new administration. Although many C.D.U. leaders, particularly in Bavaria, denounced the reorganized bizonal administration as too centralistic, the C.D.U. agreed to take the responsibility of operating it. The Communists for their part opposed the whole existence of Bizonia on the ground that it was an illegitimate division of Germany. As a result, the Chief Executive and all the members of the Executive Committee were elected with almost exclusively C.D.U. support.

It is interesting to note that despite the theoretically nonpolitical character of Bizonia's functions the members of all parties consistently voted as solid blocks and to a large extent under the direction of party headquarters. Although in the state legislatures the C.D.U. in particular is somewhat less united, it is clear that the more or less amorphous parties of the early postwar period have given place to highly centralized organizations.

Both the S.P.D. and C.D.U., especially the former, have urged the Allies to promulgate an "occupation statute" which would clearly define the boundaries between the powers of Military Government and those of German institutions. They have pointed out that at present there can be no real democracy in Western Germany because all German organs of self-government can act only with the approval of Military Government and indeed depend on its will for their very existence.

The parties in the West were faced with a humiliating dilemma. If they advanced proposals for a West German government they were exposing themselves to the charge of being responsible for the division of Germany. If they cooperated unreservedly in working administrative machinery devised and installed by Military Government without their participation, they could be accused of being Quislings. But if they merely abstained from doing anything, they could have no influence on the course of events. At best, the decision would have been an extremely difficult one. Under the circumstances, the parties attempted to compromise by combining the three courses in varying degrees. They disclaimed responsibility for the form and even the existence of the bizonal administration. They emphasized that Germany had been divided not by their will but by the failure of the Allies to agree among themselves. The Christian Democrats agreed to operate the administration; the Social Democrats assumed the role of loyal opposition. Both left the next step to the Allies, who in turn were just as eager to pass the responsibility right back to the Germans.

Meanwhile, however, events were forcing the issue. On the one hand, the inclusion of Western Germany in the Marshall Plan made it necessary to think in longer-range terms than were consistent with the purely provisional organization of the Western zones. On the other, the Russians were bringing ever increasing pressure for the incorporation of Berlin into their zone, in which at the same time they were completing the skeleton of a totalitarian German state. The Berlin parties, for their part, reacted to this by emphasizing the differentiation between Berlin and the Russian Zone. In the case of both the C.D.U. and the L.D.P., the Berlin organizations had been from the beginning sections of those in the Eastern zone.

But when the Russians refused to recognize Jakob Kaiser's leadership in the C.D.U. of their zone, the Berlin C.D.U. declared its independence and continued to follow Kaiser. A similar development took place, for slightly different reasons in the L.D.P. Here, the zonal chairman Wilhelm Kuelz had maintained good relations with the Soviet Military Government and had participated in the setting up of the People's Congress. But the rank and file of his party in Berlin had no taste for these maneuvers and split off from the zonal organization in protest. The three Berlin non-Communist parties allied themselves in a "Freedom Front" and on March 18, the centennial anniversary of the revolution of 1848, held a tremendous joint demonstration. This was the first demonstration of its kind since the end of the war and was indeed something quite unusual in German political history. But the independence of the parties in Berlin was, of course, only possible as long as the occupation of that city was conducted in part by the Western Allies. Against this the Russians had long waged a war of nerves, charging that the creation of Bizonia involved the abandonment of the principle of four-power control and deprived the Western powers of any right to stay in Berlin. In April, 1948, Russian interference with Western military supply trains to Berlin, together with the breaking up of the Allied Control Council and the termination of quadripartite rule in Germany, convinced the Western Allies, and especially the United States, that there was no longer any reason to delay the establishment of a West German state.

In June, 1948, the London Conference of the six Western powers (United States, Great Britain, France, and the Benelux countries) published its recommendations for the reorganization of Western Germany. These recommendations included the proposal for a Constituent Assembly to prepare a constitution to which all German states could subscribe as soon as circumstances permit. This meant, under the circumstances, a constitution for the three Western zones of occupation.

Meanwhile negotiations for the long overdue all-German currency reform had broken down. Hence the day after the six-power proposals had been approved by the Western Allies (despite strong opposition in the French National Assembly) the Military Governments of the three Western powers introduced a currency reform in their zones. This reform supplied a basis for the restoration of normal economic life, and was to become a milestone in the recovery of Western Germany. But at the same time it marked a complete economic break with the Soviet Zone. The Russians answered the Western currency reform by blockading Berlin and threatening the people of the Western sectors with starvation. For a short time the position of the Western Allies in Berlin seemed untenable.

It was in this critical situation that the Military Governors issued three basic documents on the political reorganization of Western Germany to the Minister Presidents of the Western German states and asked them for an immediate decision on these proposals. The first document repeated the agreement on West German constitutional development reached by the six-power Conference. A Constituent Assembly, popularly elected or chosen by the state parliaments, was to meet by September in order to draw up a constitution for Western Germany. This constitution was to be democratic and federal, was to define and protect the rights and freedoms of the citizens, and was to provide an adequate central authority. The second document requested the Germans to work out modifications of the existing state boundaries in such a way as to reduce the existing disparities of population. The third document created the basis for an Occupation Statute by defining the powers which the occupying nations reserved to themselves. These included control of the Ruhr, in accordance with principles already laid down by the London Conference, as well as the determination of questions relating to reparations, the level of industry, demilitarization, the conduct of Germany's foreign relations and to some extent of German foreign trade.

Western German political leaders at first received these proposals very reluctantly, if not with actual hostility. They feared that acceptance would throw upon them the responsibility for the final splitting of Germany and give the Communists an effective weapon for their propaganda. They also feared that the Western Allies might give up Berlin and eventually all of Germany to the Russians.

The nominal responsibility for deciding on the Allied proposals rested on the eleven Minister Presidents of the Western German states. Of these, five were Christian Democrats, five Social Democrats, and one a Liberal Democrat. Actually, the decision was made by the political parties. The Social Democrats had originally been very hostile to the six-power proposals on the ground that they would finally foreclose the possibility of a united Germany and give the Communists a pretext for creating a government in Berlin or Leipzig. Instead of a constitution, they wanted an administrative statute establishing a temporary government. They declared that a constitution presupposes sovereignty, which no West German state, answerable to the occupation authorities, could have. The Christian Democratic Union was less reluctant but tried to play for time. It came out strongly against popular election of the Constituent Assembly. As the "government" party in the bizonal set-up it feared that discontent with economic conditions would result in a shift of votes from it to the Social Democrats. It wanted to wait for the currency reform to take effect, and even after the reform it preferred to have the state parliaments choose the delegates for the Constituent Assembly. The S.P.D. was strongly opposed to this repetition of the Economic Council set-up, but it did not press for popular elections because it felt that this would give the Assembly too much weight.

The Conference of the Prime Ministers to consider the Allied plan agreed to the proposal of the Social Democrats not to call the Assembly a Constituent Assembly and to that of the Christian Democrats not to hold popular elections. In the preamble to their counter-proposals, the Minister Presidents declared: "Full responsibility for the Occupation Statute and for the division of Germany into two spheres rests with the Allied powers." Nevertheless, they no longer objected in principle; they were critical only in details. Whatever reluctance the Germans might still show, the French were even more anxious to delay the establishment of a West German state. They interpreted the German proposals for changes in the three basic documents as refusals and for some time did not permit the Minister Presidents of their zone to attend further conferences. But the French objections were overcome and in a new conference with the Military Governors on July 26, 1948, the eleven Minister Presidents formally accepted the responsibility of initiating a central government for a West German state. The firm attitude of the Western powers in Berlin had made a deep impression in Western Germany, while the reaction of the German people to the blockade had made successful Communist maneuvers in the West improbable. The long-existing conflict between the former Allies seemed to have become irreconcilable, so that it was scarcely possible even to hope any longer for a united Germany. Hence there was no longer anything to be lost by an independent and positive policy for Western Germany. All non-Communist parties had come to accept the reorganization of the Western zones of occupation as preferable to the existing provisional set-up. The Communists—who by this time were no longer included in any of the state governments of Western Gemany—declared that the Assembly was illegal, but nevertheless took part in it.

On September 1, the date suggested by the Western powers, the Assembly met in Bonn as a "Parliamentary Council" to work out a "Basic Law" for Western Germany. The sixty-five delegates had been chosen by the state parliaments on a basis of proportional representation. The C.D.U./C.S.U. and the S.P.D. had twenty-seven delegates each, the L.D.P./F.D.P. five, and the Deutsche Partei, Zentrum, and K.P.D. two each. Five Berlin representatives, three of the S.P.D. and one each of the C.D.U. and the L.D.P., participated with a voice but no vote. The presence of the Berlin delegates was important because it emphasized that the people of Berlin and the Eastern zone—far from regarding the members of the Parliamentary Council as Quislings and splitters of Germany— were looking forward to the creation of a viable state and a strong government in the West which could become the nucleus of a future all-German republic.

The Western political parties, of course, carried over their differences into the Parliamentary Council, but from the very beginning they showed a greater willingness to compromise than was usual in German political life. There was a tacit agreement that, as far as possible, controversial issues would be kept out of the Basic Law. On one important problem, the degree of federalism, a compromise had to be found between the attitudes of the C.D.U. and S.P.D. But basic economic decisions, such as the degree of socialization, and cultural and religious questions, such as the relation of state and church and the role of the church in schools, were to be omitted from the Basic Law, lest it prove inacceptable to one of the major parties.

But postponement has not removed these differences, and the fight between the main parties already going on in the West German states and the Bizonal Council indicated clearly the main lines of division. Since the currency reform, the economic conflicts between the C.D.U. and the S.P.D. have become even sharper. Immediately following the reform, the C.D.U.-controlled Bizonal Administration, over the opposition of the S.P.D., removed almost all commodities except basic foodstuffs and raw materials from price control and rationing. The effect of this return to a free economy was a sharp rise in prices, while wages remained stationary. Against the wishes of the S.P.D., Military Government had introduced the currency reform before the main parties had agreed upon the so-called *Lastenausgleich* (equalization of burdens), generally regarded as a necessary component of an equitable reorganization of the economy. Again, the question of private or public ownership of basic industries, which has up to now been impossible to settle (partly because of the attitude of the occupation authorities), will continue to be one of the basic problems of the new West German state and one of the most difficult issues for the C.D.U. to face without risking a shift of its labor vote to the S.P.D.

At the same time that West German political leaders were taking the first steps toward the establishment of a central government, the Communist-dominated People's Council of the Soviet Zone approved a draft constitution for a centralized all-German "People's Republic." The creation of an all-German government under Russian auspices seemed imminent. But it did not materialize. Apparently the Russians first delayed its proclamation because of the four-power negotiations in Moscow, Berlin, and Paris which, they hoped, would lead either to an agreement on their terms or to the withdrawal of the Western powers from Berlin. In the former case, they would probably have dropped their plan for a German government; in the latter, they would have been able to proclaim it in the traditional German capital. But when the American and British airlift defeated the Soviet effort to conquer Berlin by starvation, the blockade became a boomerang for the Russians. Anti-Soviet feeling in Berlin grew so strong that it was no longer feasible to proclaim a Russian-sponsored government in that city. The division between Eastern and Western sectors had become almost complete, and one could scarcely declare two-fifths of Berlin the capital of the united Germany.

Russian propaganda for an all-German government had long been coupled with the proposal that the occupation of all powers withdraw from Germany. The Soviet Military Government had hoped to establish a dependable "friendly" government which would make an overt Russian occupation superfluous. Now it became clear that the Socialist Unity party no longer had sufficient popular support to make it an adequate instrument of Russian policy by itself. It had not even dared to attempt a general strike against the introduction of West German currency in Berlin. In the Soviet Zone it had lost so much prestige that the Russian Military Government found it necessary to postpone indefinitely the elections due in the fall of 1948. But in Berlin the majority of the City Assembly, with the backing of the Western powers, insisted on new elections in accordance with the City Constitution. In the hope of preventing the scheduled elections, the Russians resorted to a violent propaganda campaign culminating in the slogan that to participate in the elections was to support fascism and war, as well as to threats of reprisals, the splitting of all branches of the city administration, the disruption of city-wide services, and finally the establishment of a separate City Council for the Eastern sector. But they failed to intimidate the population. On December 5, the elections took place in Western Berlin. Although every man who voted was exposing himself to possible reprisals, only about 3 per cent fewer voters went to the polls than in 1946, when the Socialist Unity party, which now boycotted the elections, had participated. The Social Democrats received 64.5 per cent of the vote, the Christian Democratic Union 19.4, and the Liberal Democratic party 16.1 per cent. As compared to the 1946 election results for Western Berlin, the C.D.U. lost rather heavily to the L.D.P., while the S.P.D. received about two thirds of the votes which two years ago had been cast for the Socialist Unity party. If one attributes the entire decrease in the percentage who voted to S.E.D. supporters and adds those who intentionally spoiled their ballots, total Communist strength in Western Berlin can be estimated at about 4 per cent as compared to over 13 per cent in 1946. Even though no elections were permitted in the Soviet sector, there was ample evidence that the political sentiment of its population was similar to that in the Western sectors. The Russian blockade of Berlin had effectively kept Communist influence out of the minds of the people of the traditionally "red" city.

Three years after the fall of the Nazi Reich, the German political parties are emerging from a shadow existence into reality. Organizationally they are well established. They have the resigned and hardly enthusiastic loyalty of a great part of the German population. But until the summer of 1948 all German activities in the field of "higher politics"—be it the drafting of constitutions for the various states, the formation of coalition governments, or the making of decisions on the degree of socialization—were confined to matters of secondary importance. All political life was overshadowed by the fact that German economic and political unification was made impossible by the increasing tension among the occupying powers. On this vital question the German parties had no power of decision. Under these circumstances it was not surprising that they were slow to show initiative or to develop a strong sense of responsibility.

As long as the occupying powers presented even a semblance of a joint policy towards the defeated Reich, the German parties were relegated to a relatively unimportant role and their programs remained pious wishes or abstract declamations. When increasing tension between the former Allies made Germany one of the most important political battlefields both sides began to grant the German political organizations a greater measure of responsibility—varying, to be sure, according to their concepts of what constituted political responsibility. In the West, the parties were called upon to exercise a higher degree of genuine self-government, although still under the supervision of the occupation authorities. In the East, Soviet Military Government tried to transform the Socialist Unity party into the ruling state party of a "People's Democracy." In the course of this process, the political parties—except the Communists—ceased to be all-German organizations. They had to adapt themselves to the existence of two basically different Germanies. Parties of the Eastern and the Western zones, even if they still preserved the same names, had come to represent very different policies. The four-party system, as originally set up by the Russians in Berlin, had, with some variations, become well established in the Western zones. In the Soviet Zone it had lasted less than one year. The forced merger of S.P.D. and K.P.D. in the East, which was to create one united German labor party, did have that effect—but in an unintended way. For in free elections the S.P.D. developed more and more into *the* German labor party.

The struggle between the concepts of laissez-faire capitalism, democratic socialism, and totalitarian communism, as represented by the most important German parties, has resulted in an overwhelming victory for the Western-oriented parties, indisputable in the Western zones and in Berlin, but clearly discernible even in the Russian zone. General disappointment at the failure of the Allies to devise an adequate answer to the problems of Germany's future has undoubtedly led to disillusionment with democracy and a resurgence of nationalist sentiment. But the often voiced opinion that a new German nationalism would inevitably strengthen the Soviet position has, at least up to now, not proved to be correct. Communism has been rejected wherever the Germans have had an opportunity to express their political opinions freely. But this, of course, has not prevented the establishment of a near-totalitarian dictatorship in Eastern Germany.

In Western Germany, the issue between a new form of democratic socialism and a system based, as far as conditions in Germany permit, on private property and free enterprise remains to be fought out. With the establishment of a West German state, the political parties of two-thirds of Germany will for the first time since the breakdown of the Weimar Republic be able to present the German people with genuine alternative policies. It remains to be seen whether they will be able to evolve an adequate program for the solution of the difficult problems which face Western Germany today—and whether if they do, international developments will permit them to put it into effect.

Chap. 7 The Problem of Reorientation

CLARA MENCK

THE GREAT POWERS AT POTSDAM agreed on the necessity of denazifying and democratizing Germany, but there was only a limited common understanding of what these goals implied. There was agreement on the more obvious and negative aspects of the problem. The first proclamations of the occupation authorities abrogated the various Nazi laws and dissolved the Nazi organizations. The surviving top Nazis were tried at Nuremberg under a four-power charter. The general principles of denazification were agreed upon; but in the administration of these principles each power went its own way.

For the positive side of the program—democratization—the years which have elapsed since the occupation have seen a great deal of formal progress. The machinery for a working democracy—electoral systems, constitutions, parliaments, political parties, and trade unions—has been established. In spite of all of this activity there is a distinct feeling of disappointment on both sides. Disappointed German anti-Nazis, Military Government officials, and journalists frequently observe that the spirit of Nazism still lives on or has been revived in Germany.[1] Actually there are relatively few convinced Nazis left in Germany. At the same time it is true that democracy has failed thus far to become a desirable and common aim, and a dangerous spiritual vacuum exists which is apt to foster new forms of nationalism and totalitarianism.

Many factors have contributed to this situation. The essential difficulty of the problem has been gravely enhanced by the deterioration in relations between Russia and the Western powers which has diverted attention away from social and political reconstruction. The economic crisis, the expulsion of millions of Germans from the Eastern territories, and the consequent social disorganization and demoralization have also seriously hampered the democratization effort.

Before examining the reasons for these disappointing results and describing the efforts thus far made in the program of democratization, it is necessary to explain why National Socialism succeeded in infiltrating the German people and how strong these attitudes were at the time of the occupation.

SOCIAL-PSYCHOLOGICAL CONSEQUENCES OF NAZISM

It is well known that the Nazis perverted the minds of Germans by inculcating such doctrines as anti-Semitism and racial superiority. The less obvious effects of the terror are often overlooked. What the Nazis left behind in 1945 may best be described as an atomized social structure. All natural and traditional rights, ties, and groups had been systematically destroyed in order to produce an easily controlled amorphous mass in which each individual was helpless and lost. Only the names of older institutions survived; from stamp-collectors associations to trade unions, each social group had been turned into an instrument of centralized power. The war furthered this development by separating families, shifting workers from their homes, and by the evacuation of whole towns.[2] The Nazis and the war had eroded the ties of family, church, and neighborhood—the foundations of the social fabric.

On the other hand the Nazis had ingeniously succeeded in satisfying the most striking and disparate features of the German character—the belief in authority and the romantic longing for boundless freedom. These tendencies to the extreme were exploited with cunning by Hitler, who built a rigidly centralized regime in his Reich and at the same time directed this romantic expansiveness into external aggression, particularly to the "boundless plains of the east." It was this *romantic imperialism* plus a dim sort of idealism which captured the imagination of the German youth, and not *nationalism* in the traditional German sense. And it is the ignominious degeneration and collapse of this romanticism which lies behind the present indifference and cynicism of large numbers of the younger generation. This lack of balance and rationality has been described by the Swiss Protestant theologian, Karl Barth, in a sentence that may be one of the best clues to German behavior, ". . . in order to escape responsibility to himself in his political thought and action the German inclines to give up, to descend into the abyss of the unconscious."[3]

These general considerations suggest the following criteria for a long-range program of German reorientation:

1. The aim of re-education should be defined as a strengthening of the general capacity for rationality, rather than in combatting specific doctrines.[4]

2. Institutional reorganization should not be content with formal conformity to democratic standards, but should insure genuine opportunity for individual responsibility and active participation in civic life.

3. The problem of economic and social reconstruction should not be narrowly defined in terms of better physical conditions of life, but should include the reintegration of atomized individuals into a new social structure.

The problem of tackling the Nazi-inculcated attitudes still surviving among the German people is a matter of great difficulty. The publicity given to the persistence of anti-Semitism has perhaps been somewhat exaggerated.[5] In a comparative study it would probably be found that anti-German-evacuee attitudes are at least as strong as anti-Semitic ones. Scarce living accomodations have had to be shared with Jewish refugees and German evacuees and have produced serious resentment not on racial grounds, but on the basis of an undifferentiated bitterness.

The problem of tackling the remnants of *nationalism* appears to be much more serious since German nationalism was one of the preconditions of Nazism. At the time of the collapse of Germany there seemed to be an opportunity to heal the old evil and to build up a healthy nonaggressive patriotic feeling of the Swiss type. Many Germans, particularly in the South, welcomed "the retreat from world history" that was to be the consequence of the collapse. But this would have required a maximum of forbearance on the part of the Allies, an attitude hardly to be expected after the ravages of the Nazi domination in the occupied territories. Had it been possible to avoid too sharp an attack on German national feeling, such a balanced attitude might have been achieved. As matters have developed there has been a vehement nationalist reaction. It will be the task of years, if not of decades, to heal the wounds of Nazism both in Germany and in the countries which suffered at her hand, thereby opening possibilities for the development of a German patriotism which will not be a threat to her neighbors.

The difficulties with regard to nationalism which have developed since 1945 have been as follows:

1. In the early period after the occupation there were tendencies which were influenced by the "Wendell Wilkie Mood." These anticipations proved too vain and idealistic in the light of the development which followed. The disappointment of these hopes for "One World" produced a most dangerous reaction among the young people. Such humanitarian beliefs came to be viewed as mere propaganda.

2. The policies of Poland, Czechoslovakia, and Russia in the eastern territorial settlement and the expulsion of Germans produced a lasting "irredentist" reaction. The effort to explain these policies as consequences of German oppression was not successful. The policies of at least two of the occupation forces, the French and the Russian, in removing property and industrial installations strengthened these attitudes.

3. At the same time the denazification laws in the Western zones provided no opportunity of getting rid of the former German Nationalists who often had quite "clean questionnaires," or who could even prove that they had been persecuted in the last years of the Nazi regime. These nationalist elements still have influence in the schools, universities, and churches. They are mainly to be found today in the C.D.U. and the Liberal parties.

4. In the Russian Zone the Communist-dominated S.E.D. took up the cry of national unity and thus attracted many of the extreme nationalists under a new slogan.

5. Federalism as an antidote to nationalism might have been welcomed by many German elements, but the new *Länder* were not the successors of the historical states. These were cut by the zonal boundaries. But even more serious was the fact that the zonal division of Germany by breaking up the German economy tended to discredit the idea of federalism itself. The present state of chronic economic emergency cries out for central planning and central administration and has greatly overshadowed the issue of regional decentralization. It had been hoped that nationalism might have been weakened by political federalism. Instead it has been strengthened by "economic federalism." There is some danger of a new nationalistic longing for the re-establishment of the Reich. The fact that the Communists have taken up the slogan of unity for very conspicuous purposes has depreciated the slogan on the right. On the other hand, the linkage of extremism and nationalism is a tremendous temptation for the younger generation.

6. While nationalism, for the Nazis, was primarily a propaganda device aimed primarily at the middle classes, *totalitarianism*, the very essence of National Socialism, was not preached but practiced. For the public the absolute state was camouflaged as *the people*. Its theory was an esoteric affair; but the practice was vigorous and ruthless in centralizing all corporative and private activities, and making them tools in the hand of the state. The tendency toward bigger and more powerful organizations has survived the belief in Nazism itself, and is quite independent of its doctrines. Strongly encouraged in the Russian Zone, this tendency can be noticed in the Western Zones too, and may be found in nearly all branches of administration.

7. The problem of present-day German militarism is often oversimplified by confusing it with the old-style militarism of the Prussian Junker. As a matter of fact it was mostly in the pre-1914 period that the glamor of the military officer played an important part in the average German's love for military things. Today this is far

less important than the attraction of the military way of life with its dangers, its irresponsibility, and its strong corporate loyalty. The fact that a very large part of the younger generation has been accustomed to such a form of life is a very serious obstacle to the spread of civilian and democratic values. The successful efforts of the French to enlist young Germans in the Foreign Legion is not to be attributed only to the bad economic situation or a love of war as such; a military organization satisfies the excessive longing for status, security, and irresponsibility which so deeply pervades the younger generation.

PROBLEMS AND ACCOMPLISHMENTS OF REORIENTATION

In order to define the problems and survey the accomplishments of the reorientation program it will be necessary to consider first the effect of the war and the occupation on the German family pattern and the younger generation. This will be followed by a discussion of education, religion, the media of communication, and the arts as instruments in the reorientation program. The study will conclude with an analysis of the influence of personal contacts with the occupation forces, the attitudes of Germans towards the new German governments, and the problem of German guilt.

THE FAMILY PATTERN

Obviously it is the main task of all policy in Germany to strengthen the power of resistance of the individual against the totalitarian tendencies of the state—whatever state or states will be built up in the future Germany. The primary means in this task is the restoration and reconstruction of family life. In Germany the family has always played an extremely important role in character education, but the fabric of family life was deeply shaken by the influence of Nazi totalitarianism. The Nazi "family propaganda" did not in the long run conceal the fact that marriage and child-rearing were being subordinated to the economic and military values of the state. After the defeat it was still impossible in the majority of cases to resume normal family life. The reasons were lack of housing, financial insecurity, the absence of millions of

German prisoners of war, and the insecurity growing out of the denazification program. The many long separations and the lack of housing have been responsible for a large increase in divorces. On the other hand there has been a great increase in marriages especially among the younger age groups.

On the whole the tendency toward early marriages is desirable as a means of reintegrating the younger generation in a normal civil life. But there are problems in this connection which are most difficult to solve. On the one hand the large number of unmarried women (there are 170 to 180 women to 100 men in the marriageable ages) demand equal pay and equal opportunity for work. On the other hand the men, in order to commence family life, have to be in a position to support a family. This problem of the economic basis of family life will continue as long as there is large-scale unemployment and severe economic hardship.

The inner structure of family life has lost much of the authoritarian character it formerly possessed especially among the middle classes. Almost everywhere one observes a much freer relationship between parents and children, although there is evidence that fathers in many cases have strongly resisted these threats to their status. The defeat of Germany has, of course, had its most severe psychological impact on the adult males. There is a tendency as a consequence for fathers and husbands to try to reassert their authority as a means of bolstering shaken self-esteem. The position of women and children has been greatly altered. The compulsory employment of women and youths during the war was in part responsible for this change. Perhaps more important is the fact that the real income of the family today is only partly covered by the income of the father. Women and dependents play an important role in queues and black markets. Thus the family where it has not been destroyed, has become a new form of communal existence. It has been greatly changed from the traditional patriarchal German form.

There has been a great development of women's leagues in all the occupation zones which are attempting to educate women for their civic tasks.[6] On the whole the vitality of women has suffered

less through the stress of war than that of men. But this fact has
been reflected in family life rather than in increased activity in
politics. The average German woman still views politics as a foreign
sphere. The development of greater political responsibility among
women will depend on their being granted a greater share in professional life, and in the opening of higher political and administrative posts in conformity with their numbers and competence.

The real political problem which the German woman presents,
grows out of the need of developing a new feminine type which
lays more stress on common sense and less on depth of feeling.
What role the new women's leagues will play in this process cannot as yet be determined. In any event they are making efforts to
give women a new self-assurance, and the necessity of fighting for
their share in professional life may lead to increased political activity as a means of protection against discrimination.

But the various programs of political re-education of women
have thus far had no great success. Here as in the case of German
youth all efforts at direct re-education will play a minor role compared to the question of whether the new institutions will offer
opportunities enough to be attractive.

Youth and Youth Activities

The report of the American educational mission to Germany
describes the formation of youth groups outside of the educational
system as an "old German tradition."[7] It is true that the German
youth movement produced a large number of anti-Nazis, especially
among the Socialist and Catholic groups. At the same time it should
not be overlooked that the youth movement had originated out of
the spirit of rebellion against the middle-class German world, and
that this spirit of revolt had degenerated in some sectors of the
movement into a romantic and nihilistic rejection of political
reality.[8] The Nazis skilfully exploited these attitudes in drawing on
the youth movement for the formation of the Hitler Youth.

After the capitulation the Military Governments authorized the
formation of youth groups, and set up agencies to supervise their
activities. In the American Zone nearly a third of all young people

between the ages of ten and twenty-five are registered as members of youth groups.[9] The figures obviously include all persons registered as members. The number of those taking an active part is considerably smaller, perhaps only 10 per cent of the young people. In the British and French zones there are a variety of youth groups. In the Russian Zone there is a single organization, the *Freie Deutsche Jugend,* which has many of the characteristics of a totalitarian youth organization.[10]

The positive value of the work of the youth organizations in Germany is obvious.[11] To some extent the vacuum left by the Hitler Youth has been filled in. Those in danger of becoming waifs and strays are supported in some kind of group environment. A general sense of comradeship and responsibility is being cultivated. There is, however, some danger in bringing together young people who are mainly united by negative experiences and influences. They easily yield to the desire of being continuously led by others, and they may lose the desire to grow up and take over mature responsibilities.[12] These young people may set the bond of "being the young generation" at a higher value than the task of growing up to take their share in adult political life. The rejection of the shams and corruptions of political and economic life today may become a slogan against democracy in general.[13]

In general, young people show a widespread aversion to joining the existing political parties. At the same time a minority shows keen interest in the political discussions and forums arranged by the occupation powers and the German authorities.

In general, the generation of fifteen to twenty-five years shows a very heterogeneous picture with regard to attitudes and interests.[14] Can one say that a future democratic leadership is developing among them? To cite the obvious political indifference[15] of contemporary German youth to the present political parties as conclusive evidence would perhaps be unwarranted. There may be an element of health in the present tendency of indifference to political party activity. It may reflect a sturdy individualism in many cases, a disinclination to become "suckers" again, after the catastrophic disillusionments and humiliations of the Hitler epoch. This individualism and independence is most marked among the intelligent boys and girls, many of whom had become critical of National Socialism long before the defeat.

The confusing and disturbing impression which we gain from studies of the attitudes of German young people may be understood if one places it against the background of their former life. Under the Nazi regime only those children whose parents were articulately anti-Nazi had an opportunity of choosing between Nazism and opposition. The remainder, the great majority, had become accustomed to viewing only certain facts and overlooking others. The question of Nazism and anti-Nazism among the youth was not a matter of character but of intelligence and information. In order to choose an anti-Nazi position they had to build up a picture of the world outside Nazism step by step and with the utmost difficulty. The educational system deliberately crippled their intellectual faculties. While religious instruction was not forbidden it was greatly overshadowed by the inculcation of the Nazi *Weltanschauung*. As a consequence most young people had become religious illiterates. Life in the Hitler Youth discouraged personal friendship (always an important character-building and educational influence) in favor of group life. These tendencies were greatly strengthened by the evacuation of young children into camps during the war.

The effects of these experiences cannot be overrated; they are much more important and more lasting than any belief or disbelief in specific doctrines. This camp life of a more or less military character was an overwhelming experience of an almighty state which feeds and protects the individual, shifts him as it likes, and has rights, powers, and purposes which he can never see through. For this generation the idea of a normal life was meaningless; they had lost contact with the past and were handed over like puppets from one institution to another—evacuation camps, Labor Service camps, military camps. The utter toughness of this generation (some of whom have lived through more adventures than the standard hero of a wild West tale) and their lack of elementary knowledge of so much that is important gives them that grotesque mixture of independence and helplessness so characteristic of soldiers and prisoners. They have developed either into the type of the eternal soldier or, on the other hand, into extreme individualists who try to make up now for what they were deprived of in the past. Between these extremes there is a mass of confused young people who are either disillusioned and without any spiritual foundation or who try to overcome the emptiness which the collapse of Germany has left them with by seeking in a random and careless fashion for whatever knowledge they can lay their hands on.

This emptiness explains the apathy and distrust on the one hand and, on the other, the eagerness to learn that has been so often observed in the universities and in the adult education centers. It has become a common experience of educators that audiences and groups of young people at first show the utmost docility. But the moment their pride is hurt they respond with the utmost stubbornness. They lay much stress on their not being guilty for the deeds of the Nazi regime, but they are not aware of the remnants of Nazi doctrines still in their minds. If a new Nazi leader would appear they would not follow him because he is a Nazi, but because he is a leader.

EDUCATION

As many as 70 per cent of the schoolteachers had to be dismissed after the occupation because of party membership. All textbooks were confiscated, and new ministries of education were set up in the various *Länder*. As soon as physical facilities and teaching staffs were available school began again. At first only the three R's could be taught because there were no non-Nazi materials in such subjects as history and geography. The new teaching staff was hastily recruited from among the young people and members of other professions. Gradually new syllabi and texts were forthcoming so that the full curriculum could be reinstituted. The teaching of civics and the social sciences in the secondary schools is still in its very beginning because of the lack of curricula and trained teachers.

One of the problems of the new school administrations was whether or not to continue the two separate public-school systems; the one requiring fees and the other free. The free schools generally were staffed by less well-paid teachers with less adequate training and with a larger teaching load. The maintenance of these separate school systems, separating after the fourth year, has been criticized as contributing to class consciousness and preventing the social ascent of the gifted children of the poor. In the Russian Zone free and uniform education has been instituted; in the Western zones the issue is still pending.

In the Russian Zone the period of common education has been extended to eight years, after which vocational specialization or further general education may be followed. In the American Zone the occupation authorities support a reform on the American pattern with a universal primary school of six years.[16] These decisions are to be left up to the German authorities, subject to Military Government approval.[17]

The kernel of the problem, however, is not the reform of the educational structure but of the spirit of the German schools. To transform the German educational pattern from an authoritarian one to a relatively free one, means changing the spirit and approach of the teachers. And the shortage of teachers, to say nothing of the shortage of well-trained, democratically inclined teachers, is the gravest problem confronting German education today. Some of the teachers removed for Nazi party membership have been reinstated after clearance by the Denazification Tribunals. Many others have been hastily trained and given jobs. As a consequence the contemporary German teachers are of a very uneven quality. The problem cannot be solved short of a long program of teacher training coupled with an improvement in the salary scales for teachers. And since future teachers are recruited from the younger generation the problem of recruiting a democratic teaching staff is simply one aspect of the general problem of the democratization of German youth.

Two great problems of German education are very much a matter of controversy at the present time. The first is the question of the emphasis on humanistic or classical education versus a more contemporary and practical orientation. Critics of classical education argue that it tends to produce nonpolitical types of men. Proponents of the system claim that during the Nazi period the humanistic gymnasia were strongholds of anti-Nazi thinking. A second problem is the issue of secular versus denominational schools. In the Russian Zone all schools are secular. In the Western zone the pattern varies from the denominational schools of Bavaria and South Baden, to the secular schools of Greater Hesse. Everywhere in the Western zones parents are guaranteed the right to have their children receive religious instruction during school time under the tutelage of teachers of their own denomination.

Very little real contact has been established between parents and the primary and secondary schools. The American authorities hope to strengthen the influence of the parents and the town councils on the schools, but this program has not achieved much success because the demands of daily life are so exacting as to leave little time or energy for such "parent-teacher association" activity. At the same time the schools show a somewhat authoritarian aversion to interference.

THE UNIVERSITIES

Nazism had a particularly strong hold on the German universities even before 1933.[18] The faculties were largely made up of conservative nationalists, and the student bodies were particularly susceptible to romantic idealism. The "revolution of 1918" had failed to affect the German universities since the state did not interfere with the appointment of the faculties. The universities chose their own professors, who served for life. As a consequence of this principle of co-option the old German conservative spirit of the time of the Monarchy was perpetuated under the Weimar Republic. Only universities with old democratic traditions like Heidelberg, the newer ones like Hamburg and Cologne, and some individual faculties of philosophy, history, and sociology were at all liberal. The old conservative student fraternities survived in the Weimar period, and the left-wing groups were unable to build sturdy organizations of their own.

When the Nazis came to power there was little resistance in university circles. Professors and students fell an easy prey to the temptations of nationalism and idealism contained in the first Nazi slogans. All democratic and left-wing tendencies in the universities were eliminated under the Nazis.

As a consequence the problem of re-staffing the universities is a far more serious problem than in 1918. Party members on the faculties and professors whose writings incriminated them were removed from office after the occupation. But many of them have been reinstated after clearance by the Denazification Tribunals as "nominal" Party members. Roughly speaking the contemporary university faculties are made up of the following groups: (1) the old nationalist professors who avoided joining the Party; (2) the nonpolitical professors who had great reputations and who had not been removed by the Nazis; (3) a small number of liberal professors like Jaspers, Radbruch, and Guardini who had been removed by the Nazis but have now been reinstated; (4) a fourth group consisting of Party members who, after removal, were given a clean bill of health and reinstated.

There is no reserve of intellectuals who are both competent and politically reliable to fill up the great gaps in the university faculties. The training and selection of new professors is a long-range problem. The immediate inadequacy in the university programs can only be remedied by the return of some of the emigrant professors or the appointment of foreigners as visiting professors. Conditions of life in Germany discourage any hope that the lack will be sufficiently remedied by intellectuals from outside Germany.

There is some discussion of the reform of the constitutions of the German universities.[19] It has been proposed that they be made independent of government interference by placing them under the control of autonomous boards of trustees. It has also been suggested that a probationary period be instituted before permanent tenure is granted in order to eliminate the old system which favored the nonpolitical types, remote from public affairs. Both of these proposals are of American inspiration.

The special problem of German students grows out of the large disproportion between the numbers of applicants for university education and the availability of university facilities. Shortages of consumers goods and the monetary inflation has left plenty of cash available among Germans for educational purposes. The returned prisoners of war are in a great number of cases eager for higher and professional education. Several systems of selection have been worked out to cut down on the number of applicants. In the American Zone the Military Government has set limits on the number of former army officers and nominal Party members who may be admitted. The regulations in the British and French zones are similar. In the Russian Zone former active officers are entirely excluded. Everyone applying for university admission has to write a composition on a political theme which is used as a basis for acceptance or rejection. The Russians have also introduced the practice of admitting young workers nominated by the trade unions, after a preparatory training of only a few months.

Figures on the social composition of the university student bodies are not comprehensive. In the Western zones some 50 per cent are dependent on the support of parents or their own savings. Forty per cent are working their way, while 10 per cent admit to supporting themselves by black market operations. In Berlin and the Russian Zone the proportion of workers and farmers among the students is 22 per cent. In the Western zones the number of students of working class origins is quite small.

Despite the various efforts which have been made, there has been little real progress in developing political interest among students. Even in the Russian Zone only some five hundred belong to S.E.D. student organizations. In the Western zones only 1 per cent of the students are members of socialist groups, while the Communist organizations are much smaller. There are quite a few clubs which use the term "democracy" in their names, but the main emphasis in most of these organizations is on recreational and convivial activities. On the other hand religious student societies have quite large memberships. The Catholic groups claim a membership of more than fifteen thousand; the Protestants around ten thousand.

The lack of political activity among students may in part be the result of a general debunking of politics after the propaganda of the Nazi era. Another factor is the fear of making political commitments in the light of the general conflict between Russia and the West. Political indifference and neutrality appear to be the relatively safe course of action.

In general university campus life in Germany is characterized by great concentration on study and the passing of examinations. On the whole intellectual standards are reported to be high. But the destruction of libraries, laboratories, and other university facilities and the extreme housing shortage constitute serious obstacles to effective work.

The speedy re-establishment of educational contacts abroad would be one way of remedying some of the glaring deficiencies of contemporary German student life. The French Zone has gone farther in this regard than the other zones. The French have invited German students to participate in short summer sessions in France. Groups of German students have been admitted to English universities, while individual scholarships have been granted by Swiss institutions. American military authorities have recently begun to encourage a program of cultural exchange between the United States and Germany. Some German students and intellectuals have been invited to the United States for study. American professors have been invited to teach at German universities. During 1948, as a consequence of the initiative of the University of Chicago, an American faculty was assembled and gave lectures at Frankfurt a/M.

ADULT EDUCATION

A number of people's academies (*Volkshochschulen*) have been re-established in the larger towns.[20] These institutions have proven to be quite popular among adults interested in vocational and professional training, filling in educational gaps, cultivation of the arts, and civic education. The adult education centers are local institutions but sponsored and supervised by the ministries of education of the *Länder*. In the Russian Zone the Adult Education centers operate under curricula published by a central office. In the Western zones their programs are developed and largely controlled locally. Instructors are largely on a part-time basis. Fees are low and many scholarships are granted.

Statistics for Wuerttemberg show that 80 per cent of the students are under the age of thirty-five. The social composition of the student bodies is mainly middle class. Even in the Russian Zone the proportion of workers is under 20 per cent. Classes in the social sciences are not particularly popular,[21] although serious political discussion takes place in other courses. In the adult education centers as in other educational levels, young people tend to shy away from direct discussions of German political questions, particularly those pertaining to the Nazi period. The relative lack of interest of the working classes cannot be explained in economic terms. Salaried employees do not get higher salaries, and the trade unions provide scholarships for interested workers.

RELIGION

The Nazi campaign against the churches was postponed when war broke out in order to avoid provocation of public opinion. Pressure on Nazi party members to leave the church, of course, continued; and the evacuation of children from towns threatened by bombing made it possible to cut down on religious instruction. At the same time the war led to an increasing interest in religion, which became more marked as the prospects of Nazi victory declined and the hardships of war became increasingly felt. In both the Catholic and Protestant denominations Nazi barbarism and atrocities aroused opposition even among those religious circles which had made their peace with Nazism.[22] In general the power and attraction of the churches—the only non-Nazi institutions surviving in Germany—increased toward the end of the war.

After the collapse the churches continued to gain prestige by all types of relief and welfare work including that organized for the deportees from the east. Not only did church membership increase, but a number of Protestant sects (stimulated by help from abroad, particularly the United States) gained a remarkably large number of followers.

What effect this new interest in religion will have on political attitudes it is impossible to predict at this point. In many cases it is undoubtedly a form of escapism. But in both the Catholic and

Protestant denominations serious attempts are being made to deal with political problems in a genuinely Christian spirit. Active groups among the clergy and laity are attempting to overcome the stagnation of religious and clerical routine and use the experiences of the tragic past as means in a renewal of community and civic life.[23] The churches have sponsored meetings, talks, and discussions on social and political questions. The *Katholische Bildungsarbeit* in the Catholic side and the Evangelical Academies on the Protestant are examples of this activity.

One of the most important religio-political problems of postwar Germany is that of the traditional tie-up of Protestantism with political conservatism and nationalism. Karl Barth has expressed skepticism as to whether any significant progress has been made in this connection.[24] The Christian Democratic Union, representing a combination of Catholic and Protestant elements, is strongly influenced by conservative Protestant and Catholic groups. In the Protestant areas of Germany the old *Deutsch-Nationalen* have been rather successful in gaining control of the Party; while in the Catholic Rhineland and Bavaria the conservative Catholics have come to the fore in the Party. This has led to the formation of a separate Catholic party in the Rhineland, the *Zentrum*. There are, however, strong forces in both Catholicism and Protestantism which are fighting this tendency to make religion and the church serve reactionary purposes.

THE MEDIA OF COMMUNICATION

The Nazis had seized control of broadcasting facilities from the very outset, while the press was taken over step by step from 1933 until 1944. But even the formally "private" newspapers were closely controlled with regard to staffing, and were subject to the daily directives of the Propaganda Ministry. Toward the end of the war a general mistrust of "print" had developed in Germany which seriously affected attitudes toward the new German press after the occupation.

The occupation forces followed different principles in the establishment of the new German press. The Russians and the British (and later the French) gave the control of newspapers to the political parties; while the Americans attempted to build up a nonpartisan, private press.[25] In the British and American zones no censorship was instituted although destructive criticism of the occupying powers was forbidden. The press in the Russian Zone shows a startling uniformity which suggests that some system of central control is maintained.

Newsprint is more plentiful in the Russian Zone, and the newspapers of the Russian Military Forces and the pro-Soviet party are specially favored. In the British and American zones the size of editions is greatly limited by the scarcity of newsprint. As many as ten persons have to share a single copy; many of the papers can appear only two or three times a week and consist only of four to six pages.

The scarcity of paper, the deterioration of equipment, the impossibility of maintaining foreign correspondence, and, most important, the shortage of trained and reliable journalists has seriously hampered the development of a genuinely popular press. Some satisfaction has been noted in the general public at the separation of news from editorial comment, a policy which has been strongly advocated by the American Information Control officers.

Interestingly enough, the popularity of the new German newspapers was greatly increased when they began to criticize the policies of the newly established German governments. In the sharp conflicts between the *Länder* governments and the press, the latter won many friends. And for the first time general apathy gave way to some political interest among the general public. There is considerable promise in the American policy of an independent press. It may produce a group of independent and sturdy publicists which might raise the level of political controversy and contribute to a healthy criticism of governments and political parties. There is at the same time a danger that the nonparty press will degenerate into colorless and politically indifferent media. This is in part a question of the training of journalists and the development of an *esprit de corps*.

There has been a substantial development of periodicals in post-

war Germany.[26] And since they contain lengthier and more detailed discussions of social and political questions, they constitute
a better barometer of opinion and attitudes in Germany than the
press. There are few exclusively political periodicals, although
many of those in other fields treat of politics from religious,
philosophical, or cultural points of view.

Considerable stress in these new periodicals has been placed on
the discussion of the roots of Nazism, the real meaning of democracy, the relation of Christianity to politics. The intellectual standard is quite high; they appear to be directed primarily to the
educated and serious public. Popular mass periodicals are almost
entirely lacking, although there is a great demand. The periodicals
thus far developed appealing to women or young people are on
the whole rather poor. The effort in these periodicals at the education of youth and women is often rather obvious and consequently
ineffective.

The publication of books has been much delayed and not only
for technical reasons. Soon after the occupation it became apparent
that the "drawers of the spiritual emigrants" (the surviving literary
and intellectual opposition) were empty. Very few had been able
to produce anything under the stress of war and terror. The first
books to appear in Germany dealt with the most urgent questions
of the time—the concentration camps, the nature of National
Socialism, and the like. Most of them were badly written and had
little influence on the public. The translation and publication of
foreign literature on these subjects might have made a useful contribution, but there were serious bureaucratic delays in getting
copyrights for translations. The inexpensive American overseas
editions of foreign books on government and politics, and also fiction, was an encouraging development. In the Russian Zone the
standard works of Communist doctrine have been published in
large quantities.

The circulation of different types of periodicals and books cannot be taken as evidence of the reading interests of the German
public. Because of the great scarcity of reading matter in Germany,
almost anything printed is sure to be sold. The high percentage of

books with political educational purposes is significant primarily as evidence of the good will of the publishers.[27]

Most books are published in editions of only five thousand copies, far too few for the really tremendous demand. As a consequence pressure is being placed on public libraries to an extent never before experienced in Germany. Many book collections and libraries were destroyed during the war, and there is a serious shortage of trained personnel and physical facilities. U. S. Information Centers have been established in thirty towns in the U. S. Zone.[28] A few of such institutions have been established in the other zones, especially the British. The American libraries are well administered and are quite popular among the young people who can read English. The fact that the books have not been selected for propagandistic purposes has impressed the population. The cultural clubs which have been formed in the American libraries are popular and have done much useful work.

Radio broadcasting was re-instituted quite soon after the occupation. At first the broadcasting stations were run by Allied officers. But gradually Military Government control was relaxed to the point where actual operation is in German hands, while the Allied role has been reduced to supervision. In the Western zones the occupation authorities are opposed to a government owned and operated radio. There has been discussion of various forms of control as for example, municipal, institutional (church, universities, etc.) control through professional organizations. The proposal has also been made that control be exercised through public but autonomous boards of trustees. No final decisions have as yet been made with regard to these important questions. As a consequence the public does not know who is running the stations, and there is some distrust of the reliability and impartiality of the programs. The stations have made efforts to overcome this feeling by arranging round-table conferences, political discussions open to all the political parties, critical commentaries on government policy, and the like. The volume of "fan mail" suggests that these efforts have had some success.

The Nazis had been quite successful in using the highly developed German film industry for propaganda purposes. Nazi films had been quite successful with the younger generation, but the older groups had not forgotten the high quality of foreign films and eagerly looked forward to their arrival after the occupation. There was considerable disappointment with American films. The first American films shown in Germany were those which had been selected for the American Army; later they were selected by commercial interests without much consideration for political, educational, or artistic criteria. One of the greatest opportunities for mass education was lost by the poor quality of the film offerings. The French have, on the whole, imported the largest number of good films. Russian films shown in the Western zones have been of very poor quality. Another difficulty grows out of the zonal barriers which have prevented the showing of good importations and domestic films throughout Germany. The new German film industry is still in its infancy. A few of its serious products have been excellent (e.g. "The Murderers Are Among Us," "In Those Days"). These German films and a number of Swiss pictures dealing with similar themes (e.g. "The Last Chance," "Marie Louise") have had excellent receptions among the public.

The German theatre was quick to re-establish itself despite many destroyed and half-destroyed theatres and the scattering of performers during the war. Theatre control is quite decentralized, and healthy rivalry and experimentation encouraged. Foreign plays are quite popular, though there is a certain tendency for each zone to stress the plays of the occupying power. The contemporary German theatre is quite international in its offerings. In the American Zone the plays of Thornton Wilder have been overwhelmingly successful; the French playwright Anouilh is the second most popular foreign playwright. The high calibre of the American theatre was a distinct surprise to the German public and perhaps has done more to overcome prejudices than any other cultural activity. At the same time the influence of the theatre should not be overstressed; it caters only to a small public.

THE EFFECT OF CONTACT WITH THE OCCUPATION FORCES

In the very last weeks before the Nazi collapse the typical attitude in Germany was the cynical one of "wait and see." It was generally felt that the Allied countries were no better than the Nazis, that they were similarly concerned with power, and that they would exercise their power in the familiar historical style. This cynical belief in power and debunking of ideology and moral values has proven to be the most lasting and dangerous inheritance of Nazism, far more dangerous than any of the specific Nazi doctrines. These attitudes are, indeed, more widespread today than they were in 1945 and must be viewed as the great problem of the future. They provide the soil for the revival of Nazi ideas. The problem is not limited to the Russian Zone or to those areas in the French Zone where the occupation was followed by excesses by the military. Even where looting and acts of violence were the common thing for a limited period, the population soon recognized the difference between combat troops and the later occupation forces.

That there has been a distinct political deterioration in the Western zones too, is not attributable to the excesses of the occupation armies. It is primarily due to the intensifying conflict between East and West and the effects of these developments on the prospects for German recovery. The situation of world politics today makes the various statements of Allied war aims appear as so much propaganda. The red tape and indefinite delays of a complicated military government administration also have made their contribution to the development of cynicism.

Another factor contributing to German cynicism and demoralization was the Allied slogan of re-education itself. The Germans were aware of Allied plans of re-education before the occupation. Through the formulation of these moral and political standards they have provided the Germans with criteria for the criticism of Allied behavior. This is the explanation of the queer fact that the Anglo-Americans, whom many Germans had set their hopes on, are much more subject to criticism than the French and Russians, who never put much emphasis on the idea of re-education and who openly behave as victors and occupants. The French and Russians did not frustrate any hopes, while every GI was expected to be a moral delegate of American democracy.

Personal, purely human, contact between the occupation forces and the Germans is relatively rare as far as the mass of the population is concerned. They are more rare in the Anglo-American Zone than in the French and Russian zones. "Fraternization" in the narrow sense of the term—love affairs between boys and girls—is of little significance for "re-orientation." Social relations between members of the occupying forces and Germans is infrequent and generally confined to intellectuals who were already internationalists.

Some efforts have been made to provide for genuine social contact. Various clubs for social and cultural purposes have been opened recently; and valuable efforts are being made to overcome the self-consciousness prevailing between people of quite different standards and opportunities. The families of members of the occupying forces invite German children to parties. Various branches of the military government administration have formed discussion groups to which Germans are invited. Collaboration in sports has been undertaken. There have been many generous, brave, and optimistic attempts made, particularly in the American Zone, which may bear fruit in the future. Perhaps more than anything else the establishment of contact by Germans with relatives, organizations, or even with unknown persons overseas has done much in impressing those Germans who are inclined to see the occupying forces only as "conquerors." The selfless and generous spirit of so many people abroad has been an important factor in creating self-confidence—the foundation of all re-education—which politics has thus far failed to create.

THE REVIVAL OF ACTIVITY

If one adopts the thesis that the German problem is not so much a question of the persistence of specifically National Socialist attitudes, but rather the political submissiveness of the population vis-à-vis the totalitarian state, then the revival of civic activity, so marked in Germany, should be viewed as a symptom of great importance. When one enters a German town these days one is impressed by an apparently thriving cultural and political life—exhibitions, meetings, and discussions are constantly held, political posters are prominently displayed, newspapers and periodicals of high quality are available, political clubs and societies proliferate everywhere.

But when one penetrates beneath these surface manifestations and formal activities one realizes that there is a deep and fundamental apathy among the general population. Neither governments nor political parties have succeeded in winning real popularity. The actual number of party members is small. And those who vote for political parties generally admit, when questioned, that they have voted for a "lesser evil" or "against something," rather than out of any genuine conviction or enthusiasm.

This widespread apathy is not the consequence of the general destitution of the people, and cannot be disposed of simply as a heritage of National Socialism. Even hungry people can have strong political feelings if they have any hopes of a better future. Apathy and demoralization are especially noticeable among the convinced anti-Nazis who were eager in 1945 to join with the Allies in the rehabilitation of Germany. The reasons for this widespread indifferentism appears to be the following:

1. A general fear of war between the powers prevails in Germany and keeps many valuable people from committing themselves to one side or the other. The terror in the East has its paralyzing effects in the Western zones too, since the danger of war is commonly overrated. Though most people are convinced of an eventual victory of the Western powers, they fear that the Russians will occupy all of Germany in the short run.

2. The new governments as well as the agencies of the new Bizonia have no clear power, nor real responsibility. The legislative process is so complicated (the Control Council, Military Governments, Bizonal Offices, and *Länder* all have a share) that the common man is unable to see any point in his participation in the democratic process. It is also impossible to decide who is responsible for successes and failures.

3. The *Länder* parliaments were chosen at a time when only the

historical parties of the Weimar Republic were ready to compete, and under the control of the surviving "old men." The new parliaments are more like the legislative bodies of the *ancien régime*, the powers of which were confined to "remonstrances" to an absolute sovereign. There is, consequently, an element of shadowboxing and hypocrisy in the new German democratic forms. At the same time the chronic economic emergency has given the upper hand to the bureaucracy. The total state—not as a doctrine, but as a reality—has been prolonged by the impossibility of returning to a normal economic life.[29]

4. The basic precondition of all reconstruction is lacking. Denazification has not as yet succeeded in eliminating all the significant Nazi influences. In the Eastern zone denazification is the name given to what is actually a new form of party terror. In the French and English zones the program of denazification was carried out hesitatingly; while in the American Zone the scope of the program was far too large in the beginning.[30] Zonal differences, conflicts of jurisdiction, the great delays in the program due to inadequate personnel, have created a state of widespread insecurity and anxiety without bringing about a genuine purge of Nazi influences.[31]

All of the above factors have rendered the formal German "democracy" of the occupation a target of criticism not only among those who really wish for a more sound democratic society, but also for those who use its failures as a basis for camouflaged totalitarian ambitions.[32]

The struggle for democracy in Germany will only begin in earnest when normal conditions of life provide opportunities for a genuine "grass roots" democracy. These conditions will only be present when there is no longer an irreconcilable conflict between the desperate physical needs of the individual and his duties as a citizen. Much has been accomplished in many fields, but no real progress has been made in this last connection.

THE PROBLEM OF GERMAN GUILT

The effort of the occupation authorities to create among Germans a feeling of responsibility for what was done in the Nazi period has, on the whole, not been successful. The program stressed the atrocities committed but failed to make clear the nature of the connection of the average German with these events. After all the number of concentration camp executioners was relatively small. The typical German's responsibility and guilt was of another order. He could not be made to accept direct guilt for mass murder; and a great opportunity was missed by not demonstrating his guilt of political irresponsibility, of tolerance of internal and external aggression, and of permitting the establishment of a system which in its full development implied this form of terror and extermination.

The doctrine of German guilt came from the outside and without any differentiation as to degrees of responsibility. At the same time in the first phase of the occupation nothing was said about the German victims of Nazism and the German opposition. The campaign thus rested on oversimplifications which made it possible for Germans to reject not only the particular version of guilt which was propagated, but any idea of guilt at all. Another damaging consequence of the doctrine of undifferentiated German guilt is the effort of German youth to dissociate themselves from the older generation in order not to be stigmatized and included in a moral pariah status.

The problems of German guilt have been given a careful treatment in the German literature which followed the occupation.[33] Recognition and acceptance by Germans of their real responsibility for all that Nazism implied will be a slow process. But contrary to some impressions it is not a hopeless task. The Catholic Bishop of Rottenburg, Johannes Baptista, has recently proposed a formula which many have been willing to accept: that everyone must consider himself guilty in the degree to which he entertained hopes for himself in the event of Nazi victory.

A spiritual regeneration over a short period of time has been rarely known in history. It is a task requiring the greatest tact and patience. It must stress the sound members as well as the sick, and offer some hopeful prospect.

NOTES AND INDEX

Notes

CHAPTER II

1. Walter Rest, "Die Pflicht zu Entscheidung und Wagnis," *Frankfurter Hefte* (May, 1946), pp. 4 ff.
2. The following draws partly on sections of the U. S. Strategic Bombing Survey's report, *The Effects of Strategic Bombing on German Morale* (Washington, D. C.: Government Printing Office, 1947) Vol. I, Pt. II, Chap. 7, which were contributed by W. H. Kraus. Cf. also the suggestive treatment in H. R. Trevor-Roper, *The Last Days of Hitler* (New York, 1947), especially pp. 17 ff., and the mounting documentary evidence brought out by the war crimes trials—see *Nazi Conspiracy and Aggression* (Washington, 1947), *passim*.
3. The organization of Office III was indicative of the SD's sweeping concerns. The following were its major subdivisions: General Community Life (comprising legal matters, cooperation with other agencies), Public Administration, General National Life (morale aspects), Race and Racial Health (including Racial Minorities, Citizenship, Migration, Settlement, Occupied Areas), Culture (comprising Research and Education, Religion, Sports, Arts, Propaganda, Press and Literature), General Economic Policy (including Colonial Economy).
4. It should be noted, however, that no quantitative polling techniques were ever used—virtually a practical impossibility in view of the secrecy of these operations.
5. There were many other morale reporting systems. On the whole Gestapo reports were more limited in scope and more cut and dried. That the reports of the Propaganda Ministry were often at variance with those of the SD is easily understood. There were reports of the Labor Offices, mostly concerned with labor morale. We know of further morale reports compiled by the heads of the general district administration (*Regierungspraesidenten*) as well as of district attorneys who, at least since the outbreak of the war, extended considerably beyond the problems peculiar to their jurisdiction.

6. One major local branch (Bremen) handled the following subject matter
   functions, in addition to its Intelligence Division N: Communism-
   Marxism, Reaction, Churches and Sects, Free Masons, Jews, Malingering
   and Absenteeism (*Arbeitsbummelei*), Factory Protection, Counter-Intelligence.
7. Gisevius testimony, July, 1946, as reported in *Marburger Presse* of July 23,
   and *Donau-Kurier* of July 19.
8. Reichstags-Verhandlungen 1942, pp. 109 ff.
9. Cf. Hitler decree of August 20, 1942, *Reichsgesetzblatt* I, p. 535; for this
   and further relevant materials, see John H. Herz, "German Administration under the Nazi Regime," *American Political Science Review* (August,
   1946), pp. 682 ff.
10. In the secret Party bulletin *Die Lage*, August 23, 1944, cited from U. S.
    Strategic Bombing Survey, *The Effect of Strategic Bombing on German
    Morale* (1945), Vol. I, Pt. II, Chap. 6.
11. "A German of the Resistance, The Last Letters of Count Helmuth
    James von Moltke," *Round Table* (June, 1946), p. 222.
12. *Ibid.*
13. Cf. Victor Gollancz, *What Buchenwald Really Means*, (London, 1945),
    p. 4. From the mounting literature on this inferno one may mention:
    Bruno Bettelheim, "Individual and Mass Behavior in Extreme Situations,"
    Journal of Abnormal and Social Psychology (October, 1943), pp. 417 ff;
    Herbert Bloch, "The Personality of Inmates of Concentration Camps,"
    American Journal of Sociology (January, 1947), pp. 335-41; Christopher
    Burney, *The Dungeon Democracy* (New York, 1946), a striking document,
    marred by intemperate bias; *Konzentrationslager Buchenwald* (Weimar),
    a significant document from the Communist point of view; Eugen Kogon,
    Der SS-Staat (Frankfurt, 1946); David Rousset, *The Other Kingdom* (New
    York, 1947).
14. Meeting of June 8, 1944.
15. The process of pulverizing the group and paralyzing the individuals was
    fiendishly perfected in concentration camp practice: "With ruthless
    brutality thousands were murdered before the eyes of the others who could
    not weep from sheer horror. Thus thousands died in Buchenwald but there
    were no tears. There was only horrified dismay that this was possible. The
    horror was so paralyzing that almost all went to their death like lambs.
    Thus each new inmate had his moral backbone broken upon arrival and
    what was left of him was a fear-shaken individual who merely wanted to
    preserve his shred of life."—*Konzentrationslager Buchenwald, op. cit.*, p.
    107 f.
16. From Marie Luise Kaschnitz, "Von der Schuld," in *Wandlung* (Heidel-
    berg), January, 1946. See also, in a soberer vein, Kogon, *op. cit.*, pp.
    335 ff.
17. Alfred Scholz, "Die Ungenannten," *Telegraf* (Berlin), July 20, 1946.
18. In a sermon on July 13, 1941, Archbishop Count von Galen of Muenster
    dared to put it in the following terms: "Since none of us know of a way
    in which to obtain an impartial control of Gestapo measures, of its inter-

ference with liberty, its residence prohibitions [Aufenthaltsverbote], its arrests, its imprisonments of German citizens in concentration camps, a feeling of helplessness has arisen among wide groups of the German people which approaches cowardly timidity and severely injures the national community." From Joh. Neuheusler, *Kreuz und Hakenkreuz* II, (Munich, 1946), p. 16 ff.

19. Reports now appearing in the German press indicate that active resistance in the period after 1936 was on a considerable scale. One writer claiming to cite the Gestapo report for 1936 claims a total of over 20,000 arrests for resistance and subversive activity. During this same year the Gestapo is alleged to have seized more than a million and a half leaflets. See Guenther Weisenborn, "Es gab eine duetsche Wiederstandsbewegung," *Neue Zeitung*, December 9, 1946.

20. Report 245 Reichsfuhrer—SS, Der Chef des Sicherheitshauptamtes, *Erfassung fuehrender Maenner des Systemzeit*, June, 1939.

21. RSHA, *Die Kommunistische Taetigkeit im Reichsgebiet und in den besetzten Gebieten nach dem Kriegsausbruch mit der Sowjet-union* (August, 1941).

22. Compilations of Gestapo statistics for earlier years are now coming to light in Germany. Citations of these reports in newspaper articles are too imprecise to draw definite conclusions.

23. The Gestapo offices in Polish areas included Bromberg, Kattowitz, Posen, and Bialystok. Whether these offices covered the whole of former Poland is impossible to say. It is also quite likely that the Wehrmacht carried out security measures in Poland. Consequently figures for arrests of Poles (and possibly for other foreign populations as well) must be viewed as minimum figures.

24. Thus the Prague Radio of January 29, 1946 stated that 25,000 German anti-fascist families were given the option of taking German citizenship or returning to the Reich with their property. Paul Hery in *Temoignage Chretien* of October 7, 1944 in an article entitled "Des Allemands Contre Hitler" estimates that the National Committee for Free Germany had more than 2,000 members in France alone. The number of NKFD periodicals in the western regions was more than a dozen. Some of these groups rendered aid to the French resistance according to this source.

25. The existence of such combined organizations was confirmed in Luebeck, Hamburg, and Leipzig. Guenther Weisenborn, *op. cit.*, refers to the organization "European Union" which included German and foreign workers. In Munich in 1942 the Anti-Nazi German Peoples' Front included Germans, foreign workers and PW's. This group collaborated with an organization of Russian officers. The leaders of both organizations were seized in 1943 and executed in 1944.

26. A Military Government report analyzing the results of an investigation of a million Germans in the U. S. Zone found 1 per cent who gave evidence of anti-Nazi activity. If these figures are applicable to the entire German population perhaps half a million Germans had engaged in anti-Nazi activity and had survived the terror. See Harold Zink, *American Mili-*

tary Government in Germany (New York: The Macmillan Company, 1947), p. 142.

27. See Helen Peak, "Some Psychological Problems in The Re-education of Germany," *Journal of Social Issues* (August, 1946); Helen Peak, "Some Observations on the Characteristics and Distribution of German Nazis," *Psychological Monographs* (1947); Wolfgang H. Kraus, "The German Resistance Movement," *Journal of Social Issues* (August, 1946).

CHAPTER III

1. This tendency was observed among all the resistance movements. See Massimo Salvadore-Paleotti, "The Patriot Movement in Italy," *Foreign Affairs* (April, 1946), pp. 539 ff.; L. S. Stavrianos, "Greece: The War and Aftermath," *Foreign Policy Reports* (July, 1946); on Belgium see Jean Terfve, "The Communist Party," *Annals of the American Academy of Political and Social Science* (September, 1946), p. 19. For France and other countries see Gabriel A. Almond, "The Resistance and the Political Parties of Western Europe," *Political Science Quarterly* (March, 1947), pp. 27 ff.

2. Paul Sweezy, "Germany from the Ruins," *New Republic* (April 22, 1946), pp. 585 ff; Moses Moscowitz, "The Political Reeducation of the Germans," *Political Science Quarterly* (December, 1946), pp. 535 ff; Gabriel A. Almond, "The German Resistance Movement," *Current History* (May and June, 1946).

3. This period of "resistance mystique" was a characteristic phase in the early liberation period in a number of European countries, especially France. The terror forced doctrinal differences into the background.

4. Rudolf Pechel, *Deutscher Widerstand* (Zurich: Eugen Rentsch Verlag, 1947), pp. 4 ff.

5. Allen W. Dulles, *Germany's Underground* (New York: The Macmillan Company, 1947), p. 97 ff.

6. Jakob Kaiser, "Der Aufstand des Gewissens," *Neue Zeit*, February 2, 1947.

7. Pechel, *op. cit.*, pp. 86 ff. See also Adam Trott zu Solz's memorandum on the activities of Communist organizations in Germany during the war, cited in Dulles, *op. cit.*, p. 137.

8. Pechel, *op. cit.*, p. 93.

9. The movement spread throughout the Wehrmacht and was particularly strong among the German armies of occupation.

10. There were, to be sure, many efforts throughout the Nazi period to establish regional and even German-wide tie-ups of left-wing groups. Unfortunately the chances of discovery increased in proportion to the expansion of the organization. Most of these efforts at expansion resulted in the breakup of the organizations, arrests, and executions.

11. Jakob Kaiser, "Der Aufstand des Gewissens," *loc. cit.*

12. In a sample check of former leading figures, Himmler's police head-

quarters estimated in 1939 that of a sample of 82 designated as "Liberals and Pacifists" as many as 38 per cent of the 77 per cent still in Germany were recipients of retirement incomes. This is of course indicative of their high average age. Cf. *Erfassung fuehrender Maenner der Systemzeit* (June, 1939).

13. Walter Petwaidic, *Die Autoritaere Anarchie* (Hamburg, 1946), p. 29 f.

In the spring of 1943 a play (*The Parasite*) was produced in Berlin whose final words: "Justice exists only on the stage," were received, according to Hassell with frenetic applause.—Ulrich von Hassell, *Vom Anderen Deutschland* (Zurich, 1946), p. 301. On January 16, 1946 Bishop Wurm, in opening the provisional assembly in Stuttgart, said: "Never has it become as evident to us as in recent years that the idea of God and that of law are closely related. . . . It remained for the past system to change the law according to momentary needs and to posit the will of an individual as law-making without reservation. There were only rights over men and no rights of men."—Theophil Wurm, "Recht und Gerechtigkeit," *Neubau*, Vol. 1 (Munich, April, 1946), p. 7 f.

14. Illuminating observations on the attitude and outlook of the officialdom can be found throughout the writings of Hassell, *op. cit.*, and Hans Bernd Gisevius, *Bis Zum Bittern Ende* (Zurich, 1946), Vol. I, pp. 355 ff. Translated under the title *To The Bitter End* (Boston, 1947).

15. Von Hassell, *op. cit.*, p. 92.

16. "It is probably due to the German character, but also to the inspiration of the goal that the German industrialists have followed the watchwords of the leadership with such good will from the beginning. This explains, too, why the 'leadership corps' of industrial management, on the whole, required but very few changes. . . . This is the more remarkable as . . . in the beginning only a small number of leading businessmen were adherents of National Socialism. . . . Although a certain reserve remained in business circles, also the skeptics did not refuse cooperation, since official cooperation was attractive even in a business way. . . ." From a widely read German monograph by Erich Welter, *Der Weg der Deutschen Industrie* (Frankfurt am Main, 1943), p. 23 f. This modest understatement tallies with the observations of such students as Franz Neumann and much documentary material which now comes to light.

17. The situation recalls A. Morize's statement for France: "Doubtless there was hesitation and wavering, especially among the high clergy. Certainly not an adherence to the policy of 'collaboration' with the enemy but, in certain cases, a rallying to Petain's principles of 'National Revolution.' It was only a repetition of history, a resurrection of the 'Moral Order' of the most beautiful days of MacMahon. . . ." Cf. A. Morize, *Resistance, France, 1940-43* (Boston, 1943), p. 72 f.

18. Among recent critical statements, see for instance Edmond Vermeil, *Hitler et le Christianisme* (London, 1944); P. Schmid-Ammann, *Der Politische Katholizismus* (Berne, 1945), especially pp. 73 ff.; since this was written, Hans Rothfels, in *The German Opposition to Hitler* (Hinsdale, Illinois, 1948), pp. 34 ff., has suggestively dealt with the subject.

19. The whole background has been admirably analyzed recently by Carl Mayer in "The Crisis of German Protestantism," *Social Research* (November, 1945), pp. 397 ff.
20. For a record of statements by the Catholic bishops in Germany, see J. Neuhaeusler, *Kreuz und Hakenkreuz,* 2 vols. (Munich, 1946), Vol. II, especially pp. 40 ff.
21. Neuhaeusler, *op. cit.*, Vol. II, gives a first documentary record of Catholic resistance activities, although it is mostly confined to those which have an "official" character.
22. Neuhaeusler, *op. cit.*, Vol. II, p. 16. One might add that the Nazis refrained from making a martyr of any high dignitary of either church. There were vigorous demands inside the Party, to make an example of Galen. Goebbel's prudence prevailed in the inner councils.
23. Circular of Reichsleiter Bormann to Gauleiters and Reich Governors Concerning the Relations of National Socialism and Christianity," cited from Neuhaeusler, *op. cit.*, Vol. I, pp. 358 ff.
24. This and the following citations are taken from Karl Barth, *Die Evangelische Kirche in Deutschland nach dem Zusammenbruch des Dritten Reichs* (Stuttgart, 1946), p. 11 ff.
25. SD Directive of February 15, 1938, reprinted in Neuhaeusler, *op. cit.*, Vol. I, pp. 360-82; it is entirely devoted to the churches and the best methods for controlling them.
26. Hassell, *op. cit.*, p. 321. Hassell comments: "Of course it will not do any good, and may well harm Wurm personally; but it may be of great significance for the future and before history that at least the Protestant Church has openly and clearly set itself apart from the whole filthy mess— something for which our brave field marshals evidently lack the civil courage."
27. *Kirche und Welt: Eine Notwendige Besinnung auf die Aufgaben des Christen und der Kirche in unserer Zeit.* Approximately 1940.
28. Cf. his *Protestantische Rompilger* (Munich, 1937), especially pp. 64 ff., where he cites an elaborately documented memorandum on international Protestantism which had been prepared for him by one of his men.
29. Karl Barth, *op. cit.*, p. 16.
30. Max Seydewitz in *Civil Life in Wartime Germany* (New York, 1945), p. 338, believes they constituted only 10 per cent during the war period. This is probably too low an estimate.
31. Cf. *Kriminalitaet und Gefaehrdung der Jugend,* published as a "strictly confidential" document by the Jugendfuehrer des Deutschen Reiches, ed. by W. Knopp and Dr. Raetz, January 1, 1941, Chap. VI.
32. For the whole recent background see Hans Ebeling, *The German Youth Movement* (London, 1945), on resistance activities, especially pp. 20 ff. The most recent general treatment of the German youth movement as a whole is Howard Becker's, *German Youth Bond or Free* (New York, 1947).
33. The German name, "Buendische Selbstschuetzler," actually defies translation since the term "buendisch" grew out of the particular ideology of the movement.

34. In Solingen, in the Ruhr area, for instance, oppositional activity among the working class youth went on under the cover of a sports club. A former Communist youth leader was in charge while two others known as 'Gandhi' and 'Nuska' conducted discussion groups which came to an end when a Gestapo agent betrayed them.

35. Ebeling, *op. cit.*, p. 23 ff.

36. SD Bielefeld, III C 2, February 3, 1942: the same SD office complained, in another report (October 12, 1942) that the return of retired older teachers, "with their antiquated religious convictions," had the most serious effects and resulted in "confusion" among students and parents.

37. The Bielefeld SD reported in May, 1942 that censored letters indicated Catholics to be steadily gaining ground in the army at the expense of zealous Nazis. It feared the party's decline because all the best young men were in the army. A deeply religious letter written by Colonel Moelders, the flying ace, to his spiritual adviser at home was so widely circulated as an anti-Nazi statement that even a French lady wanted to show it to former Ambassador Hassell in Paris (January, 1942)—who of course already knew it. (cf. Hassell, *op. cit.*, p. 251, also p. 236).

38. From the sentence in the Schmorrell-Huber-Graf case, see note 42 below.

39. At least four of the students involved in the second trial had been members of a Catholic youth organization, "New Germany."

40. Professor Kurt Huber, a native of Switzerland, who taught philosophy at the University.

41. There were several more trials at a later date. The last known execution in this connection, that of the student Hans K. Leipelt, took place in January, 1945. Cf. K. Alt, "Wie sie Starben," *Neubau* (April, 1946), pp. 39 ff.

42. Sentence in re Schmorrell, Huber, Graf, *et al.*, 1st Senate of People's Court, April 19, 1943, 6 J 24/43, 1 H 101/43.

43. Wolfgang Lohmeyer, "Tat und Traum," *Der Ruf der Jungen Generation* (August 15, 1946), p. 12.

44. If and when they come to light, the records of German courts-martial will be highly illuminating on this point. That drastic sentences were frequent is indicated in the Moltke letter which was quoted in Chapter II above. It is of some interest that a French author estimated that in November, 1943 there were about 2000 active members of the organization "Free Germany in the West" in the German forces stationed in France. (Paul Hery, *Temoignage-Chretien* (October 7, 1944). See also *Free Germans in The French Maquis* (London, 1945), p. 23.

45. This was written as a record of conversations held with Americans during captivity, while the war was still going on. This accounts for the use of the present tense. See Alfred Andersch, "Gespraeche am Atlantik," *Der Ruf der Jungen Generation* (August 15, 1946).

46. For the general background cf. Herbert Rosinski, *The German Army* (Washington, 1944); Alfred Vagts, *History of Militarism* (New York, 1937). The most significant personal recollections or diaries hitherto published by participants in recent events are Gisevius, *op. cit.*; F. von Schlab-

rendorff, *Offiziere gegen Hitler;* Pechel, *op. cit.;* and von Hassell, *op. cit.*

47. "Moreover," Liddell Hart has observed, "keen soldiers are easily inclined to confuse professional fulfillment with patriotism." B. H. Liddell Hart, "The German Generals II," *Harpers Magazine* (February, 1946), p. 190.

48. Hammerstein appears to have been one of the earliest pessimists. He was retired as Chief of the Reichswehr Command in February, 1934 and died in 1943.

49. Gisevius, *op. cit.,* p. 373.

50. A step whose significance apparently never ceased to trouble a man like Beck. Cf. Gisevius, *op. cit.,* II, p. 18 f.

51. Thus Beck's successor, General Halder, who assured Gisevius late in 1938 that workers and soldiers were behind Hitler and would defend him. He cited as examples his own four sons-in-law, all of them captains. (Gisevius, *op. cit.,* II, p. 37.) In November, 1939, General Vogel expressed the same worry and added that the result of any open revolt would therefore be highly problematic (Hassell, *op. cit.,* p. 111). The Nazi infiltration had progressed so far by 1935 that one of the anti-Nazi officers, Colonel Siegfried Wagner, is quoted as calling the armed forces "Fachschaft Wehrmacht" at that time, in analogy to the Nazi-initiated industrial and occupational groupings which went under that designation. (Cf. Dr. P. J. Stuermer, "20 July 1944," *Stuttgarter Zeitung,* July 20, 1946.)

52. On the occasion of a coup which did not come off: *op. cit.,* p. 120 f.

53. For this and some other relevant data, F. J. Schoeningh, "Gab es ein anderes Deutschland?" *Sueddeutsche Zeitung,* July 19, 1946, cf. also Schlabrendorff, *op. cit.,* p. 52.

54. Herbert Rosinski, *German Industrial Mobilization* (Washington, D. C., 1946), p. 2; cf. also the observations of Trevor-Roper, *op. cit.* pp. 7 ff., and numerous revealing entries in *The Goebbels Diaries,* ed. by L. P. Lochner (New York, 1948).

55. As it turned out, her past was not even shady but quite unequivocal—this was promptly discovered in Berlin police files.

56. Although Fritsch had finally been completely vindicated in court-martial proceedings.

57. Keitel was soon to be known as Lakeitel, little lackey. The High Command had actually been established in 1934, but was kept secret until 1938.

58. He was removed on December 19, 1941, and Hitler assumed command himself. It was from then on that Hitler could indulge, now without check from an old soldier like Brauchitsch, in the most arbitrary and despotic treatment of his officers. For a listing of the General Staff's main grievances concerning Hitler's conduct of the war cf. "SS—Bericht über den 20 Juli," *Nordwestdeutsche Hefte* (February, 1947), pp. 10 ff.

59. His behavior during the crisis showed him up as weak and irresolute.

60. Thus F. v. Schlabrendorff, *op. cit.,* p. 24 f.

61. Schlabrendorff, *op. cit.,* p. 27. This version is based on the accounts of Gisevius and Schlabrendorff. According to other sources, which have

been available to F. L. Ford, Beck merely announced his intention at a staff meeting late in summer which was to become effective for the case that Hitler should start aggressive action against the Czechs. He reportedly obtained a pledge from all army group commanders that they would refuse appointment as his successor in such an event. Early in September Beck carried out his intention of resigning. General Franz Halder accepted appointment as his successor claiming that Chamberlain's trip to Godesberg on September 13 had created a wholly new situation and thus released him from his pledge. (Cf. Franklin L. Ford, "The Twentieth of July in the History of the German Resistance," *American Historical Review* (July, 1946), p. 616.) Only the full publication of memoirs and documents will resolve these and other discrepancies.

62. Gisevius, *op. cit.*, Vol. I, p. 402.
63. Dulles, *op. cit.*, p. 81.
64. *Ibid.*; Pechel, *op. cit.*, pp. 121 ff.
65. See *The Round Table*, *loc. cit.*, for a translation of von Moltke's last
    letter to his wife in which he makes clear that the Kreisau group was condemned not for plotting a coup, but for planning a postwar program.
66. Pechel, *op. cit.*, pp. 177 ff.
67. See Ralph H. Bowen, *German Theories of the Corporative State*, (New
    York, 1947).
68. See *inter al.* Allen Dulles, *loc. cit.* and *passim*; Pechel, *op. cit.*, pp. 209
    ff.; Jakob Kaiser, *loc. cit.*; "Ein Abschiedswort Dr. Goerdeler's," *Neue Zeit*, December 19, 1946; on his constitutional plans cf. Gerh. Ritter, "Goerdelers Verfassungspläne," *Nordwestdeutsche Hefte* (December, 1946), also Rothfels, *op. cit.*, pp. 85 ff.
69. See Dulles, *loc. cit.*, for the Nazi indictment of Popitz; cf. Pechel who
    gives a more friendly view of Popitz' policies.
70. Bonhoeffer established liaison for the conspiracy with the Bishop of
    Chichester. See Dulles, *op. cit.*, p. 142; George K. A. Bell, "Background of the Hitler Plot," *Christendom*, I (1946), 65-72.
71. Franklin Ford, *loc. cit.*, in an otherwise excellent analysis of July 20 un-
    fortunately minimizes the democratic and "left" tendencies which were present in the group.
72. The expression is not easily translatable. Literally it means "corpse-
    obedience"; it connotes the complete absence of self-will of the automaton.
73. Dulles, *op. cit.*, p. 175.
74. *Ibid.*, p. 187; see Pechel, *op. cit.*, p. 190, on the role of the oath.

CHAPTER IV

1. Quotations taken from the *Directive to the Commander in Chief of the
   United States Forces of Occupation Regarding the Military Government of Germany during the Initial Post-Surrender Period*, also known as "JCS

[Joint Chiefs of Staff] No. 1067," April, 1945. This directive is fairly representative of Allied policies in that period.

2. The base year is 1936, except for mechanical and electrical engineering (1938) and synthetic fibers (1943).
3. Hence its numerous internal inconsistencies. For an interesting account of the negotiations leading up to the Agreement, by two American participants, see B. U. Ratchford and W. D. Ross, *Berlin Reparations Assignment* (Chapel Hill: University of North Carolina Press, 1947).
4. *The Future Level of German Industry*, Memorandum by the United States Representative on the quadri-partite Level of Industry Committee, January 28, 1946.
5. John K. Galbraith, *Recovery in Europe*, National Planning Association, Planning Pamphlet No. 53 (October 1, 1946).
6. September 6, 1946.
7. Paris, Spring and Summer, 1946; Moscow, March 10-April 24, 1947; London, November 25-December 1, 1947.
8. See Molotov's statement at the London meeting of the Council of Foreign Ministers, December 8, 1947.
9. Statement of Secretary Marshall, London, December 5, 1947.
10. Statement to the Council of Foreign Ministers, July 10, 1946.
11. Statement to the Council of Foreign Ministers, July 9, 1946.
12. Statement to the Council of Foreign Ministers, July 12, 1946.
13. Statement to the Council of Foreign Ministers, Moscow, March 31, 1947.
14. Statement to the Council of Foreign Ministers, April 3, 1947.
15. *New York Times*, April 9, 1947.
16. Statement to the Council of Foreign Ministers, March 17, 1947.
17. Statement to the Council of Foreign Ministers, December 10, 1947.
18. Letter to Senator Arthur H. Vandenberg from Secretary Marshall, February 4, 1948.
19. *Manchester Guardian*, November 11, 1946.
20. See statements by Major General W. H. Draper, Berlin, May 6, 1947, and by Secretary Marshall, London, December 14, 1947.
21. From Secretary Marshall's report on the London Meeting of the Council of Foreign Ministers, December 19, 1947.
22. April 10, 1947.
23. In 1946 and 1947, the crisis was due to shortfalls in imports; in 1948, collections of indigenous foodstuffs failed to come up to expectations.
24. Report of the Hoover Mission, *New York Times*, February 28, 1947.
25. Includes the population of the American and British sectors of Berlin and displaced persons.
26. However, delays in the importations of incentive goods provided under these plans around Christmas of 1947, led to discontent among the miners and contributed to a decline of production.
27. Including brown coal, in terms of hard coal equivalent.
28. Germany's war debt was largely financed by banks and other institutions rather than by direct bond sales to the public.
29. In the fall of 1947, the official cost of living index stood at approximately 125 per cent of the 1938 level.

30. According to newspaper reports, between 60 and 80 per cent of the domestically produced food calories, one-half of the manufactured consumers' goods, and two-thirds of industrial supplies were sold in the legal market (see *New York Times*, December 7 and December 16, 1946) For high-value but low-calorie foods such as meat, fats, eggs, and fruits, the black and barter markets were probably more important than the legal market. Relatively effective controls were maintained over housing and transportation.

31. OMGUS, Manpower Division, *Second Field Report on Conditions of Industrial Labor*, March 8, 1947.

32. Before the war, the official exchange rate was maintained at 1 Reichsmark = 40 U. S. cents; but the effective exchange rate, reflecting the relative internal purchasing power of the Reichsmark and the dollar, was about 30 cents.

33. *The New York Times*, October 29, 1948.

34. *The New York Times*, November 12, 1948.

35. Some experts held that this spiraling effect of price increases could have been avoided if the necessary price adjustments had been made *prior* to currency reform, when the resistance to price and income cuts could have been minimized because money was of small importance.

36. Verwaltung für Wirtschaft des Vereinigten Wirtschaftsgebiets, *Die Deutsche Wirtschaft nach der Währungsreform*, Eighth report, period ending September 20, 1948.

37. *Revised Level of Industry Plan*, Press Release, August 29, 1947.

38. OMGUS, *Denazification and Public Safety*, Monthly Reports.

39. Statistisches Landesamt für Grosshessen, *Staat und Wirtschaft in Gross-Hessen, Statistische Mitteilungen*, December 1, 1946.

40. *New York Times*, March 21, 1948.

41. See Foreign Secretary Bevin's speech of October 22, 1946.

42. Russell Hill in *New York Herald-Tribune*, April 26, 1946. According to the Red Army paper, *Taegliche Rundschau*, December 17, 1946, however, the capacity of Soviet Zone industry still exceeds the level laid down by the Control Council, particularly in the engineering industries.

43. See *New York Times*, October 25, 26, 29, 1946; *Washington Post*, October 27, 1946.

44. *Der Deutsche Zweijahrplan für 1949-50*, Dietz Verlag, Berlin, 1948.

45. *New York Herald Tribune*, Paris Edition, June 10, 1946.

46. Compare also "Umgang mit Zahlen," *Telegraf* (Berlin), September 12, 1946.

47. Joseph Alsop reporting from Berlin, September 8, 1946, *New York Herald Tribune* of the same date.

48. *Der Deutsche Zweijahrplan*, op. cit.

49. *News Chronicle*, January 31, 1946.

50. Although seventy-four of the plants originally seized by the Soviets were allegedly returned to the German state governments in January, 1947, the share of the plants remaining under Soviet ownership in the total production of the Soviet Zone declined by only a few per cent.

51. By the time when the bulk of the expellees reached the Soviet Zone,

most of the land had already been distributed. However, in order to satisfy the claims of a chosen few among this group, an additional 300,000 hectares were distributed in the year beginning in July, 1946.

52. Assuming a per capita standard of living equal to that prevailing in the rest of Germany.

53. The lower figure is that supplied by the four powers to the Council of Foreign Ministers' Conference in Moscow in March, 1947. The Hoover Mission estimated the number of German prisoners of war still in Allied hands at more than four millions. Between March and December, 1947, about 420,000 prisoners were repatriated.

54. Population census of October 1, 1946.

55. Committee of European Economic Cooperation, Vol. I, *General Report*, Paris, September 21, 1947. U. S. Department of State, Publication 2930.

56. Including War Department appropriation for the bizonal area.

57. Report of the President's Committee on Foreign Aid, *European Recovery and American Aid* (Washington, D. C., November 7, 1947).

58. House of Representatives, Select Committee on Foreign Aid, Subcommittee on Germany, February 28, 1948.

59. U. S. Department of State, *The European Recovery Program*, Chap. XVII, "Western Germany."

60. Section 115 (f) of the Foreign Assistance Act of 1948.

61. Statement by the Department of State and the Economic Cooperation Administration, October 27, 1948. During the spring and summer of 1948, a preliminary review had already been made by a cabinet committee appointed by the Secretary of State.

62. Subsequent statements indicated that the French had not yet abandoned their more far-reaching demand for international management or some other form of international control over·the production and investment programs of these industries.

63. The *Economist*, April 17, 1948.

64. Economic Cooperation Administration, *Bizone Area of Germany, Long-Term Program*, October 29, 1948.

CHAPTER V

1. Joint Report on the Berlin Conference, August 2, 1945, A, 9, iv; hereafter referred to as Berlin Conference.

2. See statement by former Secretary of·State Byrnes in his Stuttgart speech of September 6, 1946: "So far as many vital questions are concerned, the Control Council is neither governing Germany nor allowing Germany to govern itself."

3. Berlin Conference, A, 2 and B, 14.

4. The factors, here cited, are not meant to give a historical survey, but merely to indicate a few historical references to the three main contem-

porary problems treated in the subsequent sections below, to wit, (a) the territorial structure, (b) composition and functions of the bureaucracy, and (c) the issue of centralism vs. federalism in post-Nazi Germany.

5. Prussia comprised two-thirds of the area and three fifths of the population of the Empire. It was nearly four times as large and five times as populous as Bavaria, the next largest state; and its size was totally disproportionate when compared with some of the minute, puppet principalities.

6. The original draft of the Weimar Constitution, prepared by Hugo Preuss, Minister of the Interior, included a plan for such a basic administrative reorganization of Germany revising the traditional relationship between the states and the central government and dismembering Prussia. However, this draft, as several other plans later, was rejected by the Constitutional Assembly under pressure of the state interests. Cf. Arnold Brecht, *Federalism and Regionalism in Germany* (New York: Oxford University Press, 1945).

7. The Nazis, however, greatly weakened the traditional structure of the states by superimposing upon them the territorial divisions, called *Gaue*, by which the Nazi party was organized throughout the Reich, as well as by depriving them of most of their independent governmental functions.

8. The only states in which liberal constitutional governments developed were Wuerttemberg and Baden and, to a certain extent, Bavaria.

9. See Chapter I.

10. See the Nuremberg indictment of the officials in the German Foreign Office.

11. Actually the Nazis, in order to play quite safe, introduced an interesting dual mechanism of administrative controls. Besides the traditional state machinery, they gradually built up their own party apparatus as an alternate executive agency. On the highest levels of state and provinces, these two administrative bodies were merged through personal union between the state governor (or head of the provincial administration) and the party *Gauleiter* (chief of the party *Gau*). However, in addition to this merger of state and party controls on the highest level, the party apparatus on all levels served as a most effective instrument of pressure on the state administration, insofar as the latter continued to operate independently, and even assumed the power of execution over a number of functions (especially during the war) which were considered politically too important to be left to the regular administrative agencies. For a detailed treatment of this problem, see John H. Herz, "German Administration under the Nazi Regime," *The American Political Science Review*, Vol. XL, No. 4 (August, 1946). I am also indebted to Mr. Herz for valuable assistance in the preparation of this chapter.

12. Such as the administration of justice, education, religion, police, local government, internal trade, and agriculture.

13. The most important were: citizenship, foreign affairs, customs, taxation, banking, postal affairs, railroads, army and navy, public health, and general civil and criminal law codes.

14. For the allocation of raw materials, war production, food controls, etc.

15. Bavaria was the only state which had a major political party, the Bavarian

People's party, which espoused the cause of particularism. It had separated on this issue from the Center party in 1919.

16. After the last war, there arose an outright separatist movement in the Rhineland, backed by French interests and Rhenish industrialists. But this movement subsided when the men behind the scene became known and the popular reaction throughout Germany was such as only to inflame nationalist sentiments—a reaction similar to present German attitudes on the proposals for separating the Ruhr area.

17. In Germany the lower regional units of administration, into which the states and provinces were subdivided, were known as "government districts" *(Regierungsbezirke)*, "municipal counties" *(Stadtkreise)*, "rural counties" *(Landkreise)*, and "Communes" *(Gemeinden)*.

18. According to the tentative settlement at the Berlin Conference, Prussia lost the provinces East Prussia, West Prussia, Upper and Lower Silesia, and the larger part of Pomerania.

19. The major regional units used in the Russian zone are: Mecklenburg-Pomerania, Brandenburg, the former Prussian province of Saxony, the former state of Saxony, and Thuringia.

20. The American zone consists of four states: Bavaria, Hesse (first known as Greater Hesse), North Wuerttemberg-Baden, and the Free City of Bremen which, like Hamburg, functions as a separate state.

21. The French zone of occupation is divided into three states: Rhineland-Palatinate, Baden, and Wuerttemberg-Hohenzollern.

22. a. Denazification is prescribed under Article III, A, 6;
    b. Democratization and decentralization of the administrative machinery are agreed upon in Article III, A, 9 (i-iv);
    c. References to the democratization of specific fields (education and judiciary) are in Articles III, A, 7 and III, A, 8.

23. The policy was enforced much more rigorously in the American than in the British or French zones.

24. A "Law for the Liberation from National Socialism and Militarism" was passed by the three states in the American Zone on March 5, 1946.

25. These difficulties have been freely and widely discussed by the German press in the American Zone.

26. *The New York Times,* November 6, 1946; Bad Nauheim, DANA, German Press Service, November 5, 1946.

27. This is true even though it frequently takes the form of concern (and, sometimes, genuine concern) for "justice" in the individual case. The charge that a rigid application of denazification would result in grave injustices for individual cases is the principal, overt argument used by the right-wing opponents of the denazification program.

Some of the political difficulties resulting from the position of the bureaucracy in post-Nazi Germany were also alluded to in a farewell address by Professor James K. Pollock formerly director of the Coordinating Office of Military Government at the German *Laenderrat* in Stuttgart. Professor Pollock said *inter al.:* "In the new Germany, the power of officialdom must be curbed if the people are to exercise control over the government.

. . . The role, played by the public and the people in a modern state, has never been properly recognized in Germany. The German people have always relied too much on the trained civil service in all decisions affecting basic political problems. The position of the civil servant was inviolate; and even today, there are trends towards a similar development. . . ." *Der Tagespiegel* (Berlin), August 16, 1946. For a more recent evaluation of the effects of denazification, see Mr. Drew Middleton's dispatch in *The New York Times*, October 17, 1948. The whole subject is treated exhaustively and authoritatively in an article by John H. Herz, published by *Political Science Quarterly* in December, 1948.

28. Berlin Conference, III, A, 9, i, ii, iii. The democratization of government and administration, as envisaged at the Berlin Conference, also refers specifically to the revival of democratic political parties. This phase of the democratic process in post-Nazi Germany is reviewed elsewhere (Chapter VI).

29. See previous section.

30. See Chapter VI.

31. The degree of British supervision and control is illustrated by the large number of British Military Government officers in Germany. In February, 1948, the number was still 18,000 as compared with 4,000 Military Government personnel in the American zone. The French have also employed a disproportionately high number of occupation officials.

32. Berlin Conference, III, A, 9.

33. Berlin Conference, III, A, 9, iv.

34. A chairman, two deputy chairmen, three representatives of the Free Trade Union Association, two representatives of the Peasants' Association, one representative each for the five states in the zone, and the presidents of the thirteen economic offices of the Central Administration.

35. The five economic agencies are for economics, food and agriculture, finance, transportation, and communication, respectively; a sixth central office is in charge of personnel matters.

36. For the text of three directives, see *The New York Times*, July 2, 1948.

37. See below.

38. *Neue Zeitung* (Berlin), June 17, 1946.

39. See Chapter VI.

40. There are a few separatist political groups in the Rhineland and Palatinate; but none of them has so far succeeded in gaining any popular support. Special problems which are not dealt with here arise in connection with the Saar.

41. In contrast to the Weimar Constitution, the Hesse Constitution contains a general nationalization clause (Article 41) which, on insistence by military government, was voted on separately from the constitution. It, too, was approved by about the same margin as the constitution as a whole. Its practical significance is somewhat impaired by the fact that there is comparatively little to be nationalized in Hesse.

42. Public interest in Germany is confined exclusively to professional politicians and constitutional lawyers. For a more detailed discussion of the

state constitutions, see Robert G. Neumann, "New Constitutions in Germany," *American Political Science Review*, XLII (1948), 448-68.

43. Including such clauses as "old age has the right to be respected" or "the state of 'x' renounces the waging of aggressive warfare."

44. See former Secretary Byrnes's statement in his speech at Stuttgart, September 6, 1946: "The Potsdam Agreement did not provide that there should never be a central government. It merely provided that, for the time being, there should be no central German government."

45. See the official French protests against the Anglo-American decision to turn over to the Germans limited and temporary control of the Ruhr coal, iron, and steel industries and to leave the ultimate decision concerning the ownership of these industries to a future German government, *The New York Times*, November 11, 1948. M. de Gaulle was even more critical, not only of this issue, but even of the political consolidation of the three Western zones, *The New York Times*, November 18, 1948.

46. See the statement by Prime Minister Stalin: "Speaking briefly, the politics of the Soviet Union in the German question comes down to the demilitarization and democratization of Germany." From Stalin's written interview with a correspondent of the London Sunday *Times* as reproduced in the *Washington Post*, September 26, 1946.

47. See Chapter IV.

48. The structure of the former administration of Berlin under four-power rule (the *Kommandatura*) was not discussed in these pages.

CHAPTER VI

The chief source of the material in this chapter is the German press, including party organs. Among the most important of the latter are: *Neue Zeit*, Berlin (C.D.U.); *Koelnische Rundschau*, Cologne (C.D.U.); *Rheinische Post*, Düesseldorf (C.D.U.); *Rhein-Ruhr-Zeitung*, Essen (Zentrum); *Der Morgen*, Berlin (L.D.P.); *Hamburger Freie Presse*, Hamburg (F.D.P.); *Sozialdemokrat*, Berlin (S.P.D.); *Hannoversche Presse*, Hanover (S.P.D.); *Sopade Informationsdienst*, Hanover (S.P.D.); *Deutsche Volkszeitung*, Berlin (K.P.D.); *Volksstimme*, Cologne (K.P.D.); *Neues Deutschland*, Berlin (S.E.D.); *Volksstimme*, various local editions in the Russian Zone (S.E.D.)

1. For the background of the German party system see *inter al.*: Ludwig Bergstraesser, *Geschichte der Politischen Parteien in Deutschland* (Mannheim: Bensheimer Verlag, 1924); Sigmund Neumann, *Die Deutschen Parteien: Wesen und Wandel nach dem Kriege* (Berlin: Junker und Duennhaupt, 1932). For the contemporary German party system see Karl Mahler (ed.), *Die Programme der Politischen Parteien im Neuen Deutschland* (Berlin: Druckerei-und Vertriebsgesellschaft m.b.h., 1945); Rainer Barzel, *Die Geistigen Grundlagen der Politischen Parteien* (Bonn: Verlag Goetz Schwippert, 1947); Hoyt Price and Carl E. Schorske, *The Problem of*

Notes 327

Germany (New York: Council on Foreign Relations, 1947); Robert G. Neumann, "The New Political Parties of Germany," *American Political Science Review*, Vol. XL, No. 4; Moses Moscowitz, "The Political Re-education of the Germans," *Political Science Quarterly* (December, 1946); Hans Meyerhoff, "Parties And Classes in Post-war Germany," *South Atlantic Quarterly* (January, 1947); Felix Hirsch, "German Parties—New and Old," *Current History* (June, 1946).

2. Arnold Brecht, *Federalism And Regionalism in Germany* (New York: Oxford University Press, 1945), pp. 31 ff.
3. Gabriel A. Almond, "The Resistance and The Political Parties of Western Europe," *Political Science Quarterly* (March, 1947), pp. 39 ff.
4. Karl Mahler, *loc. cit.*
5. *Ibid.*, p. 29.
6. Studies of the groups associated in the July 20 conspiracy indicate that some of the spirit and momentum of the C.D.U. had its origins in this resistance movement. See Chapter III.
7. Karl Mahler, *op. cit.*, p. 11.
8. For the policies of the Christian Socialist wing of the C.D.U. see Otto Heinrich v. d. Gablentz, "Christlichen Sozialismus," mimeographed C.D.U. report, undated; Eberhard Welty, "Christlichen Socialismus," *Die Neue Ordnung* (October, 1946); Fedor Stepun, "Die Pflicht zum Eigentum und das Recht der Enteignung," *Hochland* (November, 1946); Oswald v. Nell-Brenning S.J., "Christlichen Sozialismus," *Stimmen der Zeit* (March, 1947); Walter Dirks, "Das Abendland und der Sozialismus," *Frankfurter Hefte* (June, 1946).
9. For German election returns see Special Report of the Military Governor U. S. Zone, *Statistics of Elections in Germany, 1946* (March 15, 1947); OMGUS, *German Governmental Organization And Civil Administration*, No. 23 (April 1—May 31, 1947); American Association for a Democratic Germany, *Facts About Occupied Germany* (January, 1947).
10. Deutsche Zentrums-Partei, *Das Kultur, Wirtschafts, und Sozialprogram der Deutschen Zentrums-Partei* (November, 1946); Helene Wessel, *Der Weg der Deutschen Demokratie* (Dortmund, 1946).
11. Karl Mahler, *op. cit.*, pp. 7 ff.
12. For the doctrines of the German Liberal parties see "LDP und NLP," *Marburger Presse*, February 14, 1947; Wilhelm Kuelz, "Soziale oder Sozialistische Ordnung," *Der Morgen*, December 22, 1946; Helm Wienkotter, "Liberalsoziale Wirtschaft," *Coburg Neue Presse*, January 11, 1947; "Gegner der Sozializierung," *Der Kurier*, December 18, 1946; Theodor Heuss, "Wahlkundgebung der DVP," *Mannheimer Morgen*, November 5, 1946.
13. On the doctrines and characteristics of the Social Democratic party see Karl Schmid, *Die Forderung des Tages* (Stuttgart: Verlag Ernst Klett, 1946), pp. 50 ff.; "Sozializierungsvorschlag der SPD in Berlin," *Neue Zeit*, December 1, 1946; "Wichtige Erklaerungen-Schumachers," *Badische Neueste Nachrichten*, January 14, 1947; "Wie Sieht die SPD Unsere Wirtschaftliche und Politische Situation," *Südost-Kurier*, January 15, 1947;

"Deutschland's Kunftige Verfassung," *Telegraf*, March 24, 1947; "SPD und Nationalismus," *Sozialdemokrat*, January 13, 1947; Alfons Schoepflin, "Berliner SPD—Parteitag," *Socialdemokrat*, April 11, 1947; Kurt Schumacher, "Der Weg Deutschlands," *Schwabische Landeszeitung*, January 14, 1947.

14. For the background of the formation of the S.E.D. see American Association for A Democratic Germany, *Der Neue Kampf um Freiheit* (New York, 1946).

15. On the size, characteristics and policies of the S.E.D. see Franz Dahlem, "Die SED und Die Zukunft Deutschlands," *Neues Deutschland*, January 14 and January 15, 1947.

16. For the background of the formation of the *Unabhaengige Gewerkschafts-Opposition*, see Daily Excerpts from German Publications, OMGUS, Manpower Division, Reports and Statistics Branch (March-May, 1948); American Association for a Democratic Germany, *Facts About Occupied Germany* (August, 1948).

CHAPTER VII

1. A summary of the polls of German opinion are to be found in Information Controls Division OMGUS, *Trends in German Public Opinion*, Report No. 60 (April, 1947). A growing literature based on military government experience in the program of democratization and reorientation should also be consulted. See *inter al.*, Marshall Knappen, *And Call It Peace* (Chicago: University of Chicago Press, 1947); Bertram Schallner, *Father Land* (New York: Columbia University Press, 1948); David Rodnick, *Postwar Germans, An Anthropologist's Account* (New Haven: Yale University Press, 1948).

2. The degree to which the after-effects of the war have contributed to this social disintegration is reflected in the following figures: 15 to 20 per cent of the population are deportees from the east; 30 per cent are "aliens," i.e. persons who were removed from their homes owing to evacuations or expulsions and have lived in their present homes for no longer than the past ten years. About twenty millions have lost their personal belongings.

3. Karl Barth, *Zur Genesung des Deutschen Wesens* (Stuttgart: Mittelbach, 1945).

4. The question of the roots of National Socialism in German history is a matter of considerable controversy in the postwar German literature. Right-wing politicians of the Weimar Republic period emphasize the last fatal events that led to the Nazi seizure of power and the decline of conservatism due to the influence of Hugenberg. See Hans von Schlange-Schöningen, *Am Tage danach* (Hamburg: Hammerich und Lesser, 1946). The liberal-nationalist Friedrich Meinecke sees the critical point in the splitting of politics from humanitarian liberalism at the end of the nine-

teenth century. See Meinecke, *Die Deutsche Katastrophe* (Wiesbaden: Brockhaus, 1946). A considerable number of writers lay stress on the fatal Prussian spirit with its mechanical thinking and regard Hitler as the last consequence of Frederick II. See Rudolf Degkwitz, *Das Alte und das Neue Deutschland* (Hamburg: Claassen und Goverts, 1946); Fritz Harzendorf, *So kam es* (Konstanz: Sudverlag, 1946); Fritz Kramer, *Vor den Ruinen Deutschland* (Berlin: Wedding-Verlag, 1946). A Marxist point of view sees the turning point in the failure of the peasants' revolt and Luther's propagation of the doctrine of submissiveness to authority. See Arthur Niekisch, *Deutsche Daseins-verfehlung* (Berlin: Aufbau-Verlag, 1946). The German problem is attributed to a viciousness of German history by Paul Distelbarth who contrasts Germans as "warriors" with Frenchmen as "farmers." See *Deutsche und Franzosen* (Stuttgart: Rohwohlt, 1946). There is no lack of metaphysical explanation as for example Alfred Weber, *Abschied von der bisherigen Geschichte* (Hamburg: Claassen und Goverts, 1946), who dissolves the German problem into a European one. See also Hans Windisch, *Führer und Verführte* (Seebruck: Heering-Verlag, 1946). Max Pribilla in *Deutschland nach dem Zusammenbruch* (Frankfurt: Josef Knecht Verlag, 1947) gives a very clear and considerate representation of the problems from a Christian point of view and is remarkably free of all self-pity.

5. For an objective study of this topic see Koppel S. Pinson, *Essays on Anti-semitism* (New York: Conference on Jewish Relations, 1946) especially the contribution of Waldemar Gurian.

6. The part played by women in the Nazi seizure of power is a matter of considerable controversy. Statistics for the few places where the female vote was separately counted are contradictory. At the same time, it is obvious that Hitler succeeded in swaying the German woman to a greater extent than men. Among Nazi married couples it was often the case that the women were the more fanatical and "Nazi idealist" partners. See *Wandlung* (Heidelberg, 1947), Number 3/4, p. 265 ff.

7. For a summary of the report of the American educational mission see George F. Zook, *Japan and Germany: Problems in Education* (New York: Carnegie Endowment for International Peace, 1947).

8. See Waldemar Gurian, *Die Deutsche Jugendbewegung* (Habelschwerdt-Franke, 1923).

9. Youth groups may be sponsored and assisted financially and otherwise by the political parties provided they are not dominated by such parties. As late as May, 1947 only Socialist and Communist youth groups had applied for permission to organize in the American Zone.

10. Statistics on the size of youth groups in the various zones are as follows: British Zone: 13,846 youth groups with a total of 758,054 members. French Zone: 1900 groups with 93,000 members. The Communist-dominated *Freie Deutsche Jugend* had a total of 405,000 members as of August, 1946. The following statistics are for the U. S. Zone as of March, 1947.

Total population in U. S. Zone 17,688,518
Number in Age Groups 10-18........................ 2,299,507
Members of Youth Groups........................ 890,416

330   *Notes*

Religious Groups ....358,696 or 40.2%
Sport Groups ....280,454 or 31.6%
Handicraft Groups ....12,616 or 1.4%
Cultural Groups ....121,579 or 13.7%
Trade Union Groups .... 65,547 or 7.3%
Miscellaneous Groups .... 51,524 or 5.8%. See OMGUS,
Education and Religion (Cumulative Review) No. 22, pp. 40 ff.

11. The American Army has set up seventy-seven youth centers which have provided important material help for the youth program.

12. This was a well-known consequence of the pre-Nazi youth movement with its artificial prolongation of youthful romanticism.

13. Indications of such tendencies are to be found in some of the contributions to such youth periodicals as *Der Ruf* (Munich) *Die Zukunft* (Reutlingen), *Das Junge Wort* (Stuttgart), Der *Horizont* (Berlin). See also the article by Alfred Andersch in *Frankfurter Hefte* (September, 1947).

14. Their state of mind is described in a selection from four hundred replies to an essay contest conducted by the German newspaper *Mannheimer Morgen*. The theme of the contest was "Jugend! Weisst du den Weg?" ("Youth! Do you Know The Way?")

15. On this point see OMGUS, *Education And Religion* (Cumulative Review), No. 22, p. 34.

16. On this point the current controversy in Bavaria is of interest. The German educational administration prepared a program which was strongly censured by the American authorities because of its traditional conservative bias, *New York Times*, November 28, 1947.

17. Information on these and other developments may be found in OMGUS, *Education And Religion* (Cumulative Review), No. 22.

18. All the German universities have now been opened, although some of them are still limited to only a few of their former faculties. A new university has been established at Mainz in the French Zone. In the American Zone there are now six universities and fourteen technical academies (*Hochschulen*) serving a total of more than 49,000 students. In the British Zone there are six universities and nine academies and technical colleges with a total of almost 32,000 students. In the Russian Zone there are six universities and two technical colleges with a total of almost 13,000 students. In the French Zone there are three universities, one technical academy, and more than 11,000 students. The total figure for students at the university level as of the summer of 1947 was 105,865. Twenty per cent are women, and 10 per cent are foreigners. The Russians are planning an international university for 12,000 students on the island of Ruegen in the gigantic hotel built under the Nazi *Kraft Durch Freude* program. The British are planning to open an English style university near Hanover. Most of the greater German universities have been more or less seriously damaged. As a condition of admission students in some cases are required to give several weeks of physical labor in the effort at physical reconstruction.

19. An interesting general view on the problems of the German university is to be found in Karl H. Bauer, *Vom Neuen Geist der Universität* (Heidelberg, 1947).

Notes   331

20. Among the new adult education periodicals are *Freie Volksbildung* (Munich), *Denkendes Volk* (Berlin).

21. Only 10.2 per cent of the students in the Wuerttemberg *Volkshochschulen* have taken social science courses.

22. Waldemar Gurian, *Hitler And The Christians* (New York: Sheed & Ward, 1936).

23. There has been an important development of religious periodical publication. Among the Catholic periodicals perhaps the most significant from a social and political point of view are *Neues Abendland* (Augsburg), *Faehrmann* (Freiburg), *Stimmen der Zeit* (Freiburg), *Hochland* (Munich), *Frankfurter Hefte* (Frankfurt). Important Protestant periodicals are *Zeitwende* (Munich), *Der Sonntag* (Hanover), *Christ und Welt* (Stuttgart).

24. Karl Barth, *Der Weg der Evangelischen Kirche in Deutschland* (Stuttgart: Mittelbach, 1946).

25. The political parties in the American Zone are permitted to publish small weeklies, most of them quite poor in quality. The nonparty press seems to be preferred by the German public. About 75 per cent of the people questioned in the U. S. Zone favored nonparty papers.

26. A few of the current periodicals are *Wandlung* (Heidelberg), *Sammlung* (Gottingen), *Frankfurter Hefte* (Frankfurt), *Gegenwart* (Freiburg), *Sie* (Berlin), *Berliner Hefte* (Berlin), *Deutsche Rundschau* (Berlin), *Weltbühne* (Berlin), *Aufbau* (Berlin), *Volk und Zeit* (Karlsruhe), *Rheinische Merkur* (Koblenz), *Wirtschaftzeitung* (Stuttgart), *Nordwestdeutsche Hefte* (Hamburg), *Der Spiegel* (Hanover), *Hochland* (Munich), *Deutsche Beiträge* (Munich), *Stimmen der Zeit* (Freiburg). The total number of periodicals in the U. S. Zone is 309, of which 30 are youth publications, 72 religious, 144 professional, 36 literary, and only 13 political. See OMGUS, *Information Control*, No. 26.

27. Among the more important political books to appear in postwar Germany are Eugen Kogon, *Der SS Staat* (Frankfurt: Frankfurter Hefte Verlag, 1946) and Dolf Sternberger, *Dreizehn Politische Radio Reden* (Heidelberg: Schneider, 1946). The latter is rather effectively couched in language suitable for a large public.

28. OMGUS, *Information Control*, No. 26.

29. This vicious circle has been best described in the contribution of Senator Borgner of Hamburg in the *Report of The Munich Conference of Prime Ministers* (Munich, 1947). As for the main social problem of Germany, that of the expellees and refugees, the paradoxical situation is described by Friedrich Mayer-Reifferscheidt in "Dem Geringsten Meiner Bruder," *Hochland* (Munich, 1947). He points out that it was only by means of authoritarian, undemocratic measures that it was possible to help the victims of the totalitarian state.

30. The Denazification Law as first formulated in the American Zone affected about 80 per cent of the population if one takes families into consideration.

31. In this connection it should be noted that the internment camps for arrested Nazis have become dangerous centers of Nazi propaganda, and

the bases for a new myth of the "martyrs of democracy." At the same time the fact that the rations of the Nazi internees were better than those of the civilians is one of the bases of criticism among the anti-Nazis of the American Military Government.

32. The best critic of democratic formalism is Dolf Sternberger, editor of the *Wandlung*. He stresses the danger of giving shelter to undemocratic forces in a formal democratic structure which has not been able to consolidate itself as yet.

33. The literature cited in note 4 above (p. 283) deals with this problem.

For more detailed discussions see Hannah Arendt, *Organized Guilt*, published in translation in *Wandlung* (Heidelberg); Eugen Kogon, *Der SS Staat* (Frankfurt: Frankfurter Hefte Verlag, 1946); Karl Jaspers, *Die Schuldfrage* (Heidelberg: Schneider Verlag, 1946). It is a matter of considerable interest that the standard works on the German resistance have not been published in Germany, and can be acquired only with great difficulty.

Index

333

Women's League, 262
Works' Councils, 198
World War I, 15, 16, 22-23, 191
World War II, 17
Wuerttemberg, 195. *See also*
 Wuerttemberg-Baden
Wuerttemberg-Baden, formation
 of, 195; constitution for, 212;
 mentioned, 224, 225, 236, 239, 240,
 244, 246, 251
Wuerzburg, 235
Wuppertal, 75
Wurm, Bishop, 83-84

Y

Yalta Agreement, and partitioning

of Germany, 112; violation of,
 126
Youth, and anti-Nazi resistance, 85-
 90; and reorientation of Germany, 288-91

Z

Zentralverband der Angestellten,
 73
Zentrum, 298
Zhukow, Marshal, 164, 226, 227
Zinnkann, 67
Zonal Advisory Council, 206
Zonenbeirat. See Zonal Advisory
 Council